THE GREAT HUMANIST

RAMASWAMI VENKATARAMAN

The Great Humanist
Ramaswami Venkataraman

ATTAR CHAND

Gian Publishing House
Delhi-110 007

GIAN PUBLISHING HOUSE
29/6 Shakti Nagar, Delhi-110007

ISBN 81-212- 0106-3

PRINTED IN INDIA

Pub lished by Gian Publishing House, Delhi (India) and
Printed by (Godw al Printers), Delhi.

PREFACE

Biography is commonly considered a branch of history with its own peculiarities. In some respects, it is more lively and interesting than the chronicle of events and movements; in others it is slightly more difficult and liable to errors of excess and defects. Dealing with men and women like ourselves it is full of drama and engage our feelings of sympathy or antipathy. These very feelings are apt to warp our judgements and by reason of partiality or the opposite, lead us away from the truth. In India the tendency is to endow the subject with exaggerated qualities. Writers generally choose those persons in whom they are profoundly interested and for whom they entertain great love and esteem. Defects of temper, and oddities of manner are either slurred or singled out for affectionate tolerance. Bad qualities and their consequenses in actual life are generally ignored and non-existent virtues, installed in their place. Of our legendary heroes and saints the accounts that survive are hardly credible. Even dates are lost in confusion.

Today there is an astonishing amount of biography both in English and in the vernaculars of the country.

It is perhaps premature to expect a high level of excellence, but our achievement is full of promise and our standards of accuracy and attention to detail are developing fast.

The aspiring biographer, still needs unfortunately to be warned against extravagant leniency towards his subject and over-emphasis of the brighter side.

Men and women are, as our ancient books say, the creatures of the three *gunas—sattva*, *rajas* and *tamas*—in infinite combination and inter-play. What they are and what they do—is not to be judged by our limited vision as we know and assess them in our brief day. It is the large vision and perspective of extended recognition as an able and rising member of the Lok Sabha. In most instances Venkataraman hewed to the Congress party line.

Venkataraman has never been what is called a popular leader. Partly, that is because of his Brahmin birth. Tamil Nadu politics began as a fight between the Brahmins and the well-off non-Brahmins organised under the banner of the Justice Party. While the Brahmins captured the Congress party with stalwarts like S. Srinivasa Ayyangar, C. Rajagopalachari and S. Satyamurti, the Justice Party was led by stalwarts like Dr. T.M. Menon, Sir K.V. Reddy Naidu and the Rajah of Panagal. At one time Dr. P. Subbaroyan, whose forte was cricket not politics, was a leader of the Justice Party but he soon left it and joined the Congress. From the beginning caste friction was the bane of the Tamil Nadu Congress. E.V. Ramaswami Naicker left the Congress when he was not allowed to eat with Brahmin Congress leaders.

The tall, silver-haired and smiling figure of Venkataraman was sworn-in as the 8th President, of our Republic on July 25, 1987.

More a statesman than a politician, Venkataraman is one of the few leaders whose image remains untarnished even after having been in the thick of politics for five decades. An able administrator, good parliamentarian, successful presiding officer of the Rajya Sabha and, above all, gentleman to the core, he has the requisite qualities to become President of the Indian Republic. Though his political career began in Madras where he rose to the position of Finance Minister, he has never identified himself with any particular region or community. On the contrary, he watched with sorrow the rise of parochial forces in his State. When he found himself catapulted to the national stage, he admirably measured up to his tasks. As Union Minister, whatever his portfolios, he left a mark on the administration. His role as Vice-President has been equally commendable. After taking oath as Vice-President of India, on August 31, 1984, Venkataraman pledged that he would work for communal harmony and national integration. It is, therefore, in the fitness of things that the ruling Congress party selected him for the highest office.

Venkataraman's performance in New Delhi as Ministers of Finance and Defence was quite in character of the man. He read his briefs and spoke less than others. He never strayed out of line. When he was asked to defend the trusts of A.R. Antulay, he unhesitatingly did as he was told. That, did not save Antulay in the end. But that is not Venkataraman's business. In the Congress Parliamentary Party he had hardly ever opened his mouth. According to Valmiki, in the Kaliyuga Brahmins will not only lose their tufts but take to fighting. Venkataraman must have familiarised himself with strategy and tactics and gone over the niceties of the MIG-21 over F-16s. The point is that he was found adequate for the job. At least the Chiefs had no complaints.

A keen debater and a painstaking parliamentarian, Venkataraman has had a trouble-free rise in politics. He has been in Parliament for about two decades, of course with a gap of two decades, a minister in the Tamil Nadu government for a decade, a Member of the Planning Commission and Chairman of the UN Administrative Tribunal. From an almost insignificant position in the fifties in the matter of industrial development, Tamil Nadu has now emerged as one of the industrially advanced states in the country. And he has wound up his innings as a successful politician by holding charge of two of the most prestigious portfolios of Finance and Defence in the central cabinet, after being con-sidered for the office of the Vice-President in August 1984. By his integrity Venkataraman has set high standards. A disarming smile and sincerity suggest a simplicity of character to the undiscerning. But a closer acquaintance reveals a shrewd politician as well as a sensitive and deeply religious man. He is forceful and determined but avoids the temptation of becoming dogmatic.

A man of experience—a lawyer by training (and therefore he knows the Constitution well), a former diplomat, politician and specialist in economic affairs, Venkataraman is knowledge-able and knows a lot of people. It is said he knows most senior Indian Foreign Service men because he spent around ten years at the UN, besides leaders of other countries. Because of his long years of experience and his objective attitude, his advice is likely to be invaluable—something the government of India at the highest level so really needs today. But all those who know him well say that he never advises unless his advice is sought for and he would rather make his advice stick through persuasion than imposel it on anyone. His roots are embedded in the Congress Party but he is capable of rising above Party affiliations in matters concerning the nation. When the Congress split into two in 1978 Venkataraman was not quite happy about it. For a few months he remained out of both calling himself an independent Congressman. He was quite vocal in Parliament during those months. But even his friends in the Press ignored his speeches. He was persuaded to throw in his lot with Congress (I) which he did.

Venkataraman has a mind of his own on various matters. Anyone who has had private conversations with him or listened to his public speeches knows he won't be a rubber-stamp President. There will, however, be no confrontation. Differences of opinion will be ironed out but the world may never get to know what differences, if any, there were between the President and the Prime Minister. The style of functioning at Rashtrapati Bhavan will change radically during Venkataraman's Presidentship.

There is no doubt that Ramaswami Venkataraman (77) has been in the public eye for over five decades and enjoys his common touch. He has shown the easiness of good manners. He is fluent without being brash and modest without seeming false. Over the five decades the camaraderie has certainly made friends and influenced people.

Venkataraman explains when India became independent forty years ago there was a shortage of everything including food, textiles, housing, power and even transport. "We tried to telescope the development process, which had taken nearly 200 years of industrial revolution in the west, into a few decades. So a great deal of pressure was generated affecting the

* Promila Kalhan RV—a portrant. *Hindustan Times* 22 June 1987 p. 6.

country's polity, which in its turn had its impact on the development process. It was not even."*

In the social field there was a rigid caste system and efforts to change it after independence led to increased tension. Similarly, in the economic field the effort was to have more equitable distribution of wealth, but that again brought all kinds of social tensions and pressures. In the political field, India opted for a federal constitution which inevitably raised questions of the respective powers of the states and the Centre. As time passed it became a cause of constant friction.

Venkataraman summed up the present situation in the country thus : "Since we were trying or grow in all directions, certain explosions kept occurring at various points. Today fanatical religionists think their rights are being eroded. The propertied classes think we are cutting into their domain. The underdog and the havenots think the progress has not been sufficient and fast enough. And finally the states think they are not having their full rights." "Despite all this I am an optimist," Venkataraman asserted and hoped that the country would progress as it has beendoing in the past.

But when asked about his views of on India's role in the World of tomorrow, he sadly admitted that "my optimism gives way because the threat of a nuclear holocaust is very real." He felt that unless the big powers with nuclear capability come to some agreement to eliminate nuclear weapons a catastrophe could occur even by mistake.

In this context Venkataraman dismissed the deterrent theory. Granted that it might have created a balance of terror, if such destructive weapons go on being accumulated, the danger of a conflagration too increases in the same proportion. Then the whole world would be destroyed. At least in conventional wars destruction was confined to certain specific areas and they could be rebuilt as was done after World War II. He appreciated the efforts of the present Soviet leaders primarily because peace was essential for improving the quality of life in the country.

---

*PM-President differences may only be temperamental—Venkataraman, An interview with C.S. Pandit. *Amrita Bazar Patrika*, 26 June, 1987.

Any biographical study of Venkataraman would be incomplete without a reference to his great sympathy for and friendship with the fraternity of working journalists. He was a member of the first wage board for journalists and made a signal contribution to its outcome. In fact, he delayed his entry into the Kamaraj Cabinet in 1957 for three months since the report of the Wage Board was not ready. On account of this, he attracted the wrath of the press barons in Madras but the long arm of Kamaraj extended him enough protection. As in the Capital too, he was an unfailing presence, in the central Hall, even when there was no Parliament session, to have a cup of coffee with journalists and fellow Members of Parliament.

Venkataraman belongs to a generation steeped in values that are perhaps not cherished by the new breed of politicians. Though not aggressive he has also been a very successful trade unionist. He looks venerable in his silverly hair. He seems just the man for the presidentship. In today's bitter atmosphere the president will have to be a man who can bring peace between warring politicians, warring political parties.

When asked what he looked forward to if and when he enters the Rashtrapati Bhavan, Venkataraman modestly remarked : "Only to see India continue to make progress at the same rate." He had no fears of any disintegration of the country despite all the tensions.

July 1987 ATTAR CHAND

ACKNOWLEDGEMENTS

One of the more pleasant tasks associated with writing a book is to acknowledge the assistance so necessary for its completion. The basic research was done in Delhi Libraries and Institutes, as was the writing of the first draft of the manuscript. My friends in the libraries gave assistance far beyond the normally extended limits set by Chief Librarians and Head of the Departments.

I have tried to be as objective as I could. There are some affairs of national and international importance in which Ramaswami Venkataraman was deeply involved, but which do not find "adequate place" in the book, but a time may come when I would like to devote one or more additional chapters to them. I am much obliged to writers from whose books and articles I have taken passages freely.

This study, however, could not have reached fruition without the help of my well-wishers : Jagmohan, Governor, Jammu and Kashmir, Dr. V.P. Dutt, Professor, Delhi University, and Lalit Bhasin, Advocate, Supreme Court of India, Dr. M.K. Saini, University of Delhi, H.S. Wadhwa, FICCI, New Delhi, Nandrajog, PHDCCI, New Delhi, M.K. Dhar (Hindustan Times), Dr. R. P. Dua, Dr. K. R. Sharma, Dr. Harjinder Singh, Delhi University, A.N. Dar, Editor-in-Chief, National Herald, Vinay Rai (Industrialist), V. D. Chopra (Patriot), B. K. Batra (Advocate) and my sons, Dr. Harish Kumar and Gulshan Kumar suggested sundry improvements and provided nourishing guidance and inspiration.

Finally, a large number of persons who are friends or associates of Venkataraman have offered valuable information. But none of them is responsible for any opinions or conclusions of the author. As a result, this study is essentially a study in public opinion, party politics and public relations.

ATTAR CHAND

CONTENTS

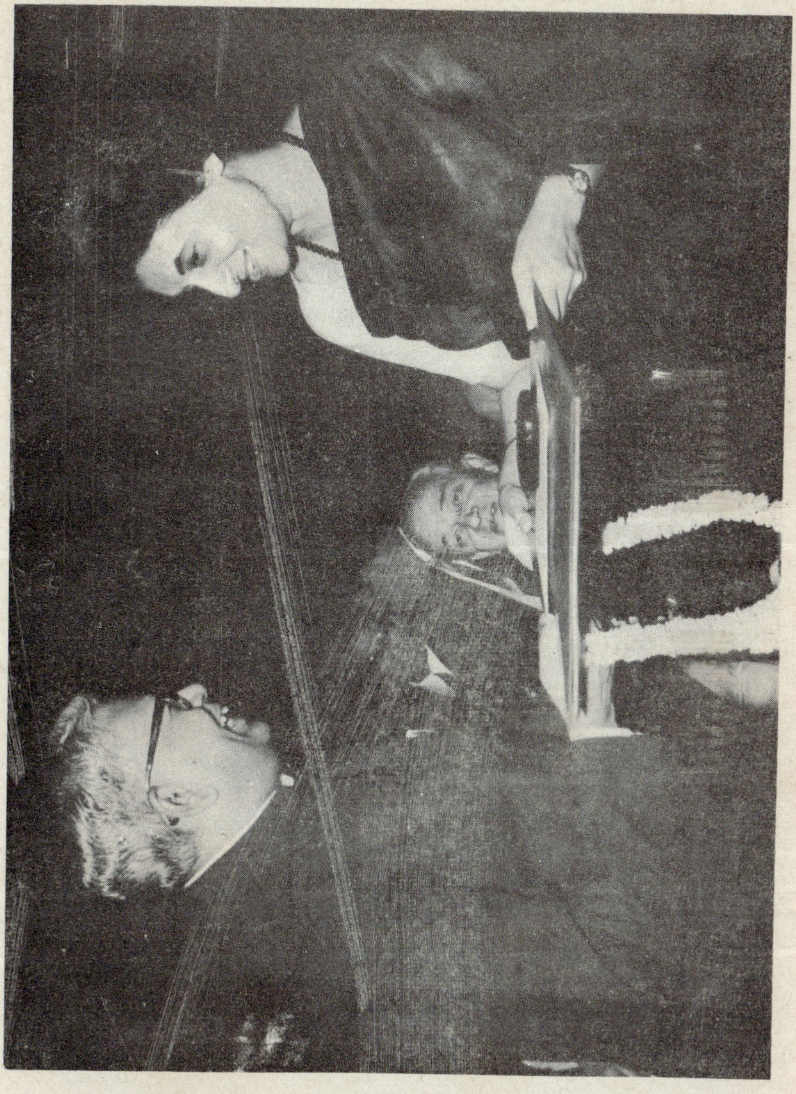

R. Venkataraman, receiving "Soviet Land" Nehru Award for 1967 for journalist work from late Prime Minister Mrs. Indira Gandhi at a function in New Delhi on November 15 1967

R. Venkataraman with Rajiv Gandhi, Zail Singh and Balram Jhakhar.

1

THE COMMITMENT

Like Oliver Goldsmith, there is nothing that President Venkataraman has touched without adorning it in his five decades of public life. A clear thinker, and above all, a great humanist and friend of the poor is how the millions of people in Tamil Nadu know Venkataraman, (RV) as he is affectionately called. K. Kamaraj under whose political tutelage he came in the early forties was mainly responsible for shaping his career. Perhaps no other Congress leader in Tamil Nadu can surpass his commitment to the high moral values and progressive policies that Kamaraj had stood for and for life-long loyalty to his political mentor.

The State of Tamil Nadu, previously popularly known to the world as Madras, its erstwhile name, is situated at the south-eastern extremity of the Indian peninsula, bordered by three States on its west and north. The blue waters of the Bay of Bengal and Indian Ocean skirt her eastern and southern land territory. With an area of 1,29,966 sq. kms., it accounts for a little over 4 per cent of the country's total area and is the tenth largest State (total 45 million). A notable feature is that the density of population is appreciably higher than the national level, being 316 per sq. km. as against 182 for the country as a whole.

The political history of Tamil Nadu is unique in the sense that the kings and chieftains of this region were never brought under complete suzerainty of the conquerers and invaders who ravaged northern India and even reached the borders of the State.

In the distant past, the Tamil region was ruled by three royal houses of Cheras, Cholas, and Pandyas. They ruled wisely, were great builders and munificent patrons of art and architecture and acted as guardians of the people.

The Pallavas who ruled in 4th century too were well-known patrons of arts and letters and built Mamallapuram (Mahabalipuram), reputed for its monolithic structures and rock-reliefs, besides the seven Pagodas which continue to attract chroniclers and tourists. They are standing monuments of a peerless and artistic style of architecture in the South. Remnants of Tamil culture and religious concepts which spread far and wide are still found in some of the south-eastern lands. The village administrative system that the Cholas built up and the ethical and religious ideals which they propagated constitute a priceless legacy of the Tamils. Trade and commerce flourished in the area and the seafaring Tamils had brisk overseas trade with far eastern countries and Egypt, Greece and Rome. Ancient ports like Puhar, Mamallapuram and Kayal were imortant and thriving centres of foreign trade. Foreign dignitaries and travellers like Ptolemy, Plimy and Macro Polo have depicted the glory of the Tamils in vivid colours in their travelogues and diaries.

Tamil ranks among the oldest languages of the world. It is remarkable that while many languages which flourished in the centuries before Christ are no longer alive in their traditional style, Tamil has lived on, with its full vitality, and has continued to be the vibrant vehicle of thoughts and feelings of over 45 million people. A distinguishing feature of the language is its vitality and resilience and its capacity to enrich itself without borrowing. Tamil is a living language with an inexhaustible treasure for development and growth.

With ingrained essentials of Indian culture, Tamil Nadu's is, perhaps, one of the oldest cultural traditions in the world. Tamils are altruistic in their approach, and their philosophy of life is based on the principle of universal brotherhood and tolerance and harmony characterise the relations between different sects, which never fell a prey to bigotry. Thus today people fell a prey to bigotry. And so today people professing Christianity, Islam, Jainism and Buddhism or other faiths live together in peace and brotherhood.

The modern State of Tamil Nadu was born on November 1, 1956, as a unilingual State, consequent on the reorganisation of the Indian States, losing its earlier form of being one of the most polyglot of India's great administrative divisions. It continued to be known as the State of Madras till it took the present name on January 14, 1969. Tamil Nadu enjoys the reputation of being efficiently administered, with well organised administrative machinery from Block level upwards.

Tamil Nadu is often called as the land of temples. Rising into the skies, these marvels in stone with sculptured intricate patterns of art, symbolise the quest of man for spiritual peace. An endless feast for the eye, and the mind, these monuments, intriguing and inspiring, link the present with the hoary past and stand witness to the faith and love of their creators who were at once supreme artists and devotees.

The temple cities of Madurai, Tiruchirapalli and Kanchipuram and Thanjavur (district of Venkataraman's birth) constitute important chapters of the history of Tamil architecture and town planning. The Sri Meenakshi Temple, and the Golden Lotus Tank, the Musical Pillar, the thousand pillared mandapam, enclaved by this temple which has tall towered gopurams tell a tale of the fertile imagination and astute engineering skill of the Tamils. The temple of Thanjavur keeps one wondering about the angelic hand of the man who raised granite and brick so high. This temple, built about a thousand years ago has a 14-storey gopuram, the highest in India.

Several hill stations in the State have earned wide popularity for their bracing climate and splendid natural beauty. Ooty, the "Queen of hill stations" in India, nestling at the meeting point of the Eastern and Western Ghats is an all-season hill resort which is robed by verdant forests and green meadows. The Mudumalai Wild Life Sanctuary is an abode of rare wild animals. Coonoor and Kothagiri, situated on the Nilgiris ranges attract endless streams of tourists. Kodaikanal, the other hill station in Madurai district with its wooded slopes, mighty rocks, exciting waterfalls, and beautiful lake, would delight any visitor. The Silver Cascade, the Glen Falls, the Pambar and Bear Shola Falls and the Fairy Falls are some of Kodaikanal's glories.

Tamil Nadu is a major repository of all that is elegant and beautiful in fine arts, especially music and dance. Traditions in Karnatic Music and Bharatha Natyam rooted in the Shastras date back to ancient times. Most of the music of Tamil poet-saints has been set in ancient 'Panns' (Ragas). The 'Thevaram', the 'Thiruvachagam', the 'Thiruppugazh' and other sacred hymns represent the cream of ancient Tamil devotional music. Bharatha Natyam is in essence the communication of meaningful emotion, sentiment and mood by expression and gesture accompanied all the time by a scientific exposition of skilled dancing movements wherein intricate footwork and rhythm patterns predominate.

The community in Tamil Nadu at large has risen to the call of progress. Life is no longer dull or stale even in the remote interior. The community development programme has revolutionised the rural scene. The village folk are growing increasingly eager to catch up with the times, of course without cutting themselves away from old moorings.

The Indian scene which is a harmonious blend of the old and the new is beautiful at all times. Its variegated life, so rich and full of colour, presents an exquisite tapestry. The entire structure of her industry and commerce has undergone a tremendous change in keeping with the times. Tamil Nadu has played its part in no small measure in the shaping of a new society-based on rational socialism and will continue to do so in the progress and development of the nation.

All this is Tamil Nadu, lush, colour drenched, sunburnt and romantic. A rare mix of old and new, proud preserver of cultural life. Land where life is still gracious and time never hurried.

Even as Venkataraman rose higher and higher in the political ladder, he suffered from no inebriety of power. His friends know him as an administrator, who follows "the rule of the rules" and the "rule of law". Even if he were to help anyone in hardship, he will amend the relevant rules, so that other similarly handicapped would also benefit. After two-years incarceration during the Quit India Movement of 1942, he was entrusted by Kamaraj with the task of organising the labour community under the auspices of the Tamil Nadu Congress Committee. By his assiduous work he built up a powerful organisation the branch of the Indian National Trade Union Congress which Kamaraj, for reasons best known to him, did not encourage in the State.

Kamaraj brought Venkataraman to the Lok Sabha in 1952 where he caught the eye of the then Prime Minister Jawaharlal Nehru, following his significant contribution to debates on a variety of subjects. That was a time of a lot of ideological controversy in the Congress Party, with many paying only lip-service to Nehru's resolve to establish a democratic socialist State and the captains of industry and trade openly challenging it. Venkataraman, along with the late K.P. Tripathi of Assam and others had formed "a ginger group" to mobilise support for Nehru's forward-looking programmes and policies. Not infrequently, he came into clash with a titan from the South then in the Cabinet,—T.T. Krishnamachari (TTK)—specially on automatisation of looms. He won the day by his principled crusade in favour of the handloom sector. His contribution the reconstruction of Article 31 to make compensation for acquisition of all types of property non-justiciable would always be remembered. The original Bill introduced in the Lok Sabha sought to take the compensation issue out of purview of the judiciary only in regard to agricultural property. But Venkataraman, as the general secretary of the Congress Party and assisted by M. K. Ramamurty, a research officer of the party then (and now a leading advocate of the Supreme Court) mustered enough support among the members for bringing industrial and urban property also under its scope. Nehru, who always bowed down to the consensus in the party, agreed to amend the Bill in the teeth of opposition from TTK.[1]

Hewever, being shy to advance his claims, he never hit the jackpot and missed inclusion in the Council of Ministers despite frequent mention in press forecasts. But Nehru found other ways of utilising his talent. He was sent to the United Nations as part of the Indian delegation, where too he made a mark.

Venkataraman was chosen as chairman of the UN Administrative Tribunal, a post he held for a long period. Venkataraman was one of those who successfully prevailed on Kamaraj to take over the Chief Ministership of Tamil Nadu in 1954, the latter being sceptical whether he would do as well in the administration as in the organisation. "We are all there to help you" he told him. Venkataraman joined the Kamaraj Cabinet after 1957 as Minister for Industry and Labour. His record was the most distinguished not only in speeding up industrial growth but in maintaining harmonious labour-management relations. For 10 years, he laboured hard and the State came to occupy the first rank in the country in regard to industrial development, specially in the medium and small-scale sectors.

After the fall of the Congress from power in 1967. Indira Gandhi requisitioned his services as a member of the Planning Commission where too he brought to bear his pragmatic approach on the formulation and implementation of the plan. He, however, resigned later and took to prolific writing till 1977, when he bounced back to the Lok Sabha. From 1980 onwards, he had been a Central Minister in charge of Finance and then of Defence.

The last four years of his tenure in the Centre marked him out as the most soft-spoken but the ablest debater in the treasury benches. The way he established that the conditionality imposed by the IMF for its $ 5.6 billion loan cohered with the priorities and policies of the Sixth Plan was a marvellous sophistry in presentation. For his good luck, the country also emerged unscathed from the calculated risk, thanks to the massive oil discovery in off-shore areas. Venkataraman's performance in the Antulay Trust debate in the two Houses also established his pre-eminence in advocacy. The point to note is that Venkataraman steered clear without provoking personal bitterness or indulging in paroxysmal outbursts as a TTK or C. Subramaniam would do.

However sharp might be the attack from the Opposition benches, Venkataraman never lost his cool nor cast dobule doubts on the bonafides of the critics. He was loathe to label any section of the Opposition as "anti-national", "reactionary", "pro-imperialist", "pro-Moscow" and the like While being a firm believer in socialism and in friendship with the Soviet Union, he let others go by their own convictions.

Venkataraman is rarely baffled by complexity of problems, because he has an uncanny knack of getting, at their pith and substance. He reminds one of the Hindu mythological bird, "hams" which could from a bowl of milk take only the milk content and leave behind the water. In his presentation, he scrupulously avoids any high-sounding shibboleths or jargon, remniscent of the late R.K. Shanmukam Chetty, the first Finance Minister of free India. This explains how Rajaji as Chief Minister of Madras in 1952 summoned his services to study the agrarian unrest in Thanjavur, the rice-bowl of Tamil Nadu, despite his close affiliation with Kamaraj. And his report helped in ending the seething discontent among the landless labour and tenants in the area. However, if Venkataraman shared Rajaji's perspicacity, his high intellectual faculty suffered from no curve or bend which could revolt against the general will. Having put forward his views clearly, he was always willing to abide by the consensus even if it went against his opinion. Venkataraman is also deeply religious and an ardent follower of Kanchi Kamakot Shankaracharya. At his bidding, he organised the construction of a temple at Vasant Vihar in New Delhi for "Kathikeya" (known as Lord Subramania in Tamil scriptures). He attributes his imperturbability and complete equanimity of mind to the benevolence of the

"Shankaracharya" regarded by the Tamils as "nadamadum deivam"—"god trodding on earth". The repeated statements by opposition leaders that they were not fielding a Harijan candidate against Venkataraman for Vice-Presidentship because of their personal hostility to him showed the high esteem in which he was held by all segments of opinion in Parliament. No wonder the Prime Minister did not want Venkataraman to retire, which he had openly declared to do, and opted to utilise his services as the President of the Indian Union.

Ramaswami Venkataraman was born on December 4, 1910 in the Rajamadam village in Tamil Nadu's Thanjavur district. Son of the late K. Ramaswami Iyer, he was educated at Madras University. He was enrolled as an advocate of the Madras High Court in 1935-about three years before his marriage with Janaki Venkataraman.

The old temples of India, particularly those of Tamil Nadu many of which have a thousand year living history, have a triple-value religious appeal. They are magnificent monuments to the heritage of man : rich with sculptures and murals, alive with colourful rituals. They are wreathed in mystery, myth and legend : the miracles of gods, goddesses and gurus ; the largesse of ancient kings with heraldic names ; the dark doings of demons providing a weird counterpoint to all the bright glory of a multi-faceted faith. And thirdly, as possibly happened around the medieval cathedrals of Europe, the great temples provided a focal point for the arts and crafts, around which whole families of traditional artisans thrived in peace, protected by the powerful patronage of the deity, and painstakingly developed individual moes of expression that, in course of time, became associated with the name of the temple. We can find no better example of this socio-economic phenomenon than in the town and around the temple of Thanjavur. It is more commonly known as Tanjore. We could have come to Tanjore by train, along with the pilgrims, but we preferred the road route from the nearest airport town of Tiruchirapalli. This town of the Rock Fort used to be called Trichinapoly and is still referred to by the diminutive Trichy. The 56 kms. drive is pleasant, though often glare-filled if you do it in the late morning and afternoon, as we did. But the state Tourism

Development Corporation's Tourist Bungalow is delightfully cool and soon restores one's exposure-strained eyes. Formerly the residence of a nawab, this two-storey bungalow is built around a tree-shaded courtyard which chimes with flocks of birds at dusk and dawn : a green retreat from a rather dusty town. And for those who are travelling on a budget, the railway station is just a ten minute walk away, the bus station is five minutes away, and the ITDC's Traveller's Lodge is one km. from the Tourist Bungalow.[2]

The strange vimana over the sanctum is not the only odd thing about the Brihadiswara temple ; its very origins are enshrouded with ancient tales. One legend has it that the town was once the haunt of a terrible demon named Tanjam. Just before he was destroyed by Lord Vishnu he requested the Preserver to commemorate his name in a great city: thus Tanjore was born. In some historic times (850 A.D.), Vijayalaya Chola conquered the town and made it the capital of a dynasty that would rule Tamil Nadu till 1279. In 999 the great Raja (Emperor) Raja Chola I, who was afflicted by a discolouring skin ailment, learnt that he could be cured of it if he brought a Sivalingam from the river Narmada and built a temple over it. He did so and, because the lingam kept growing, he called his temple Brihadiswara. The 23-1/4 feet lingam stands in a 14 storey 215 ft. high vimana making the temple the tallest in south India. Unlike other southern temples, the vimana is taller than the gate towers or gopurams. And right on top of the vimana is an 80 ton block of granite which was taken to the top along a four-mile long ramp starting at the village of Vayalur. And since we are on Statistics, the beautifully carved Nandi bull is sculpted from a single stone and is 12 ft. high, 19-1/2 ft. long, 8-1/2 ft. broad and weighs 24 tons. According to legend, the Nandi too kept growing, so a restraining nail was driven into its back.[3]

But no statistics can do justice to the massive overpowering grandeur of the place. It rises and spreads across its open grounds, decorated with sculptures, embellished with inscriptions, attended by the shrines of lesser deities. And amongst its numerous nurals is that of a European who could have been Marco Polo. For those who liked their religion mixed with a bit of scholarship, there is a well-managed little museum run by the Archaeological Survey of India where you can see the work that has gone into restoring the temple to its once and present, glory. We spent a great deal of time at the Brihadiswara Temple, and would gladly have extended our tour, but time was hemming us into a tight schedule. And so we drove away from the great monument to an ancient king and to the palace of a more recent one. The Saraswati Mahal was built by the 19th century Nayak ruler, Maharaja Sarabhoji. There is a good collection of bronzes in the Museum and an outstanding collection of manuscripts, including 33,000 palm-leaf ones, in the Saraswati Mahal Library. For the casual visitor with rather outre tastes, the sketches made by a French-man might be of interest : he has brought out the distinct similarity between the features of humans and those of animals. They are quite disturbing. And for those with more Gothic horror incilinations, there are illustrations of ancient Chinese tortures. We had no desire to go through the entire series.

We advise visitors not to be led astray by the Tanjore Plate Cooperative sign displayed near the Museum ; it is only a sales outlet ; you cannot see workers engaged in their esoteric craft, Tanjore plates, as many people know, are beautifully decorative brass and silver work; gods and goddesses, animals or intricate floral motifs. Eventually, ofter many false starts and miles of winding, aromatic, by-lanes, we located a spectacled crafts-man and sat and watched him enthralled. The creation of a Tanjore plate, is a delicately balanced blend of precision and art. The brass base-plate is seldom decorated ; its job is to serve as a firm receptacle for the designs crafted on the other two metals. But the two softer metals need the most sensitive chisel-touch : too light a tap and the impression will not rise, too heavy and the metal will be pierced. Finally, the tiny embossed silver and copper panels are pressed onto the brass plate's grooves and indentations and the plate is ready. "How long will the panels hold ?" We asked a knowledgeable by-stander who had followed us to the craftsman's house. He frowned and the Saivite bars wrinkled on his domed forehead. "Their forefathers protably built the temple", he affirmed. Nodding to himself, his face lit by the shadow of a smile,

"Their work is not touched by time", he said softly, serene in his timeless confidence.[4]

The tall, silver-haired and similing figure Venkataraman, a post-graduate in Economics and a bachelor of law, evinced keen interest in labour laws early in his career. In 1946, he was deputed by the Government of India to serve on the panel of lawyers to defend Indian nationals charged with collaborating with the Japanese during the Second World War in Malaya and Singapore. After serving as Secretary of the Madras Provincial Bar Federation from 1947 to 1950, he was enrolled in 1951 as an advocate of the Supreme Court.

There is no better place to begin one's descovery of the ageless south of India than in the colourful historic state of Tamil Nadu. A land of proud cultural heritage, of sunshine and warmth, temples and legends, silver lined beaches, dazzling gold-edged silks pouring out of shops, delicate strains of veena and flute, of graceful movements of Bharat Natyam.

A window to the modern south as much as it is a wide open archieve of ancient legacies, Tamil Nadu amazingly for all its modern progress retains its old world charm. The giant symbols of an industrial upsurge, unspoilt hill resorts, beaches and forest sanctuaries, majestic palaces and exquisitely hewn temples all go to make one see a rare commixture of the ancient, the new and the picturesque.

He was drawn into the movement for India's freedom struggle from Britain's colonial subjugation while he was practising law. He actively participated in the "Quit India" movement of 1942 for which he was detained for two years under the Defence of India rules. He was elected to the Provisional Parliament in 1950 and to the Lok Sabha in 1952 and 1957. He functioned as the Minister of Industries, Labour, Cooperation, Power, Transport and Commercial Taxes in the Tamil Nadu Government and Leader of the House in the Madras Legislative Council from 1959 to 1967.

He became the Member of Planning Commission in charge, of Industry, Labour, Power, Transport, Communications and Railways in 1967 and remained so until 1971. He was elected to the Lok Sabha in 1977 from Madras and served as an Opposition Member of Parliament. He was re-elected to the

Lok Sabha from the same constituency in 1980 and was appointed the Minister of Finance in the Cabinet, headed by late Prime Minister Indira Gandhi. He also functioned as the Defence Minister for sometime before his election for the post of Vice-President in August 1984.

A keen debater and a painstaking Parliamentarian but one with a sound grasp of economic problems, Venkataraman was the Indian delegate to the United Nations General Assemby in 1953, 1955, 1958, 1959, 1960, and 1961. He was leader of the Indian delegation to the 42nd session of the International Labour Conference at Geneva in 1958.

Venkataraman belongs to the land of Mahakavi (the great poet) Subramaniyam Bharathi who remained for the people of India. In Tamil Nadu a legend He, by his patriotism and dedication has written himself into the pages of history. As a poet and a fiery political journalist he has contributed much towards India's freedom struggle.

The British poets Lord Byron and P.B. Shelley were the ones who inspired Bharathi. He, in all humility, called himself 'Shelleydasan". In this course of the starting from Shelleydasan he gradually described himself as 'Shakthi Dasan', Seeing his firy dedication and patriotism sister Nivedita, the spiritual daughter of Swami Vivekananda, took him under her wings. In her, he saw Goddess Shakthi (power) herself. Receiving a silent blessing from her he moved nearer to 'sathya' and 'dharma'.

Bharathi's political master was Bala Gangadhar Tilak. Tilak's "Swaraj (freedom) is my birth right", always haunted Bharathi. He wrote two poems 'Vazhga Tilakan Namam' and 'Tilaka Munivar Kone', dedicated to Tilam meaning 'Long Live Tilak' and 'King Tilak'. He was also a close follower of Sankara Bhagvad Pada.

Sarojini Naidu described Bharathi as a 'fiery soul of patriotism'. She said "Bharathi kindled the soul of men by the million to a more passionate love of freedom and a richer dedication to the service of the country". Jawaharlal Nehru had said, "Bharathi not only belongs to Tamil Nadu but to the whole of India and the world at large."

As Minister for Industry in the Tamil Nadu Government, he inspired the industrialisation of the State. His accessibility is a byword in Madras. He was extra-ordinarily friendly with the Press. But then he had no political responsibility. This was borne by the doughty Kamaraj who spent most of his time touring the State while C. Subramaniam and Venkataraman held the Fort St. George.

Kamaraj, who was a disciple of Congress Party Stalwart S. Satyamurti, was the first non-Brahmin Congress Chief Minister of Madras, Kamaraj himself had no caste feelings and held no prejudice against the Brahmins. Venkataraman flourished under him. But so far as political work was concerned Kamaraja, personally oversaw it. As a result, when the DMK displaced the Congress in office, there were few Congress leaders available for reconstituting the party machinery. Finally, when Kamaraj himself broke away to form his own party, the Congress was bereft of all leadership. Luckily for Venkataraman, Karunanidhi and later M.G. Ramachandran, for their own reasons decided to support Congress leaders for the Lok Sabha in exchange for Congress support of DMK and AIDMK candidates for the State Assembly. That arrangement brought Venkataraman to the Centre.

To an enlightened person like Venkataraman a temple is a divine place where our wishes are fulfilled.

In India, we believe that our past deeds shape present conditions. The first among the fundamental postulates of Hinduism points out that there should be some casue for every event—good or bad. That can be traced through self-endeavour. But there are also happenings which baffle a human being as no reason can be attributable to them. A boy may be studious but yet he fails in his examination, a puzzle indeed. For certain acts, no explanation can be provided at all. The mysterious ways of God cannot be interpreted. Yet in some other cases, a man might have contributed his labour sincerely, hoping to achieve what he desired but the outcome may be quite contrary to what he expected. Here too, the man will be dazed by the unexpected turn of events.

There are equally bewildering phenomena where from out of the same efforts, two exactly opposite results may flow. Two persons travel in a train which meets with a derailment. One dies but the other survives. God's dispensation is un-understandable. Hence, we are asked to submit to His will. The theory advanced for these diverse results is that they are based on one's past deeds. If a person has upheld the rules of morality and obeyed God's dictates, he is bound to be rewarded. Likewise, evil deeds cannot go unpunished. To get reconciled to this theory, the mind has to be duly conditioned.

In his discourse a priest elaborated this doctrine of destiny by pointing out how a dog gets special treatment in a rich man's house while another of its tribe gets hit by stones in public places. People may then ask : why worship God if everthing is pre-determined and pre-ordained.

Life is compared to an ocean. A person may swim across it but is sure to be devoured by sharks. But, he can have a safe voyage if he gets into a ship. One who aspires to get rid of worldly bondage can gain entry into this 'vessel', which is captained by God. He should treat praise and abuse alike.

An example to elaborate the idea that man gets what he deserves, often cited, is about a person directed to look into the placid waters in a huge well. The reflections of both the sun in the sky and of the dilapidated well nearby were noticed, to indicate that good and bad are inside a man. Each one experiences the consequences in accordance with the manner in which he functions. Worship of God and spiritual discipline will help an aspirant to face difficulties and to remain unaffected.

Man's conduct should not be judged solely by external appearance. He may pose as if he is the paragon of virtue, wear religious symbols and even conduct elaborate rites. But with all these pompous show, he may still harbour bad thoughts. Unless he is found to be free from impurities and vicious influences which corrupt the mind, he will ever remain a hypocrite.

Desire, anger, lust and other wicked propensities should have no room in the heart. Such a clean man will not seek property or power but will discharge the responsibilities entrusted to him sincerely. The Mahabharatham presents many characters, representing a cross-section of the then society, but their behaviour was no different than what one witnesses among many these days. Jealousy, hatred and quarrel between brothers were to be found.

Likewise, some people attempting to forge unity even suffering personal discomfiture was also not uncommon. One among the greatest characters was Bhishma who did his best to keep the word given to his forbears. At the same time, it was baffling that a man of his stature, upholding the principles of righteousness, should have supported wicked men on the plea of repaying the debt of gratitude. The main theme of the Epic is that so long as there is divine surveillance, there can be no violation of the law of virtue and that vice can never thrive.

In a discourse in temple, a priest said: "man pursues the objects of his desire madly until he gets them. Once he is in possession of them instead being sated, he becomes a slave to other longings. The Epic reflects how armed with the power of chastity, even God in human form could be sentenced for a default."

The Mahabharatəm through Yudhishtirar, pinpoints how after a particular stage in life. elders, who are running, the home, should hand over the reins of management to the youngsters. Yudhishtirar entrusted the administration to his grandson and along with his brothers and wife, left the world. God's law can never be circumvented and evil cannot thrive for all time are the major lessons from the Mahabharatam. From the Epic Venkataraman has adopted right characters in his life.

Venkataarman's coffee club, which lost its spontaneity, after he occupied the Vice-President's office in August 1984 might be revived. He nostalgically recalled on June 14, 1987, the coffee club gathering in the Central Hall of Parliament when he was the Finance Minister and the Defence Minister.

Members of Venkataraman's coffee club were basically journalists with whom the former Finance Minister would sit and chat quite frequently. A regular visitor to the Central Hall, he named his sessions with journalists as "coffee club'.

Everyone in the Central Hall was welcome to have a cup of coffee when Venkataraman was around.

Venkataraman did much to increase the nations defence preparedness. His speeches, as Defence Minister, showed his insight into the ominous developments in India's neighbourhood.

People of Andhra Pradesh are glad that it was during his term as Defence Minister that Prime Minister Indira Gandhi laid the foundation for a quiet ordnance factory in their State.

About 6 years ago no one would have thought of Venkataraman as a likely vice-presidential candidate. He was then known to very few people outside Tamil Nadu. He belonged to the Congress (O) which was but a very feeble political force in Tamil Nadu. Two things were against him. He lacked the temperament to fight his way to the limelight; did not possess the zest for political life. He was also handicapped by being a Brahmin. After Rajagopalachari no Brahmin has mattered politically in Tamil Nadu as perhaps in most parts of peninsular India. T.T. Krishnamachari was the only Brahmin to occupy a position of importance at the Centre after men like Rajaji and Gopalaswami Ayyangar. Though without a following himself and only marginally associated with the freedom struggle, T.T.K. owed his rise to Kamaraj. Venkataraman has also been known as one of Kamaraj's men and it was under the latter that he became minister for industries in Madras.

The word "loyalist" has a special political connotation in the country nowadays. It means one who had stood by Indira Gandhi through thick and thin. Judged by this definition Venkataraman could not be regarded as a loyalist. He was a critic of the emergency and was at the time editor of Swarajya. His editorship, of this weekly paper, founded by Rajaji, itself proclaimed that he did not belong to the same persuasion as Indira Gandhi. It must also be remembered that during the emergency he challenged the censorship regulations before the Madras high court. Later he became a convert to Indira Gandhi. Following the death of Kamaraj

During the official visit to Moscow June 21 to 27, 1983 Defence Minister R. Venkataraman was received by V.V Kuznestsov, Alternate Member of the Politbureau of the CPSU Central Committee, First Vice-President of the Presidium of the USSR Supreme Soviet.

R. Venkatarman with the Soviet Defence MInister Mr. Ustonov, 1983.

he supported the move for the merger of the Tamil Nadu Congress (O) in the Congress led by D.K. Barooah.

On her return to power in 1980 Indira Gandhi included at least two former non-loyalists in her cabinet: Venkataraman and Veerendra Patil. The latter had been a bitter opponent of hers and had unsuccessfully contested the Chikmagalur Lok Sabha election against her. Why did she induct the two, Venkataraman and Patil, into her Government? One must remember, that experienced administrators were hard to come by then—as they are still. Both Venkataraman and Patil were men of proven ability. Venkataraman has had a very distinguished record in Tamil Nadu--he brought that state to the third position on the industrial map of the country. He had also experience in a number of world bodies and had earned the admiration of Kurt Waldheim.

A warm welcome was accorded to Venkataraman as the new Chairman of the Rajya Sabha by all sections of the House on January 19, 1985.

Prime Minister Rajiv Gandhi led the members in expressing the hope that he would live up to the "distinguished tradition" set by persons like Dr. S. Radhakrishnan and with his dignity and sense of humour would maintain the high standard which the Upper House needed. He looked forward to cooperation with the Opposition anti the Chairman.

Others who welcomed the Chairman included Dipen Ghosh (C.P.M) M.S. Gurupadaswamy (Janata), Jaswant Singh (B.J.P.), Virendra Verma (D.M.K.P.), Chaturanan Mishra (C.P.I.), P. Upendra (Telugu Desam), Mursali Maran (D.M.K.), S.W. Dhabe (Cong-S) and Ghulam Rasool Matto (N.C.F.).

Responding to their sentiments. Venkataraman said he was aware of the tradition set by persons like Dr. Zakir Hussain and Dr. S. Radhakrishnan and would endeavour to walk in their footsteps.

He said that India was one of the biggest democracies, but it was not enough to be the biggest in size. It had to be so in quality and it was possible only if the members maintained a very high standard of deliberations.

He appreciated their anxiety for restoration of the pristine glory by the House and said he looked forward to a fruitful and pleasant association with them.

Rajiv Gandhi introduced his Cabinet colleagues to the members of the Rajya Sabha.

As Rajiv Gandhi called out the names of his colleagues, they rose and bowed to the Chairman and members.

Members from the ruling party as well as the opposition welcomed them with loud cheers, thumping their desks.

The Vice-Presidency of India is one of those positions which become what the incumbent makes of them. Venkataraman, on being elected to this office, had the obligation to make of the position what several of his predecessors done undone. The first incumbent of this post was Dr. S. Radhakrishnan, and he created by his duct a tradition which honours Indian democracy. His example was followed by such illustrious names as Dr. Zakir Husain and V.V. Giri, B.D. Jatti, though not in the same mould, came out with distinction from the ordeal of working with a Janata Government (1977-80) divided against itself. Venkataraman came to the Vice-Presidency with rich political experience and with a record which was enviably free of blemishes and scars. An additional asset is that he has, in his long political career, created many friends and hardly any enemy that one knows of.

Despite the popular impression of an innocuous office, the Vice-Presidency carries with it solemn responsibilities. The routine of course is to preside over the Rajya Sabha, a job which is not a bed of roses even in the best of times. But there are several non-routine chores which require shouldering heavy responsibilities and taking difficult decisions. When and if, an incumbent President of India resigns, he does so "by writing under his hand addressed to the Vice-President". Venkataraman was eminently qualified by temperament, experience and ability to discharge his duties as a Vice-President. It was appropriate that he adorned the position of Vice-President after doing with distinction two of the most difficult jobs in India managing the nation's finances, and then handling its defence. Venkataraman succeeded M. Hidayatullah an outstanding jurist who combined scholarship with judicious wisdom as the Vice-President and as the Chairman of the Rajya Sabha.

Though Venkataraman was as successful in Defence as he had been earlier in Finance, his choice as Vice-President came as no surprise. He was already 74. His eyesight was poor and he expressed a desire to retire from politics. The offer of Vice-President was a fitting reward for the services he had rendered. But there could be another reason why he was being kicked up. He had been albowed out of Tamil Nadu politics by the Moopanar group which enjoyed the backing of Indira Gandhi and Rajiv and his elevation to a non-political office was considered convenient.

In spite of the token fight that the opposition parties were giving him, Venkataraman's choice was the best that they could have expected. He knew parliamentary procedure was well versed in law and was a genial person whose friendships transcend political barriers. When Annadorai became the Tamil Nadu chief minister he wanted to have him as chairman of the State Planning Board. Chief Minister M.G. Ramachandran had written a letter to the prime minister recommending his elevation to the presidentship. He was one of the few ministers in the cabinet who was regular visitor to the Central Hall and his informal coffee club attracted both MPs and journalists alike. The latter had a soft corner for him. As a member of the Working Journalists' Wage Board he delayed his joining the Tamil Nadu government in 1957 as a minister as the report of the Wage Board was not ready.

Venkataraman is a lawyer by profession but he hardly measured up to those legal luminaries of Madras who go by the name of "Mylapore lawyers." Though not aggressive by temperament he has been a very successful trade unionist. Indeed he should be an example to today's labour leaders who do not know the art of negotiation. He is conversant with Marxism but the communist philosophy has little appeal for him.

The Vice-President is also chairman or the presiding officer of the Rajya Sabha and Venkataraman performed this task with exemplary patience, tact and skill. With his personal attributes of reasonableness and maturity he made an excellent moderator between warring groups of legislators. He established a reputation for fair play and political even-handedness, the two qualities, for most non-congress parties should find attractive. It would be a tall order for the opposition parties to come up with a candidate who can match Venkataraman's appeal. Few politicians can be said be to free from blemish, but he has never been associated with any controversy to reflect discredit on his character.

Like Caeser's wife those holding the office of the President and Vice-President, should be above suspicion. Venkataraman after his election to the office of the President of the Republic had made it clear that though he was dedicated Congress man he would remain above partisan politics while holding this august office.

Some questions were raised whether the then Vice-President Venkataraman had adhered to the spirit of this well established convention. It was alleged that following the rift between Tamil film star Sivaji Ganeshan and the Congress (I) strongman G.K. Moopnar over allocations, of party tickets, Venkataraman, who is close to Sivaji Ganeshan is reported to have played a mediator's role to bring him round. Venkataraman promptly denied the insinuation but used unconventional means to do so. It appears that instead of using the official machinery for calling the press conference, the task was left to a Congress (I) member of the Rajya Sabha. Vishwa Bandhu Gupta who sent a list of correspondent to be invited for the press conference.[5]

Even otherwise there is world of difference between the style of functioning of Venkataraman and his predecessor M. Hidayatullah. Hidayatullah had come from the judiciary and was somewhat reserved. Venkataraman being a dyed in the wool politician is more outgoing. One of the announcements that he made soon after his election was that he would keep his "coffee club" going. It was his practice as a minister to visit the central hall of Parliament from time to time whether the Lok Sabha was in session or not and invite Members of Parliament and media men to have a cup of coffee, he was not very communicative about news but a storehouse of Parliamentary lore.

Vice-President Venkataraman, on [September 2, 1984 said the Indian Air Force was second to none in the world and it could boast of possessing the Jaguars, Miraj and advanced version of the MIG—three very effective instruments—which no other country does.

Laying the foundation stone for the Air Force golden jubilee auditorium in New Delhi, his first public function after he assumed office of Vice-President, Venkataraman said the Indian Air Force had a glorious record of service and a bright future.

He said the performance of the Air Force at Hindon during the golden jubilee celebrations displayed its extraordinary capacity and ability.

Venkataraman, who was defence minister before he was elected to the second highest office in the country, said the record of the Air Force during 1965 and 1971 war should be written in letters of gold.

He said when he hesitantly approached Prime Minister Indira Gandhi, for grants she had generously given Rs. 54 lakh for the auditorium.

The then Defence Minister S.B. Chavan, said with the induction of sophisticated arms in the country's neighbourhood and in the Indian ocean, there was no alternative for the Air Force but to equip itself with the most modern aircraft and weapon system.

Chavan said the Air Force was the youngest and most modern among the three services and for such a modern force a modern auditorium was necessary here for delibrations on updating its technology. In this context he said Venkataraman had suggested a permanent asset in connection with the golden jubilee celebrations on November 27, 1982.

Vice-President Venkataraman had a special word of praise for the Air Chief Marshal Dilbagh Singh who, he said, had a distinguished career for 40 years, only ten years less than the age of Air Force itself. The Air Chief Marshal Dilbagh Singh brought in a lot of innovations, he said and added that he was sure this tradition would be carried forward.

Speaking about the auditorium Venkataraman said as Defence Minister he thought there should be something as a "permanent remembrance" of the golden jubilee celebrations. He preferred an auditorium to medals which he said would "disappear" in the course of time.

Vice-President Venkataraman, said on September 7, 1984 that politicians should strive to become statesmen so that they could serve the nation better.

"A politician is one who thinks of the next election and a statesman is one who thinks of the next generation", he said while replying to a felicitation by the citizens committee in Madras on his election to the august office.

Calling for a national spirit and pride. Venkataraman said it should be instilled at a very early stage in life. Children should be educated on the strengths and weaknesses of the country and made to feel proud about the country's cultural heritage as well as its standing in the comity of nations and the role it was playing.

Venkataraman said although India was ranked 10th in the world for GNP, the impression was India was a poor and weak nation.

Venkataraman said India was a nation to reckon with and people should stop denigrating it as poor and weak. "If we pool our strength and intelligence, we may emerge as a stronger nation with a much better international respect" he said.

The Vice-President commended the role played by India in the non-aligned movement which, he said, had prevented a third world war against the background of superpower rivalry.

Venkataraman said he felt like a "prisoner" as his new post imposed several curbs on his movements and speeches.

Opening the institution of the Rs. 35,000 Dr MGR education-cum-art endowment at the Madras University, he said the gag on indulging in politics posed problems for him as he had been a politician for several decades.

"I feel like a prisoner. I am not free to go anywhere I want to", he said. Protocol had to be followed and security ensured. "If I want to visit a friend, the security officer earlier inspects the house", he added.

Though he should not comment on the Tamil Nadu Chief

Minister, he would not be prevented from calling "a good person as good", Venkataraman said.

Tamil Nadu Chief Minister M.G. Ramachandran described Venkataraman as a "true statesman", belonging to the rare breed of politicians who did not hanker after positions. "We should thank Mrs. Indira Gandhi for selecting him to the high post", he said.

C. Subramaniam, the former Union Minister, hoped that a new chapter would begin in the Rajya Sabha under his stewardship as the Chairman.

A voracious reader of books on philosophy, religion and economics among other subjects, he counts photography among his hobbies. A tennis player, Venkataraman has settled for badminton which he plays almost regularly. His interest in the performing arts is known. He helps artists whenever he can. His wife Janaki takes interest in whatever he does. She speaks Hindi fluentily. Her parents were settled in Burma.

Venkataraman's life with his wife Janaki has been a work of love and partnership. At this age she is not at all a retiring woman. He speaks of her with admiration.

It is characteristic of Venkataraman, that newshounds have not bothered to find out what his background, his family or his achievements have been. He is almost faceless, placid by temperament with a low profile approach to life and politics, and looks like a plodder. But in fact he is not.[6]

Venkataraman believes in a simple life-style. Anyone who is honest must need do so. Even so, it has not been all plain sailing for him. He has had his share of tragedy. Venkataraman lost his son when he was only seventeen. He has three daughters, one of them living in Kanpur, Uttar Pradesh where her husband is a professor with Indian Institute of Technology, and two who are residing in foreign lands.

Despite his busy schedule he found time to pursue his hobbies i.e. tennis, photography and music, especially classical.

REFERENCES

1. R. Rangarajan. VR no victim of inebriety of power. *Patriot* 6 August 1984 ; 5.
2. Hugh and Colleen Gantzer. Timeless Thanjavur. *Indian Express* (New Delhi) 12 April 1980.
3. *Ibid.*
4. *Ibid.*
5. See *Free Press Journal* (Bombay) 30 December, 1984.
6. C.P. Ramachandran. He will be in his element. *Hindustan Times* 2 September 1984.

2

THE SOCIALIST : PATRIOTISM AND NATIONALISM

Venkataraman is great, as a lawyer, as a politician and patriot, but more so as a man. For everyone who came to contact with him acknowledged his inimitable superiority. He is a veritable king among men and his leadership is supreme in its strength. He is a man of courage, daring faithfulness and loyalty. He remained a clean administrator for this even his opponents admired him.

Venkataraman really is amongst the finest products of the great upsurge which overwhelmed the nation with the entry of Mahatma Gandhi and Jawaharlal Nehru on the scene. He has literally grown with the Congress Party to which he has contributed his heart and soul. Ideologically as well, he has matured with the maturity of Congress Socialist policies and programmes under Nehru's great leadership saw its full flowering with the acceptance of the socialist objective at Avadi Congress in 1955.

Socialism is no longer an issue but definite policy which we have chosen in the context of our undeveloped economy. Then also, it is not a mere economic doctrine with us but a moral compulsion to enforce certain human values which we have learnt to cherish. Indeed, in the economic doctrine of equitable distribution of national product is also the pursuit of human values like social justice, love and co-operation without which the augmentation of production, which is also our aim, will mean nothing. As a means to achieve socialism we have not only been aiming at greater production so that people might share the increasing prosperity of the land, but also at elimination of great concentrations of wealth leading to exploitation and the abolition of economic disparities. These aims form the nucleus of social justice which we want to achieve. Therefore, to think socialism is meant only to bring about an equitable distribution of national wealth, or is only a process of economic levelling up by the State assuming control of all productive sources or resources is wrong.

This would no doubt involve an upsetting of the structure of society as it has been existing for centuries. But centuries of habit should be broken if a new society has to be set up where the economic and human factors have to play a just and fair role so that we might build up a new nation where the stronger sections are not allowed to exploit and suppress the weaker sections. No doubt, the building up of a nation where social justice should prevail is a stupendous job, considering the vast vested interest and long-standing customs and conservative thoughts which dominate the social set-up. But in the interests of the large majority this has to be done.

We cannot, however, build up this society by force or violent means. We have chosen the democratic method by which we want to bring about this salutary revolution. Therefore, we have to educate our party men whose minds are still not steeped in the Socialist ideal and are still haunted by a large amount of vagueness. No democracy can thrive on ignorance.

Socialism which, from the Second Five Year Plan onwards, has been proclaimed to be our long-term objective, and which did not find a place in the draft of the old Sixth Plan has been brought back and given a prominent place in the opening sentence itself. It is affirmed that in the decade of the eighties 'our major goal should be the realisation of an economic and social order based on principles of socialism, secularism and self-reliance."

But the socialism of the eighties is to be different from the socialism of the fifties and early sixties. A quarter of a century ago we thought that the route to socialism was via controls, public sector enterprises and nationalisation. The novel feature of the Framework of the Sixth Plan is that it has a very different conception of socialism. Socialism to be effective must reach every household in the country, particularly the poorer households asserts the *Framework*.

The section is worth reproducing in full : 'An increase in the productive potential of the economy is an essential condition for finding effective solutions to the problems of poverty. At the same time, recognising the constraints which limit the scope for higher growth rate in the medium-term, more direct means of reducing the incidence of poverty in the stage of transition would have to be employed. It is well known that the hard core of poverty is to be found in rural areas. The poorest sections belong to the families of landless labour, small and marginal farmers, rural artisans, scheduled castes, scheduled tribes and socially and economically backward classes. The household will remain the basic unit of poverty eradication in target group oriented programmes. Families differ in such vital respects as dependency ratios, asset holdings, skills and even the ability to perform manual labour on public works. Hence each household below the poverty line will have to be assisted through an appropriate package of technologies, services and asset transfer programmes"

The country, and particularly Congressmen, must beware of the vested interests of the few privileged rich who were standing as barriers in the way of socialism. Congressman who believed in socialism should keep a constant vigil on these few privileged rich who are out to destroy socialism. Rich people could not relish the ideas that the wealth they had earned so long should be shared with the poorer sections of the people. The vested group believed that it was their birth-right to concentrate all the wealth of the nation in their hands and waste it on shameful luxuries of life when crores of people were still sharing the burden of unending miseries.

The Congress was determined to break through the vicious circle of the rich and bring about true socialism in the country. This could be done by non-violent means taught by Mahatma Gandhi, and not by violence and bloodshed.

Patriotism and love of one's own country are universal virtues. Nationalism, in fact, has been an impelling motive and compulsive force that has led to movements for freedom from colonial rule and emergence of independent sovereign countries. Nationalism is in every sense a healthy growth and a natural one, especially, in countries that are under foreign yoke. No wonder nationalist forces, dominated the Indian sea during the British regime. Any nation that has a rich tradition and sense of self-respect and commendable goals, will be wholly nationalistic in out-look and patriotic fervour colours all its activities. Nationalism is thus a healthy vital force in countries striving for liberation. But this does not mean that the intensity and vigour of nationalism, in its true meaning loses its intensity, when a country becomes free and independent. It is not a feeling on an urge that can be switched on or off at one's will, a nationalist remains a nationalist all through. Every true citizen cherishes his country's traditions and realizes his country's problems social economic and political. In this sense, therefore, nationalism never becomes an oboslete concept it is a persistent quality. Eternal Vigilance is the price of liberty. But several people associate nationalism with a narrow outlook, limited vision and petty mindedness, that is unpardonable. The advocates of broad vision of a sense of university and of the extension of outlook beyond the country's frontiers assert that there is a conflict between nationalism and internationalism.[1]

Internationalism implies a broader approach and a universal out-look. There is no denying the fact that the world today is essentially international. An internationalist is a person, who advocates community of interests and friendly co-operation between nations, internationalism implies the spread and advocacy of such friendly co-operation. Once Jawahar Lal

Nehru said, if we want to know something about the story of the world, we must think of all countries and all the people that have inhabited it and not merely of one country where we have been born.

Of course, all Indians have to live and work in this country barring a few but we have to remember that we belong to the larger family of the world. In a sense, people living in other countries are not total aliens but our cousins. It is the duty of every person, having true feeling of nationalism to strive for the happiness of all the people and make the world a happier place to live in. Seen in this light there can be no conflict between nationalism and in internationalism, between one country and the world. The question is not other the nation or the world, rather it is how to serve the world by serving the nation. The belief that nationalism dictates isolation from the rest of the world is absolutely unwarranted. One can be a good and true nationalist. There is no conflict or incompatibility involved. This is particularly evident in a progressive civilization, in which the latest technological changes, have created a new kind of interdependence among nations.

The people of the world have been brought much closer by the modern means of communication the mass media, especially through radio and television.. As a result, practicably the whole mankind must be regarded as one unit economically, technically and even politically. In the new era of global village through the radio, nothing less than a fuller and friendlier understanding between man and man will make the task of building a new society a practical proposition. The latest inventions in communication promote internationalism and facilitiate the unity of mankind and hence the promotion of internationalism through closer contracts virtually eliminates physical distance. The people of various distant countries and for long period inaccessible regions have been brought together and are coming nearer in respect of time and space. No country is an island in itself events in one country have their repercussions in others like ripples and waves in rivers and seas. In a global village international organisations devoted to mass communication will of course, have to prepare grounds for an atmosphere of friendly co-operation and healthy under-standing among all nations. This is implicit in true internationalism.[2]

In this connection the conception in the minds of those who feel that their country with its traditions and treasures can be preserved by protecting it from all sorts of international contract contacts need to be removed. Internationalism and international contact, diplomatic and economic, always enrich both parties. International organisations are designed to benefit mankind in many ways. Let us take for example the United Nations which is an expression of the will of the people of various continents to find a synthesis between the nations and the world. The organization is an attempt to provide a frame-work through which is possible to serve humanity by serving one's own national cause and simultaneously promote the global interest and strive for a better world. It is also to be borne in mind that prosperity cannot for long be confined to one region. A rich country must realize that neither affluence nor destitution can be confind to a certain people, whatever their stage of advancement. Both prosperity and poverty are divisible and for this internationalism is vital.

It is now recognised that wars can not be limited to a single area. Wars and conflicts have wide repercussions. A nuclear explosion or warfare will destrory a great part of the world and its civilization. It is through internationalism and not through intense exclusive nationalism that wars and conflicts can be avoided. Destruction may be global in a terrific way just as constructive measures and policies can be highly beneficial to entire humanity. Strong dynamic states can co-exist with others which are equally strong and dynamic, so long as there is no aggression or militancy. Internationalism promotes such peace and seeks to avoid conflicts of any kind social economical or political or militaristic. Again inter-nationalism must from the basis of world organisation, if civili-zation is to be saved just as mutual tolerance can help resolve internal discord and differences, similarly, internationalism can resolve all sorts of international misunderstandings.[3]

Socialism itself will reach its true dimensions and achieve its principal goals when strictly national, selfish and narrow policies give way to broader views and a greater understanding as befits civilized human beings. If man cannot live all by himself and must live in society for various reasons, nations also must live in associations for various reasons with other nations.

A tremendous task awaits us. We have to devote ourselves to fulfil our development plans which alone will bring plenty and prosperity to our country and root out poverty which has been the curse of our country. Ignorance, ill-health, inequality which have haunted our people and made us backward should be wiped out. The freedom and integrity of our country have been threatened and we have to defend them. We have also to defend overselves against internal schisms which impede the building up of our nation. Problems that face us are enormous and innumerable. Let us take a solemn and firm pledge that we will fight these problems in a spirit of crusading zeal, and remember that we will not be forgiven by posterity if we do not at this juncture in the life of the nation act unitedly and steadfastly to march forward in realizing our objective of a Democratic Socialist Society.

REFERENCES

1. Shyama Charan. Nationalism and Internationalism. *Indian Nation* (Patna) 1 December 1986 ; p. 4.
2. *Ibid.*
3. *Ibid.*

3

THE UNIVERSAL BROTHERHOOD

It is difficult to docket, Venkataraman and brand him in respect of isms. But perhaps he can he said to be somewhat left of Centre. He started out as a trade union worker at the behest of Kamaraj, his mentor, Venkataraman is a Brahmin and Kamaraj was not. Also, for long years, Venkataraman had a *Harijan* for his secretary. Deeply religious Venkataraman is a follower of Shankaracharya but he is not orthodox. He received the title of *Sat Seva Ratna* from Shankaracharya. Religion to him is philosophy. It is also conscience and humanity. In it there is no place for hatred of fellow human beings, but only of evil. On June 14, 1987 when the announcement of his candidature for Presidentship was published it was open to house at No. 6 Maulana Azad Road, New Delhi. But he was not open to granting interviews to the Press, not even to members of his old "coffee club" who used to sit anound with him in Central Hall when he was Minister of Finance and whose coffee bills were paid for by him. We urged him to talk but he refused to be persuaded saying he was as yet only a candidate. He had not been elected. His reply was quite in character for he is a person with a high sense of propriety. And that brings us to the crucial question : What sort of a President will he make ? "You will be taking over at a difficult time" we remarked. But Venkataraman reminded us again "I have not been elected so far."[1]

Kanchipuram for the spiritually minded, it is well-known as the temple town of Tamil Nadu. This is in recognition of the innumerable temples dotting the town dedicated to Shiva, Shakti and Vishnu as also the other Gods of the Hindu pantheon. But to one and all belonging to various parts of India and of distant lands in Europe and Asia, Kanchipuram is known for the rare—personality the Paramacharya of Kanchi Kamakoti, divine and yet human, whose ministering grace is universal in its sweep, and whose concern is for all. And by combining religious authority with reformist zeal, he has endeared himself to countless devotees, Indian and foreign alike.

Frail of body and frugal with food, many marvel at his ceaseless activities for the spiritual upliftment of people through inner awakening. This marvel becomes all the greater when it is realised that this great crusader celebrated his 94th birthday on May 20, 1987.

Indeed it can well and truly be said that age has not in the least lessened his round-the-clock spiritual ministrations. For the past eight decades His Holiness Sri Chandrasekharendra Saraswathi, the Paramacharya of Kanchi Kamakoti Peetham, has been pursuing the noble mission started by Adi Shankaracharya and carried on by an unbroken line of successors since 400 B.C.

At the ancient Kanchi Matam building, located amidst the crowded market centre of the city, people from all walks of life and clime can be seen flocking to His Holiness from dawn to midnight to seek his guidance as well as blessings, on matters spiritual as also temporal.

But he says modestly : "There is nothing to feel elated about people seeking my blessings, even in regard to everday problems." Explains the Paramacharya : "When I reflect that it is worship of God, who, these people think is approached through me, I feel glad there are so many who believe in a compassionate God. Far from bothering, it cheers me. Far from weakening me, as many mistakenly feel, it is my source of strength."

Such adoration over the decades has yielded remarkable results all over India. It was the result of his constant *pada yatra* (walking on feet) throughout the length and breadth of the country though of late failing eyesight has restricted his activities to Kanchi city.

Scores of new temples and prayer halls have been erected in Maharashtra and other States where none existed before. And old temples, remaining neglected and uncared for were renovated on the Paramacharya's initiative.

More important he constantly encouraged the launching of special programmes to attend to the sick and disabled, and for the promotion of universal welfare.

The enduring message behind such beneficial actions is that religion is the basis of Hindu culture, Spirituality is its backbone. Sculpture and dancing, regarded elsewhere as secular arts are considered as sacred in India. And the temple is the centre of ancient arts and crafts. Architecture, sculpture and inconography go into the building of temples and the making of images.

Such tireless activity at 94 is a remarkable achivement indeed for the 68th pontiff of Kamakoti Peetham. And it has been a long way from his very obscure origin as the son of a poor school teacher. Swaminathan, as he was named by his parents, was born in June 1894 in Villupuram, 100 miles from Madras city. His father belonged to the Hoysala Karnataka family which migrated to Tamil Nadu.

Strange as it may seem young Swaminathan had his early education in a mission school. And he was very much admired for his proficiency in the Bible. He was a talented actor too, winning acclaim for his part as Prince Arthur in Shakespeare's King John. He was then in the eighth class.

It was about this time that the unexpected happened. When the 66th Shankaracharya attained *samadhi* (departed for heaven) young Swaminathan's maternal cousin was installed as the pontiff. He was the only son of the family.

Therefore, Swaminathan and his parents travelled to Kanchipuram to console the mother of the boy. As it happened, the newly installed pontiff suffered a fatal stroke. And to the surprise of all, Swaminathan was selected as the 68th pontiff. It was on February 13, 1907. He was barely 13.

What he lacked in normal scholastic preparation, the 68th pontiff made up for with special courses in classical and modern thought and constant travel to meet his counterparts in other religions. It was learning by *pada yatra* as did the Adi Shankaracharya long, long ago. There have been numerous incidents that highlighted the unique qualities of His Holiness Sri Chandrasekharenda Saraswathi.

In one village, among the people who saw the Acharya off were some Muslims also. But one of them followed the party, touching the Sankaracharya's palanquin with his hands as a mark of respect. After some distance, the Acharya stopped and talked to the Muslim devotee. He placed before the saint some personal problems for advice. When taking leave, he told others : To my eyes, the Shankaracharya appears as the embodiment of *Allah* (the Almighty God) himself !

The pontiff's intense nationalism was equally obvious as far back as the 1920s. Quietly, he switched to wearing *khadi* right from the days of Mahatma Gandhi's call to boycott foreign cloth. He missed no opportunity to meet ardent patriots. Prominent among these were Chittaranjan Das, Seth Jamnalal Bajaj, Rajaji and Satyamurthy.

An interesting incident is worth recalling in this context. Once Rajaji accompained Jamnalal Bajaj, but stayed away from the meeting. The Acharya sent for Rajaji and enquired why. When Rajaji explained that he had not bathed yet, the Acharya told him that those who were engaged in national work might not find the necessary time for the daily bath ; that Rajaji who had dedicated his life for the service of the nation was at liberty to meet all religious heads at any time and in any condition.

Much later, when the Shankaracharya met Mahatma Gandhi late in 1927 in Palghat, the two conferred in a cattle shed in the Acharya's camp. The Acharya sat on the floor and spoke in Sanskrit. The Mahatma replied in Hindi.

The meeting scheduled for half-an-houı went on and on. When the secretary reminded Gandhi that he was missing his evening meal, the Mahatma declared : The conversation I am having with the Shankaracharya is my evening meal for today.

Not just prominent people but the lowly animal too was respected by the Paramacharya. While touring, on a hot day as the water flowed in droplets during the guru's *anushthana* (master's body) down the slopes behind his seat, a thirsty dog tried to quench its thirst by licking the drops, enraged at this, one of the followers picked a stone and hit the dog. Without waiting for any explanation, he told his disciples : *Ahimsa* (non-violence) the greatest of virtues and there is no greater charitable gift than food and water to the hungry and thirsty. The soul of the body of a dog and in any human frame are one and the same. It will be good if whoever hit the dog can take a little water in wooden plate used for my *anushthana* locate the dog and place the water before the creature to drink.

Recently, an incident that attracted countrywide attention also highlights the Shankaracharya's universal outlook. The Samprokshanam on March 25, 1987 of the 236-foot tallest temple tower at Srirangam in south India.

It was while visiting Srirangam in the sixties, that the Kanchi Paramacharya lamented at the incomplete gopuram that had stayed so for decades and invoked the blessing of Lord Ranganatha to identify a builder for completing the gopuram.

After a few days of this prayer, the Jeer of the Ahobila Mutt, His Holiness Srimad Azhagiasingar, declared publicly he had a dream in which Lord Ranganatha ordained him (the Jeer) to proceed from his base at Andhra Pradesh to Srirangam and take up the construction work of the incomplete temple tower and make it the grand Rajagopuram.

The capacity to quietly inspire great deeds is the secret of the Paramacharya's physical strength at 94.

For the music lovers, the 94th birthday observance was of special significance. The Acharya's premier disciple, Madam M. S. Subbalakshmi recorded three special cassettes—one of Tamil Patriot Bharati's inspiring songs the second in Hindi of Surdas, and the third in Sanskrit on Shankaracharya. And the sale proceeds went to *Shankaracharya Netralaya* (eyes hospital) for treatment of the poor.

The conduct of men, particularly in respect of their religious fervour, has been divided into three categories. Some men who are absolutely unconcerned about the need to arrange their activities properly and in a disciplined manner, are compared to pebbles in a well, which get dry the moment they are thrown on the surface. The second type of men are likened to dolls stuffed with cotton which when dipped in water get bloated and when dry, resume their original form. These men may assimilate scriputral knowledge when taught but may relapse into the humdrum life after a time. The third classification is like camphor which shoots into flames in the very presence of a lighted matchstick. Man should start the process of God-realisation with self-introspection. This will lead him to develop desirelessness and detachment. With these two traits, he can face problems and get over the problems of life. He should conduct himself like a bee that collects honey very carefully from the lillies in the pond. The frog that remains in the water may not know the flowers' usefulness or their fragrance.

Swami Ramakrishna has referred to the attitude that a man has to cultivate—threat a gold coin and a potsherd alike. Lure of the lucre or of lust should not disturb him. One who wants to reach the goal of salvation should not hate any religion. A person can reach the first floor of his house either by climbing the steps or by using a rope or through an escalator. God too can be approached in different ways. Religion is like the cotton inside a pillow ; only the covers are changed. Each can pursue his religion but God is one ; this is the catholic outlook of Hinduism where there is no scope for hatred. The man who entrusts himself to God can go about his duties without any hindrance even as a temporary visitor to a city keeps his luggage in safe custody in a cloakroom before his sight-seeing trip. "Do your duty sincerely but never presume that you have done it. Remember the unseen guidance of God", were the words of the Saint.

Religion is becoming a terror in India. At least, the way it is understood and practised, is, while everyone—leader, preacher, teacher and layman—depicts religion as a binding force, in fact it is proving a blinding one. Far from providing the healing touch, it is making its partisans bloodthirsty, literally. It consumed the Father of the Nation, Mahatma Gandhi, whose killer thought the Mahatma was benefiting a country that professed another faith. It devoured Indira Gandhi, who fell to the bullets of religious fanatics. It killed unknown numbers in Punjab, is striking Bihar, Meerut, Delhi, is killing unknown numbers in Punjab, is striking innocent men and women in the skies, in streets, houses, buses, everwhere. It bids fair to disintegrate the nation.

In the pre-independence years we blamed the colonial ruling power for the Hindu-Muslim disturbances. That was the foreign hand right inside our borders. Now we still blame a foreign hand (or more than one of the same), not publicly identified, masterminding the operations from outside. But are we so helpless that we cannot take care of so vital an aspect of our polity ? In all the years since we got scent of the foreign hand, have we not been able to think of a counter to its depredations on our own home grounds ? The time has come when, foreign hand or no, we need to concern ourselves with the handiwork of our own native hands and find out what they are up to.

In a way the formal declaration of India as a secular state and the constant emphasis laid on this aspect has had an effect not entirely beneficial to the polity. It has tended to create a cycle of minority hopes, majority resistance, minority distrust and majority resentment, taking the system in a direction other than the one intended by the Constitution makers. It has led to an atmosphere of suspicion, rivalry and even bitterness in place of the mutual confidence and camaraderie that was visualised. The mistake was to make such great play of the secular element, which should have been left to strike spontaneous roots and to grow naturally without hothouse aids.

With the result that every act, big or small, is viewed with tinted glasses. If some Muslims wish to rejoice over Pakistan's victories at cricket by bursting crackers, let them. Hindus also do (as well as some Muslims) not only when India wins a match but when it "saves" one. Some Muslims are among the "mourners" when India loses. The entire exercise is absurd. But let both explode crackers if they must, just so long as they do not explode bombs and do not shed blood.

The majority community has the major share of responsibility for keeping the peace. It should not be easily provoked into a throwback to fundamentalism and let it guide its behaviour. It is a curious thing that as we race into the 21st century, hi-tech and religion too are staging their own race, with places of worship keeping pace with industrial and nuclear their own race, with places of worship keeping pace with industrial and nuclear plants. Worship of God is becoming increasingly exhibitionist. But Gandhi told us God resides in man.

According to Venkataraman, "Service of our weaker brethren is service of God." It might do us all a great deal of good to confine religion to our shrines or our homes or, best of all, to our hearts. The temples, mosques, churches and other places of worship so released could shelter millions of houseless people—Hindus, Muslims, Christians and others alike. Even God might be pleased as he would be relieved of a part of his responsibility to mankind. True religion is humanity. And humanity is the god-head.

REFERENCES

1. Promila Kalhan *op. cit.*

4

THE FRATERNITY

Defence Minister R. Venkataraman assumed office as the nation's seventh Vice-President on August 31, 1984 for a five-year term. He succeeded M. Hidayatullah.

Venkataraman, who was elevated to the Vice-Presidency on August 22 as a Congress (I) candidate, took his oath in English. President Zail Singh administered the oath to him at a formal ceremony at Rashtrapati Bhawan. The Prime Minister Indira Gandhi, central ministers, the three service chiefs and senior officials were present at the brief ceremony. Hidayatullah, accompanied by his wife, was also present.

Later, Venkataraman said he would work for communal harmony and national integration. He hoped he would get maximum co-operation in this task from the opposition.

On general issues facing the country, Venkataraman was quite forthcoming. Optimism ran through his replies to questions such as growth of regionalism and communalism as a threat to the country's unity and integrity. All such developments, according to him, were indicative of the fact that the country was still growing.

Communalism has become what it is, in the various parts of the country, not because of threats from one religion to another. The communal hysteria is whipped up over small incidents with which the vast majority of our people is not concerned. Small groups that fan communalism are the conscious, or may be unwitting, tools of reactionary political opportunists who would not want to see India, free and united, marching towards the goal of socialism. Such groups become powerful only when they succeed in misleading the common people with sectarian slogans. The majority of our people knows that its economic and political progress depends on the growth of a united India. This majority is also convinced that a truly united India can be built only on the foundation of secularism : communal divisions help only those who want to stall the country's march towards progress and a new society.

It is unfortunate that no national leader of importance after Mahatma Gandhi, Jawaharlal Nehru and Indira Gandhi considered it necessary to awaken the Indian people to face this challenge, though Prime Minister Rajiv Gandhi has been countering the rise of communalism. But can an individual single-handed kill the menace ? Had progressive political parties realised the mischievous role that communal forces of the various types have been playing, reaction would not have been able to spread itself the way it has. What is important is a concerted effort to warn the people against the virus of communalism.

Ours is a country steeped in religious traditions and customs. The old and original religion of Indians, is Hinduism which is more a way of life than an organised religion. It is a conglomeration of diverse faiths with no single prophet as a source but has a number of renovators along its long path of history. The evolution has made Hinduism quite flexible to accommodate diverse, and often contradictory faiths. But this does not mean that Hinduism has no fanatic groups. In fact, Hindu communalism has been the major roadblock in the way of India's progress and resurgence into modernity. Though India had sizeable populations of other communities like Muslims, Christians, Buddhists, Jains etc., only a section of Muslims had been politicalised to communal dimensions. Communal politics brought about the split of the Indian nation. But the major part of the subcontinent that emerged as India after partition was a secular state, unlike the other part declared as the Islamic Republic of Pakistan. Independent India was no Hindustan in the literal meaning of the term ; it now has more Muslims than in Pakistan. Here political power did not go into the hands of communal leaders. The national leaders of India did not put religions before the nation. India's first Prime Minister, Jawaharlal Nehru, was an agnostic, if not an atheist.

The Indian Constitution declared India a sovereign democratic state with secularism as its mainstay. Religious freedom found a place in the Fundamental Rights. But the clause of "Right to Freedom of Religion" in the Constitution is more to curb the undesirable activities in the name of religion than to promote religion : "subject to public order, morality and health and to the other provisions of this part, all persons are equally entitled to freedom of conscience and the right freely to profess, practise and propagate religion."[1]

However, like all freedoms, religious freedom too could deteriorate into communal licence. This paves the way to violence, religious riots, separatism and even disintegration of a nation. It is the duty of the secular forces and Government to see that the communication of different communities does not gain ground.

Communal forces, which had been held back by the united strength of secular and nationalist forces in Tamil Nadu since Independence, have of late begun to rear their ugly heads over the horizon. The aim is clearly to divide the people on communal lines with a view of crippling the State's development, which has registered an uneasy deterioration during the last two decades. Admittedly, these forces have achieved considerable success in this direction. The conclusion of any unprejudiced political observer, after the undivided DMK takeover from the Congress in 1967, is that communal forces have found favourable conditions for their growth and statewide subversive activities. Which took a serious turn with the Janata conglomeration assuming power at the Centre in 1977. Notwithstanding their statements to the contrary, as also their pious resolutions against the mushrooming communal forces, the Dravidian parties, namely Dravida Kazhagam, Dravida Munnetra Kazhagam and the All-India Anna Dravida Munnetra Kazhagam have overtly, or covertly, helped them revive and preserve their feudal practices and customs. All three parties may have changed their politico-organisational and teactical strategy, but their ideology, inherited from the Justice Party of the erstwhile Maharajas and landlords, remains unaltered. The activities, of front line organisations, like Tamil Nadu Hindu Front, Hindu Unity Centre, Hindu Temple Protection Committee, Hindu People's Divine Rule Association were co-ordinated by the RSS, and the Viswa Hindu Parishad. Organisations with overseas connections; like the ISKCON and the Anand Marg, also set up their district units and city branches.[2]

Any country which has got a heterogenous character by way of religion or language is bound to have problems arising out of intolerance. The economically advanced countries and the nascent republics of Asia and Africa have faced this problem some time or the other in the last few decades. India is no exception. But our problems are on a much larger scale and more complex. We have a vast terrain, a massive population and an astounding variety of languages, dialects, castes and creeds, rituals and observances over all of which lie a thick pall of obscurantism and, in many cases, the dust-sheets of colonial rule.

In the advanced countries, the threat to nation's security may often have their origins in fiscal motives of unlawful and criminal organisations like the Mafia. The efforts to put them down will be in the form of day-to-day, fire-fighting operations like quelling of mob violence or tracking down and liquidating the criminals.

Our problems are entirely different from this. The experience is that the inroads into the national edifice are made by well-motivated groups who often act not for money but for a cause which they unfortunately think is a noble one. The hands and brains behind such motives may not necessarily be 'criminal'. On the contrary, they must have worked up enough mass support for their misguided and quixotic ventures.

In tracking them down the Government has to see that not only criminal activity be stopped but the gullible crowd of followers have to be weaned away without the stigma of violence and anti-social work staining them forever. The is vital for a country like India, where all the programmes of economic development have people's participation as the mainstay.

The concern for communal harmony expressed by Venkataraman has to be appreciated in the context of recent events in Uttar Pradesh, Kashmir, Gujarat, Bihar, Punjab etc. The prevailing situation in Punjab and the Bihar killings need strong condemnation. Though the opposition members in thc Parliament supported the appeal for harmony, they wanted the Union Government to take the initiative. But it should not be forgotten that if communal peace is to be ensured all political parties, including the ruling party, have to abide by a code of conduct. Communal clashes generally take place on account of non-issues. Rumour-mongers and vested interests cash in on them by fisning in troubled waters. The police can help to an extent. Whether the police is trained to perform this role is a subject which needs an in-depth study. Sometimes the failure on the part of the police is responsible for aggravating the situation. Mere transfers of key officers do not help. What is needed is a complete reorientation. The growth of different '*senas*' in the Hindi-speaking belt is fraught with danger. These '*senas*' are causing much hatred between the local communities. The standing committe of the National Integration Council should meet once in a month to formulate plans for harmony.

If Meerut is a pointer to the ugly trends that are surfacing again, the Bihar killings are a reminder of what can happen if castism is not curbed and socio-economic measures are not taken to root out violence. Those who till the land cannot be treated as bonded labour. These who acquire fortunes by engaging firm hands as slaves create conditions which lead to violence. The Bihar Government has to go deeper into the causes of the recent clashes and find a solution which will be of a lasting nature. Mere deployment of police will not help solve problems with poverty and hunger. The situation in Punjab improving. People are feeling secure. It is conceded that confidence cannot be restored all of a sudden. The process to restore normalcy has just begun. It is necessary that all political parties help in this task.

Communalism, beyond any shadow of doubt, is oating up into the vitals of the nation. Communalism is more harmful than a deadly poison. Poison kills the man who takes it ; communalism spoils generations. Under the spell of communalism we forget all about our material comfort and social progress ; we forget to distinguish good from bad ; we give up sanity and reason and start looking at things with juandiced eyes. The result is disastrous behold.[3]

There are people and politicians who associate patriotism with religion. For Heaven sake, they should never think so to think in this term will among to doing disservice to India. India is a multi-religious country. The Hindus, the Muslims, the Christians, the Sikhs, the Buddhists, the Jains, the Zorestrians etc. etc., live on this holy soil of ours. Patriots are found among all the communities living in India. Unpatriotic elements are also found in all communities living in India. Who are these unpatriotic people in our country ? These unpatriotic people are the black-marketeers, smugglers, hoarders, evaders of Govt. taxes, makers of black money, manufacturers of spurious drugs, traders in human flesh, organisers of caste and communal riots and killers of innocent people. The activities of these categories of people hinder the social development of India ; hence such people are unpatriotic. A patriot is he or she whose activities and thinking promote the social development of the country.[4]

India has all along been preaching non-violence and peace. India has always stood for the principle of peaceful co-existence. Is it not shameful that there is communal riot in the home province of Mahatma Gandhi ? So long the Hindus and the Muslims remain divided, both of them will suffer. The social, economic and political problems of the Hindu and the Muslim masses are almost the same. The Hindus and the Muslims should unitedly fight for bread, for jobs, for clothes, for shelter, for protection of health and for other amenities of life which ensure a decent living.

The Hindus in India are not responsible for the poverty of the Muslims, nor the Muslims in India are responsible for the poverty of the Hindus. It is our socio-economic system which is responsible for the poverty of the Hindus and the Muslims and the rest. The need, therefore, is to change this socio-economic system and fight unitedly foı the re-distribution of the wealth in India among the people of India.[5]

REFERENCES

1. K. Kunju Religious freedom and Communal licence. *People's Comment* (New Delhi) 16 May 1987 ; p. 22.
2. S. Dorairay. The Cancer of communalism *Link* 19 August 1984 ; p. 25.
3. Akhtar Hussain Aftab. *Fight out* Communalism. *India Nation* (Patna) 19 April 1987 ; p. 4.
4. *Ibid.*
5. *Ibid.*

5

UNITY IN DIVERSITY

India is a vast country, it is as big as the whole of Europe excluding Russia. Its varied and rare beauty is beyond description. The winding rivers, the green fields, the sky-high mountains and the sprawling plains with their veriegated flora and fauna catch the eyes of the on-lookers. On the one hand, the bright multi-coloured flowers with their refreshing fragrance arrest the notice of the common-folk and on the other, the commanding rocks and sands have a special application to the worshippers of nature. There unique varieties are to be found not only in the nature of the land, but also in language, religion and culture. The people are free to embrace any religion they like. Consequently, Hinduism, Islam and Christianity are all thriving without any prejudice to any one. The people are also free to speak their mother-tongue. There are 1100 languages and dialects in India. The people have different cultures with various food habits and clothe style. These distinctions are writ large in almost all regions. But for all these social, cultural and religious contrasts we Indian are one. Unity in diversity has been our rich heritage from ages. We are proud of having our home on such a sacred soil which produced many great personalities like Mahatma Gandhi, Guru Nanak Dev and Khwaja Moinuddin Chisti all apostles of love and peace. They preached the people to live together, making the land an abode of peace and co-existence.[1]

But with the advent of the Britishers our peaceful existence was distrubed, The Britishers made it a point to divide and rule. This was necessary because without this policy their imperialism could not have thrived for such a long-time. The British Government caused to little damage to our age-old fraternity and pristine culture. It trampled upon all our old values and gave a new curve in our life style. We made some progress in science and technology, no doubt, but our line of thin king was changed, altogether. Many anti-national forces sprang up in this abode of peace. They started working against our unity under the mask of rights and demands.

National integration is not national uniformity. National integration is not national unity, which is its consequence. National integration is not only an Indian problem. Inthe Soviet Union, there are as many linguistic states as in India. In the United States, there are more religions and sub-religion s than in India. In Malayisa and Singapore, there are three distinct ethnic groups which we do not have in India. In some individual African countries, like the Cameroons, there are more spoken languages than in all of India. In France till 1962, there were more political parties than we have in India today. Most countries thus face the problem of being a common people, with shared ideals and shared tasks. In a vast country like India, which in the size of its population is surpassed only by China, there are many religions which become the occasion for differences, sometimes violent differences. The Hindu-Muslim riots, the Hindu-Sikh violences are vivid examples. We in India call this communal differences and violence. This is Indian specialism. The term 'communal' comes from the word community; hence in all other countries when the word 'communal' is used, as in communal action or communal meeting or communal decision, the reference is to the people as a community acting or meeting or deciding. Similarly our languages become a source of violent differences, as between Hindi and non-Hindi people between Kannada and Marathi people in the Belgaum areas, between Marathi and Konkanese in Goa and so on. These differences of religion, language, culture or sub-culture, political conviction and affiliation are normal in a vast country, which will be passing the one billion mark in the number of its people as it enters the 21st century. In addition, we have the very special Indian institution of the caste system, which divides the people into various groupings, religious and proto-religious. National integration is a system which will help us maintain our various differences and yet bring us together as a people in a shared purpose, a shared task.[2]

The problem that we face in regard to national integration is that we, as a people, share certain externals, like the National Anthem, Jana Gana Mana, the Tri-colour flag, the Independence Day, Gandhi Jayanti, elections to parliament and state assemblies, etc. But we do not have behind these essential externals, a shared purpose, and an accomplished or accomplishing task.

For me, that shared purpose is to end the dualism in which our country and our people live as rapidly as possible, and become a people who with our many special features of religion, caste, language and cultures are integrated in a common shared life. With our kind of society with its mixed economy, the aim should be to alleviate poverty and keep in check our inequalities so that they do not worsen, (which involves shifts in Perspective Plan priorities) so that we can establish close and growing links between the two groups—the poor and the non-poor. I believe that all of us, educated persons in the country should work to forge and strengthen these links. That should be our life-time work, which will also give us no time to indulge in religious, langnage and other violence. (It is only we the educated who provoke violence—not poor illiterate). Thus the service of the poor and the keeping down of inequalities is the way forward, the way to national integration.

Indian society is facing a challenge as a result of the growing forces of communalism and regionalism. Presently, because of what is happening in Punjab, anger and hatred between two communities are being created. In the face of this chauvinistic wave, we must keep cool and carry on the education of our people and try to lead them in the proper direction. It is true that in the present context when atmosphere is getting surcharged with anger and hatred, this will be a cry in the wilderness. But there is no reason for frustration. This is a temporary phase and very soon situation will change. Not only Indian people, but the entire human race will welcome and act upon the teachings of Mahatma Gandhi and turn towards the path leading to national integration and to the ultimate integration of humanity as a whole. The task has to be pursued with perseverance, patience and determination.

India has so much to give to the whole civilised world and has given so much through the ages that from Indonesia and the East Indies to the West Indies, her sacred name is sought to be associated with, even by the foreigners. Her ancient language, Sanskrit, and her spiritual civilisation have become the heritage of the entire mankind. The industrialised West has only created pollution and war, or confronted the individual with the society. Will India fail to restore the balance in the world, which she has from time immemorial ? But, first, we must ourselves become Indians and think and behave like civilised and rational Homo-sapiens. Shall We?[3]

India is a country with a pluralist tradition. It is a country with many languages, many cultures and many people with different backgrounds. This, however, has not come in the way of the recognition that India constitutes a single entity—Bharatvarsha—with a basic unity in its cultural tradition. The diversity of languages and cultures need not frighten us; there is a thread of unity running through them. The traditions of the myths, the common sufferings bring the different groups together. India can be proud of its diversity, it is a diversity which encourages unity, for, it allows a great deal of cultural and linguistic autonomy. It will be a mistake if the search for aunitary state leads to a forced integration, for that will only lead to conflict and division. The basis for true integration, of unity in diversity, has been laid; with the passing of time unity will be strengthened without in any way affecting the richness of our pluralist tradition.

From the dawn of history Indian mind has been comprehensive and tolerant of very kind of thought. It admitted every kind of faith and accommodated all shades of opinion. It was ready to offer hospitality to every new-comer. New caravans of various peoples and cultures arrived here and found their resting places. Its, orbit of social life was not shut on any creed or religion.

In the advancement of nations there is no greater hindrance than narrow-mindedness. It is our duty to keep ourselves free from this disease in this new era of independence which has just begun. There is no other disease so dangerous for the healthy growth of national life. It makes its appearance in every field of thought and action. Like an action in masquerades in disguise. In the domain of religion, it appears in the form of blind faith and wants to deceive us in the name of orthodoxy. In politics it wants to over power us in the guise of nationalism. In learning and culture it makes an appeal to us in the name of our nation and country. It behoves us not to be taken in by these fictitious names. We must remember that the root cause of all this is nothing but narrow-mindedness.

The great menace which India faces today is that of communalism. After several years of Independence and at a time when we had thought that this problem was more or less solved, once communal clashes are occurring in different parts of the country.

The second menace is that of provincialism or regionalism or I believe this is evoked by the same sentiments which are behind communalism. In fact, it is an extension of the same sort of feeling. Another serious danger to national integration and perhaps one of the causes of other menaces the persistence of inequalities. In law and theory, the ancient discriminations have been abolished but opportunities have not been growing as fast as the aspirations of backward classes and tribes and minorities and other such groups. Another factor which can unite us or create barriers is that of language.

As we survey the national scene, we feel there is indeed cause for anxiety and also cause for shame that lives of Indian nationals should be threatened in their own homes and in their place of business because of their community or religion. No Indian citizen from one part of the country should be made to feel insecure in another part. The great industrial complexes like Calcutta, Bombay and Madras are a result of the investment of the capital and the skills of the country as a whole. Therefore, every citizen of India has a right to work and to live without fear in any part of the country. Killing of or attack on fellow human beings solves no problem, and those who indulge in such anti-social and anti-national acts are rather like the monkey in our old fable which, in trying to squash the fly, injured the face. Similarly, they, in the long run, injure themselves.

The need for national integration, therefore, does not arise merely from a moral purpose. Certainly the moral purpose is there but in the world as it exists today, as it is evolving today, national integration is the very conditions of our national survival. It is a practical necessity if we are to go forward with our development plans and to progress in unity and strength. It is only in the measure that we recognise this fact that we can create the right climate in the country for solving the various problems that we face. At times these problems seem insuperable but the entire story of modern India is one of overcoming the seemingly insurmountable obstacles. No thinking person should wish to weaken the unity of the country. I am convinced that the forces of integration are strong but they do need to be united and to be given some guidance.

We must find a way of harnessing the basic decency, the basic commonsense of the average citizen in order to overcome these forces which threaten his future and the future of his children.

The effort needs to be made not merely at the governmental level although the Government's responsibility is a heavy one, but at a wider level involving not merely the political parties and the administrators but also students, writers, artists, educationists, different types of cultural and other organisations and all those who work and can work in and through the media of mass communication...We have to think in terms of a concrete national programme involving every significant section of our society in a purposeful action to combat in every town and indeed in every village and every street, the dark forces which seek to disintegrate the very fabric of our social and political existence. I think we should give a call to all those who have national integration at heart to come forward and to rally together. Only such a mass movement dedicated to the cause of national integration and secularism and sustained over a long period can help to find an adequate solution of this very grave problem.

What we need is a many-pronged attack on the forces of disintegration. Merely to say that if we overcome economic disparities and attain a degree of affluence, we shall solve our problems is not enough. And since every problem ultimately has its origin in the mind of man, we have to ensure that our educational processes, the books we read, the radio we hear, the films we see, do not distort the Indian mind but lead it towards integration and solidarity.

Democracy and the participation of people mean that there must be no fear and suspicion in the minds. If any person is afraid because he belongs to a minority community or because he belongs to a lower caste or for some other reason, he cannot assert his rights and, therefore, although he is a citizen of India, he is not really enjoying the privileges of that freedom or of citizenship. And, therefore, to that extent, democracy is not real in the country. So, these are the ways which may seem small, but I think are fundamental, which can strengthen democracy and strengthen us to face those forces which today take the name of democracy but are trying to destory it in many different ways".

Communalism, whether it is Hindu or Muslim or Sikh or any other community is deplorable. And it is not true to say that we have not deplored it when it has taken place or that we have not deplored it or spoken about it strongly, when any Muslim organisation or Muslim individual has said something which is capable of inciting people or leading to any kind of outbreak outburst. But that does not mean that we can condone what a member of the majority community does. Where people are in a majority, they have a special responsibility. They are not merely one set of people. There they have a special responsibility. Anywhere where some people are stronger, they do have a responsibility towards the weaker section. In our country, in most places, the Hindus are in a majority and, therefore, they do have a responsibility towards the Muslims, the Christians and towards whoever else may be in a minority. But in those sections where the others are in a majority, it may be that the Sikhs are in a majority in a certain place—they have a responsibility to the other minorities; it may be Hindu or Muslim or something else. Similarly in Kashmir, the Muslims are in a majority, certainly, it is their responsibility to see that the small number of Hindus who live there can live in peace and security.

Communal hatred is a poisonous weed that takes no time to grow, once the seed is planted. It can sprout even amongst good people. As we found during the communal riots there were large number of innocent people who lived on the best of terms with their neighbours and worked together. But once the poison was abroad they forgot all about their having been good neighbours and having helped one another and that their children had played together. They forgot all. It is our duty to clean the places where the poison has spread ; and where the poision has spread, not ensure that it will not spread. It is only if we do this that India can be strong and a beautiful place to live in. There are still parties and individuals who mix religion with politics and exploit Hindu, Muslim, Sikh and other narrow loyalties for partisan and personal ends. The safety of our nation demands that we fight these forces with all our strength.

Basically, integration is not only an ideal, toleration is not only an ideal, all these are very practical necessities in the India of today and, I would say, in the world of today, India consists of many communities, many religions, many castes and creeds, and we have found that the more one dwells on any particular form of communalism, the narrower it becomes. In this sense, I may say, I am being educated in things that I have never heard of before in all my life as to the number of sub-castes, sub-divisions that there are practically in every religion in India. The more one thinks in these narrow terms the narrower becomes one's attitude to life, the narrower becomes our capacity to act or to think and, therefore, the narrower is our opportunity for progress or development.

India has the privilege of being the world's largest composite society, and the home of many great and ancient faiths. Communalism is an evil which divides man and fragments society ; it goes against our very genious and cultural heritage. It holds a threat to the unity and integrity of our country which must be our foremost concern. Citizenship of India is a shared citizenship. Danger to even one single citizen, to whatever community, caste, religion and linguistic group he may belong, is a danger to all of us and, what is worse, it demeans us all.

We are continuously talking about our diversity. But we have to remember one thing—that ours is a nation of great diversity and disparities and even when the disparities are narrowed, the diversity will remain. So, we must ensure that every element of the nation feels secure about fair and equal treatment and assured that it will have full opportunity to grow and retain its distinctive features. What we call national integration activity is an integral part of our administration and of strengthening and improving our society. There can be no respite in this work, nor an early completion of it.

Our concern is what kind of India shall we bequeath to future generations—a strong, harmonious, self-confident India or a feuding, weak schizophrenic India. We talk of national integration. It is not a mere phrase but an awareness of the burden and the task that history has placed on our shoulders. I have no doubt that all of us, whatever be our party or political creed, hold the freedom and integrity of our country as supreme and dear above all else. But freedom and unity cannot be taken for granted. Eternal vigilance is the price of our integrity, as it is of all liberties."

For the unity of the country it is essential that the people of all religions, castes and creeds, all languages, all States, consider their Indianness or their nationhood as first priority. Only after that does one belong to a State or speak a particular language. This in no way diminishes the local personality or local loyalty. They are all things which strengh then one another and which are enmeshed with one another. Therefore, secularism, the idea of strengthening Indian unity, the idea of giving special attention to those who are weaker than us, either because they are minorities or suffer poverty or economic backwardness because of social and historical reasons, these are accepted values of all Indians.

Sometimes, peoples who live far away think that merely because we have several religions or sixteen languages or other points of difference between us our unity is threatened or there is some danger to it. But this is not true. We have great diversity but we have equally great unity. In fact, we feel that it is the very diversity of the country which gives strength to its unity. There is, or rather I would say, there always has been a basic unity; there has been a basic feeling of Indianness which joins together Indians of different religions and different languages and even different races.

Temporarily, a least the herculean efforts of Lokmanya Balgangadhar Tilak and Mahatma Gandhi to bring about a synthesis failed. As the Islamic State of Pakistan was formed, there was a sharp reaction amongst the Hindus and a demand for a Hindu State for the rest of the country gathered momentum culminating in the assassination of Mahatma Gandhi who was considered as the impediment in their way. His marthrdom, however, instead of inflaming the public mind, softened it and the orgy of killing came to an end. The Constitutent Assembly reiterated its faith in secular nationalism and adopted a democratic Constitution bestowing equal rights on all citizens irrespective of caste, creed, race or language. Our national leaders believed that only a secular state could hold its own in the new environment and achieve development and progress.

The pledge given to the downtrodden during the struggle for Independence had to be redeemed. That is possible only if we preserve the rich heritage of our Indian society. Hindu religion is basically different from other religions. It is a way of life. Hindus are not bound by a single book as the supreme authority governing every way of life. In the Hindu way of life, it is easier to change the old order than in those religions which are governed by a single book. That is why our civilization and our society has continued to live for ages, while others have come and gone. The special characteristic of our society is our unity in diversity. We cannot give it up to satisfy the growth of dogmatism which is bound to be short-lived. We have to preserve and protect that precious heritage of the past. To that end those who believe in it must dedicate themselves to the cause of national integration with courage and determination.[4]

Under the new Constitution, due to our broadminded national leadership the country has made remarkable progress. In this part of the world, several countries became free but ours is the only country which has fought and preserved democracy as against dictatorship now prevailing in other countries. Our development and progress have attracted the attention of the world. But, unfortunately, our development and progress have also become the cause of jealousy of certain powers and they are trying to weaken us. They are once again trying to foment communal forces and to impede our development. We have to take care that we do not act as their tools. Presently there is an upsurge of communal forces. We must not play in their hands if we are determined to make rapid development and progress.

Our angry reactions to what is happening in Punjab are not helpful. It is no use getting angry and prejudiced against a particular community as such. We must not forget that today there are more Muslims in India than in Pakistan itself. They have equal rights as citizens of India. To try to create hatred against any group or community is detrimental to the interest of our country. It is anti-national. That will create separatist feelings. That is exactly our enemies want us to do. Communal chauvinism will destory us. Therefore, our traditional doctrine of unity in diversity on the basis of which Gandhi defined his concept of Indian nationalism has to be translated into action by everyone of us in our life. Separatist and chauvinistic forces have to be fought and defeated by assisting the cementing forces to grow. Those who preach and create hatred against any section on the grounds of caste, creed or region have to be fought and defeated. The Government will fight with all its strength against the external aggression and internal disruption. Temptation to take law in our hands in a fit of anger will do disservice to the cause of national integration. Our job is to unite the people by awakening in them the feelings of "Human brotherhood" Our concept of nationalism is rooted in humanism. Even some of the most powerful countries are coming round to the path blazed by Gautam Buddha and Mahatma Gandhi.[5]

Being a follower, Venkataraman was impressed by Kamaraj's views on National integration which are relevant even today : People ask, "Can we not live well separately as a Tamil Nation ?" Who can say it is impossible ? Certainly, we can live, but not like other nations. We may have to depend only on our own resources for our living and just imagine what our lives would then be. Shall we be able to produce anything in a separate Tamil Nadu at cheap rates ? There are many textile mills in Tamil Nadu and about five lakhs of people work in these mills. Can we ourselves consume all the yarn which they produce in these mills ? If we part from the rest of the country, employment prospects will be reduced to 50,000 men and will not be 5,00,000 as now. At present, we are sending surplus yarn to other parts of the country. If we become a separate nation, who will buy this yarn from us ? Will not hundreds of thousands of people lose their jobs ? The same principle applies to other industries also. Hence, it is imperative that we live as one nation—the Indian nation—in our own interests. North Indians eat wheat and we, south Indians eat rice. People of Kashmir. Assam and Bengal also eat rice. Some people say that the Aryans and the Dravidians basically differ in race and colour, Do they not possess a fair complexion in Kerala ? Are they not Dravidians ? The people who inhibit the west coast are also different from us. You cannot find any difference between a Bengali and a Madrasi in outward apperance. Why should be have these fissiparous tendencies when, in fact, all Indians are alike ?"

"Is it not because of our unity as a strong Indian nation, that we won freedom and now function under one strong central government ? Should people pay any heed to speeches of a separatist nature which seek to undermine the unity of the people ? Some mischievous politicians are trying to confuse the mind of the people. They have a master-mind in devising new ways of creating confusion and they are adepts in the art of telling lies. They are practising false propaganda as an art in itself. If we live as one nation, we may not have any necessity to go abroad in search of employment, but if we separate ourselves from the rest of the country, we shall be compelled to leave our homes and go about in search of employment elsewhere. I appeal to all Tamilians, not to pay heed to these advocates of separatism and shed that idea, if ever they were inclined towards it.

'Even from very ancient times, say from the period of Ashoka, strenous efforts were made to bring the whole country under one central rule. But they failed to do so because of limited facilities then. In those days, even Tamil Nadu had many separate divisions and could not be united at any time, but those divisions did not stand in the way of people feeling as one nation. Those days were not so difficult as now. In the present-day world, we cannot survive as a small nation and, therefore, we should instead take pride in living as citizens of a great nation, rather than thinks of separating ourselves from the rest of the country. It is only because of our living in a great country, like India, that we are able to set up new and big industries to augment our financial resource. If we because a separate Tamil Nation, we may have to send even our kith and kin to wage war with the adjoining States and all of them will die there. The feudal chieftains in the past did only such things in those days and hence we see so many battles and wars in the annals of Indian history. One great lesson taught to us by Mahatma Gandhi is that we should live united as one nation. It pains me to see that some people are preaching separatist theories, to the detriment of the nation. We can hope for our advancement only by living as one nation and by making united efforts to remove poverty from our midst. The Central Government, which is set up on the basis of one strong and unified nation, is capable of providing us security of life and property."

In the words of the great philosopher President Dr. S. Radhakrishnan : "All those who live within the limits of India are Indian, whatever may be their race, caste or community. There was practically free trade in the matter of ideas, beliefs and customs. But, unfortunately, we have not yet developed an 'All-India' outlook. We fight with each other for petty considerations and regional advantages. Such minor interests will have to be subordinated to the larger national good. The land we live in and the traditions we live by, constitute the character of our country."

National integration, is not a ready-made armour to be put on in times of wars and foreign invasions and hung up on a peg in normal times. Nor is it "in the blood" to be biologically transmitted from one generation to another. On the other hand, as Ernest Renan said, "the existence of a nation is a daily plebiscite." He defined a nation as "a soul, a spiritual principle" which is made of a rich common hertiage of memories and of "the desire to live together." In other words, national integration denotes a condition of mind among the members of a national community—a condition of mind in which all premordial loyalties are sub-ordinated to the over-arching loyalty to the nation. Pride in one's nationality and belief in its intrinsic excellence and in its "mission" are integral parts of that kind of a psyche. Such a condition of mind is the product of a perpetual dynamic process of mutual attention, sympathy and loyalty aimed at inculcating and fostering the "we-feeling" among the members of a national community. Thus national integration is a cultural product and like any cultural product can be realised by means of sound education. Therefore the role of education in national integration acquires paramount importance. The rise and spread of Indian nationalism in the nineteenth century is the best illustration of this point.

Nehru rose to great heights as he proceeded and said : "In the past conditions were different. But when a country is functioning independently, there is no alternative except to follow this (policy). The only alternative is civil conflict. We have seen as a matter of fact how far communalism in politics has led us ; all of us remember the grave dangers through which we have passed and the terrible consequences we have seen. In any event now there is no other alternative ; and we must have it clearly in our minds and in the mind of the country that the alliance of religion and politics in the shape of communalism is a most dangerous alliance, and it yields the most abnormal kind of illegitimate brood. The combination of politics and religion, resulting in communal politics is a most dangerous combination and must be put an end to. It is harmful to the country as a whole, it is harmful to the majority, but probably it is most harmful to any minority that seeks to have some advantage from it. I think even the past history of India will show that.

Nehru who had an insight into the multi-religious and cultural complexities of this country often reiterated the need for building a viable educational campaign for defences of the national integration. It is amazing that some rationalists and historians cynically laughed at his obsession with this concept, as in fact it betrayed a lack of self-confidence flowing from many centuries of foreign rule. This important dimension was neglected in our various developmental programmes and even we did not care to expose our students to the lives and works of our national heroes who had a powerful vision of India and her role in the Asian resurgence and the unification of the human race. The question which we have to address ourselves is what should be done now to consolidate the forces of oneness in the country. While building the processes of the national integration, we have to critically and creatively examine the Centre-State relationships and have to work out a clear-cut 'policy of devolution of authority' in our federal polity. It is this healthy co-operation which will strengthen the bond of comradeship between the Centre and States. Any interative perception of the viable functioning of parliamentary democracy will show that this system its many merits has also a set of contsraints. It develops inevitably as a part of its process a perpetual strifes of parties, conflicting ideas and interests and hysteric cries of regionalism, lingualism and fundamentalism at the cost of national unity. While one would welcome a healthy competition between political parties but when they adopt the path of confrontation and pose a threat to the unity of the country, one has to seriously work out an alternative to this impasse. This is precisely what is happening in Punjab. While keeping democratic framework in view, Rajiv Gandhi signed an accord with Harchand Singh Longowal and restored the democratic process in the state for tackling the problem of terrorism in a more enlightened and sane manner. This accord was highly acclaimed by the national major parties and the print media. This did not work is beside the point, but what is more important is the perception and motivation of Rajiv Gandhi who is committed to conciliatory policies and had a deep and abiding faith in the democratic norms. It is this massage which the Akali leadership and other political parties must put across by launching a massive offensive political movement in the state for building a viable united Punjub and united India. They must rise above petty parochialism and shed the shackles of superstition and obscurantist ideas and look beyond the ideals and perential values which a Buddha, a Nanak and a Kabir was able to actualise. "The incorigible prophets of doom" and gloom who are constantly 'bemoaning that the country is on the verge', of collapse are in fact weakening the social and psychological fibre of our people. Let them know that plurality of India is her strength and India is one and the unity of India must and will be achieved for it is necessary for the greatness of India's future and the future of humanity. Indira Gandhi who was trying to make India a vibrant, united and self-reliant social-economic organism was assassinated. She was operating at a razor edge and had to face gallows and bullets with the glory of a united India on her lips. There looms the reality of a crisis, which is complex and cumulative.[6]

Prime Minister Indira Gandhi said in Trivandrum on November 10, 1980 : "National integration cannot be a mere governmental movement. It has to be an all inclusive people's movement : the people of all castes, the people of all religions, the people of all regions. We are all partners in the building up of our country and we must ensure a fair opportunity to all people to realize their best potential, to make use of all their telents to develop their personality to the full. We should help people to overcome the handicaps from which they have suffered for years, and fight against every kind of deprivation, every kind of humiliation or lack of ability to take advantage of the rights which are theirs under our Constitution. To work for such a cause is the duty we owe to leaders like Mahatma Gandhi, Jawaharlal Nehru, Maulana Azad and other great leader."

With fissiparous tendencics asserting themselves in different parts of India, the need for national integration can hardly be overemphasised. But while different political parties at different times show a healthy tendency to work together to promote harmony, a collective approach to strengthen the unity which is a ditionally said to consist in the strengthen the unity which is a ditionally said to consist in the diversity of the land seldom materialises in peacetime. In the jungle law of political squabbling for [illegible], national interests are not unoften subordinated to partisan considerations which may in the long run foment disharmony. Even the most well-intentioned programmes fail to achieve the desired results in this context and annual meetings of representative national bodies serve little purpose other than letting off a stream of generalities. The discussions at the meeting of the Standing Committee of the National Integration Council would seem to bear out this fact. Prime Minister Rajiv Gandhi was not wrong when he said that not enough had been done to implement Indira Gandhi's 15-point programme for the welfare of the minorities. But it was not the whole truth either. Promotion of the interests of the minorities has perhaps been uneven and selective but the benefits that they have reaped as a body are not insignificant compared to the gains deriving from the overall development of the nation. The transfer of the subject from the Home Ministry to the Social Welfare Ministry could not have made much difference. It is generally recognised that communal tension as a rule is not causally related to the neglect of a minority community. The Sikh extremists cannot claim that they belong to a downtrodden community.

It is sad but true that communalism in India has suddenly become more menacing. One would feel that its attribution to the sudden boom in inflammatory literature is an oversimplistic explanation. Nor is it wholly credible that political parties do not exploit the minority factor in winning votes though that is not necessarily in violation of the accepted spirit of secularism. It is a simple matter of political reality. Such commonsense approaches cannot be proved or disproved by statistics. The suggestion that Government leaders should not take part in religions religious functions is not very relevant considering that secularism does not mean avoidance of religion but true catholicity in that sphere. There will be not two opinions about the statements that the word 'minority' does not mean religious minorities only. But the mere inclusion of linguistic minorities does not make the term comprehensive. More importance should be given to the economically and socially dispossessed minorities in different pockets.

Speaking of national unity, India's first President, Dr. Rajendra Prasad said : "Today when we have various kinds of differences arising and when we sometimes miss the great fundamental unity and attach importance to the apparent diversity, it is well to remember that after all fundamental unity will last because in our very nature this non-violence is ingrained, because our whole life, tradition and culture is based on that. From the time when differences of opinion were tabooed in other countries, we have tolerated differences of opinion and today when we have got a Constitution which allows freedom of speech, of expression, of thought and of religion to every-body, there is no reason why we should not have a people holding different opinions and subscribing to different ideologies, working together in co-operation with one another to the benefit of all. Our Constitution not only envisages this but it also provides for it and that is why we have secured unity of the country by insisting upon federation ; we have also ensured autonomy of the States, and the fact that one party is ruling at the Centre and another in the State has not made any difference to our relationship with one another and ought not to make any difference. This great unity has been possible because our people have from time immemorial accepted the principle of live and let live, of mutual respect and tolerance, of what may be called co-existence in modern language. We have been able to survive all these centuries and today when we have added to this cultural unity also the political unity of the country as a whole, there is no reason why our country should not rise to the greatest heights in national prosperity and service to humanity."

Looking retrospectively – it is the pathology of subcontinent, a political division on hardened communal lines indeed the expedient policy of Britishers who wanted that India should fall back into chaos of separate states and experienced continuous communal insurgencies. This assumption has proved partly true as we continue to live with a fractured state of consciousness. It is the communal bitterness and hatred which is seriously weakening the country's internal development and frustrating her role of a reconciler in the comity of nations. It is again the communal madness which has kept the successive military regimes in Pakistan on the fantastic furty of a holy war, religious hatred and bitterness against India. In retrospect, it is the obsession of the military regimes that through guerrilla war they can humiliate India which has ultimately led to their doom. Their first miscalculation was Kashmir operation in 1965 ; the second seven years later which resulted in the total defeat and break up of their country itself. Even with successive failures, Pakistan leaders have not learnt the lesson of history and have now found a new insurgency method through misguided Sikh youths to destabilise the unity of India. There are enough evidences that the anti-India movement launched by the Sikh extremists has got its bases in Pakistan and other foreign countries. This diabolical design of the Pakistan Government has been brilliantly Government has been brilliantly unmasked by Benazir Bhutto in her public educational campaign against military regime. But it is sad paradox of the Sikh extremist movement, especially the breakaway group of the Akali Dal, to become instrument of the mindless brutality of military regime of Pakistan and keep Punjab in chaos, disorderly and unstable. It is the Sikh community which has suffered maximum casualties, loss of property and rape of Sikh women during the holocaust of partition of 1947 in the hands of Muslim fanatics. One wonders why a fraction of the Sikh community which is an integral part of the national consciousness has all of a sudden turned hostile to India and has found a new master who is bound to exploit this community for the advancement of its own selfish gains. We must dig deeper.

Religious hatred is a basic element in this conflagration. The differences have been honed razor sharp by Pakistan's systematic exploitation and indoctrinating of the bewildered Sikh youths. The money and arms and ammunitions are flowing freely into Gurdwaras which have become the fortress of stock-piling of weapons. Several events catalyzed bitterness. Major decisions are made by hardiners who have the direct backing of foreign powers. Inexplicably, the responses of many foreign nations—notably, the United Kingdom, Canada and United States have failed to give much weight to the strength of the passions at work. Washington, for example, continues to talk about its dealing with terrorism with firmness and foresight but at the same time is providing the training bases in the art of guerilla technology to Sikh youth. It continues military aid to Pakistan Government on the ground that it maintains its leverage for a moderate settlement. While it champions the cause of democratic processes and the protection of civil liberties and human rights, it continues to advance the nuclear interests of military regimes. The incompatibility of Washington's so called pragmatic approach with inflamed emotions in Pakistan is difficult to explain. It eludes our comprehension and creates suspicion in the subtle nuances of the art of diplomacy practised by the foremost champions of democracy.[7]

Talking of the threats to the nation's unity, Venkataraman regrets that "the spirit of tolerance of the old days is disappearing". He traces the major divisions in the Indian society to "the colonial policy and practice of divide-and-rule".

He thinks "early education" can help tackle this problem. "I once asked people in a school ; why not teach *A* for *Allah*, *B* for *Buddha*, *C* for *Christ* and so on ? he chuckles.

REFERENCES

1. A Human Ansari. National integration *Indian Nation* (Patna) 26 January, 1987 ; p. 4.
2. Malcolm S. Adiseshiah. Reduce inequality for harmony. *Yojna* (New Delhi) 26 January 1987 ; pp. 17-18.
3. Gopal Singh. A ten-point formula to strengthen India. *Yojna* 26 January 1987, p. 31.
4. S.M. Joshi Defeat separatist forces. *Yojna* 26 January 1987; pp. 11-13.
5. *Ibid.*
6. Kishore Gandhi. Oneness of India. *Hindustan Times* 2 August 1986 ; p. 9.
7. Kishore Gandhi. Oneness of India. *Hindustan Times* 2 August 1986 ; p. 9.

6

THE SECULAR WORLD

Venkataraman is a grassroot man. He mixes with all people alike, which gives him an insight into the affairs of men. He knows well the bright and the seamy side of iife. He has the confidence to go ahead with what is good and helpful and discards the rest. He never suffers from a sense of complacency and can thus avoid pitfalls. Many political figures of late have developed a tendency to oversimplify and generalise matters, forgetting that India is a vast sub-continent in which different sections of people and different regions are affected differently. For us it would be wise to take a lesson from Venkataraman's life and base our actions on the actualities of life.

Ramaswami Venkataraman took oath as President of India, on July 25, 1987 and since then new forces and new situations have arisen. Nevertheless India's basic problems remain the same. Venkataraman's approach to economic planning and national interation—the two problems plaguing us, is not only a matter of considerable integrest but it can serve as a guideline for the nation. His broad economic planning strategy, in my opinion, holds as good today as it did when he acted upon it.

Venkataraman is so concerned with the present that he gives little thought to what Indian historians will think of him in the future. In the first three decades of his life, Venkataraman struggled for a chance to proved himself and gain recognition of his abilities. By chance, his inner self-struggle brought him closer to the then Congress stalwart K. Kamaraj who was exploring the idea of building a new Tamil Nadu—an industrial giant in the Southern part of India.

This is a secular world. True the fear is intense : religious revivalists are becoming powerful in every part of the world. And we are advised by progressives to be worried of such trends. The task is to fight religious orthodoxy and propagate secularism. Hence our original statement needs to be slightly modified. It might be wrong to say that we live in a secular world, nevertheless, it is right to proclaim that we desire to live in a secular world. Indeed, the ideal of our civilization is secular. Every new born child must undergo a process of rigorous training. From the school headmaster to the party intellectual-everyone he would encounter in the process of his 'growing up' is endowed with a great responsibility. They must induce an 'ideal' citizen to believe that not to be secular is something peculiar. Well, societies can be sufficiently tolerant; a 'non-secular' person need not necessarily be sent to a mental clinic or to a prison. But, then, they are other ways, more subtle and more effective of generating fear. This is the fear of being called a fanatic—a man without a rational progressive mind. In a secular world or in a world that desires to be secular, 'non-secular' experiences are seldom given much importance. Generally, they are considered to be obstacles; they ought to be overcome by scientific, progressive ideologies! The point is that a secular world too is hierarchical. Its commitment to science creates the boundary betwecn an ideal secular citizen and an ignorant fanatic.[1]

This duality is, however, essential. The ideals we cherish cannot he accomplished by all. What is required is a disciplined personality, an "objective consciousness" a scientific way of comprehending the world. Perhaps all these can be branded as secular consciousness. We need to preserve it in order to achieve our goals. The goals are many from neo-colonial expansion of our hegemony to ceaseless production of consumer goods. A secular mind must derive the meaning of his life from his success and victory; from the kind of work that as a technologist or as a manager he does in his office and factory.[2]

Communal violence, though not new in India, is entering a dangerous phase. It threatens to engulf not just the political terrain of parties and elections but also the deeper cultural roots and religious mainstay of this ancient civilisation whose very identity has all along been "eclectic". It is a civilization that has shown an innate capacity to sustain enormous diversity and a multiplicity of belief systems, ideologies and faiths without losing its unity and integrity. A tradition that has been built over centuries and has withstood so many jolts from within and without cannot easily be undone. But it can be severly damaged because of the new institutional setting which the civilization has chosen to manage its affairs. This is the setting of a modern nation-state with a secular political centre that, while recognizing the essential plurality based on diverse religious and cultural streams, also undertook to weave them all together into a new mode of integration that could withstand the pressures of a democratic age. The new setting proved crucial in the post-colonial, post-partition, setting in enabling the diverse entities that constituted the nation-state to find a new common core. It was able to instil a sense of belonging to a common entity called India and resrain parochial and chauvinist tendencies by channelizing social energy along "secular" lines for achieving socio-economic goals that were common to all; and in which at least theoretically everyone could participate without discrimination. Where discrimination seemed to persits, corrective measures were proposed through both constitutional entitlements and norms and conventions of accommodation and bargaining that were built into the political process.[3]

Crucial to the whole enterprise was the centrality of the democratic political process. Participation in the political process was expected to provide scope for providing justice and opening up new space to hitherto submerged peoplies through a new set of institutions that were supposed to mediate in the distribution of power and privilege in society. Political parties and elections, Parliament and state legislatures, the Courts and the civil administration, the Press and the radio and above all a large array of politicians and "social workers" operating a wide variety of local institutions and sorting out issues of stress and conflict whenever these took place provided a whole new framework to which diverse entities and populations could relate. Such a catalytic role of politics in drawing diverse social strata to it depended on two factors: the operators of the system acting in good faith vis-a-vis the people at large (despite a great deal of mutual bickering and backbiting) and the people having faith in their good faith (despite frequent let-downs and "betrayals"). There were two other conditions that were met: Willingness on the part of the politicians to play down rather than play up hostilities whenever these broke out among sections of the people and building "coalitions-of power" at the ground level consisting of diverse social strata. The broader national consensus about which one always heard during the fifties and the sixties was of course largely worked out by elite at higher levels but is was also strongly underpinned by such a culture of bargaining one's way through the complex social mosic at the grassroots.

Ours is a secular State—at least that is what the Constitution says and most of our leaders proclaim. Why is it then that religion is being misused to spread discord and hatred? Why is it that people are prepared to shed blood over a temple or a mosque in Ayodhya or elsewhere? Come to think of it, where is the piety of the Sikhs paying homage to the creator at the Golden temple and at the same time violating the lofty teachings of Guru Nanak Dev. The widening gap between precept and practice is noticeable among the followers of all religions.

The sense of insecurity discernible in a section of the majority community is as disturbing as the persecution mania haunting the minorities. The Hindu, who links the future of his religion to the future of the shrines in Ayodhya, Mathura and Kashi and is ready to fight is only a shade better than the Muslim who is ready to take up arms on hearing Syed Ahmed Bukhari's cry, "Islam is in danger". Fanatics and trouble-makers, irrespective of the religion to which they belong, are enemies of the nation. How will the nation develop the 21st century outlook if the people remain, by and large, chained mentally and spiritually to the medieval times? Religious fundamentalism is hardly the answer to our socio-economic problems. In fact fundamentalism will only deepen, not eradicate inequalities.[4]

According to Mahatma Gandhi : "All religions teach that two opposite forces act upon us and that the human endeavour consists in a series of eternal rejections and acceptances. Non-cooperation with evil is as much a duty as cooperation with good." In its broader sense a religion does not only preach a ritualistic belief in God but also teaches an ethical code of life to prepare the believer through a righteous way to achieve his goal i.e. spiritual satisfaction, salvation, nirvana, entry into heaven, union with God etc. The true aim of all world religions is one and the same, it is only the ritualistic approach for its attainment which has divided the human society into numerous religious beliefs and antagonistic faiths. The nobel theory of religion could not be blamed for this religious antagonism which has committed an countable, and unpardonable crimes against humanity. The blame must go to fanatic followers, who in their religious zeal forget the true conception of religion. No religion preaches intolerance, narrow-mindedness, disrespect to other religions and hatred for humanity. On the contrary all religions preach tolerance, open mindedness, respect for others feelings, beliefs, universal brotherhood and above all love for humanity. The fanatic followers or fundamentalists are the true culprits who show the seeds of hatred by giving more emphasize on rituals and by mis-interpretations of religious scriptures for their own wested interests. All religions have their own share of bad followers and therefore, on wonder time to time religious tensions are erupted all over the world. The religious bigots systematically play on public religious sentiments, for their vested interests and breed hatred. When the dirty game of politics is mixed up with religious favour it produces devastating repurcussions and often leads to organised annihilation of innocent human beings.[5]

On the verge of independence, the Indian sub-continent witnessed unprecedented communal conflicts which caused irreparable damage to national harmony and ultimately led to partition and that too in the name of religion. It was the saddest chapter of our history which has left an ugly scar on Indian social and moral fibre. India being a vast country of diversed cultures and religious beliefs chose a path of secularism, whereby the State adopted a natural stand towards all religions. It was the best and far sighted plan to achieve national unity in diversity. It meant religion should strictly be kept out of politics and treated as a personal affair of all citizens. It is really unfortunate to see that we, the citizens of India have not yet come up to the expectations of our Constitution-makers. It is therefore, in one of his speeches, Prime Minister Rajiv Gandhi advised the nation to fight hard against the disruptive forces of growing fundamentalism, which are certainly weakening the secularistic democratic foundation of our nation. Every sensible partriotic Indian hang his head in shame whenever a communal riot takes place in any part of the country.

Despite all precautions taken by our Constitution makers, the dirty game of politics crept into diverse Indian religious beliefs and polluted harmonious social environment. The political opportunists began to use religion to farther their ulterior motives. In collaboration with religious bigots, who had little or no place in secularistic set-up, they cultivated hatred and fear in place of love and unity. The religious sentiments of masses were exploited from time to time for political gains through a methodical inculcation of fundamentalism. Moneyed people of business community joined hands with politicians to elevate fundamentalism with ritualistic extravaganza. It is the black money amassed by dubious means often comes out for extravagant display of religious rituals without a grain of spirituality which is the life blood of a true religion. The communal disturbances are often caused by various social, economical and political causes but usually sparked off in the name of religion.

India has no option apart from following the noble path of secularism as envisaged by our constitution-makers. A firm plantation of secularistic ideal in Indian soil requires its sincere nurturing by all citizens irrespective of their caste, creed or religion. It makes imperative for the government to take effective steps to propagate secularism and educate the masses towards a broader national outlook and religious tolerance. Only lip service is not going to strengthen secularism but an organised concentrated efforts in all walks of life is required in its actual application in our day to day life. It is only then majority and minorities colud live harmoniously without any fear of subjugation or domination. No one will disagree with this fact that there is a lot of difference between theoretical propagation of an idea and its practical implementation. Fear, whether it is in majority community or minorities must be eliminated first. It is only then a proper growth of secularistic ideal could be possible.

Our secularism is still shaky even after the four decades of independence, and it is just because many of us do not practice it sincerely. A systematic inculcation of secularistic ideal right from childhood is badly needed to prepare future citizens, who could break the religious and communal barriers for the sake of national integration. Between the two World wars, the German Nazi Party systematically breed hatred and spirit of revenge through a complete mis-education and succeeded in creating a new generation of fanatic but dedicated youth who were ready to sacrifice their lives for their father-land. A lot is to be learnt from this lesson because our cause is noble. Our secularistic ideal is not for waging war but it is for the betterment of humanity.

REFERENCES

1. Avi Jit Pathak. Religion in a secular stage. *Rising Nation*. January 1987 ; p. 52.
2. *Ibid.*
3. Rajni Kothari. A new seculalturist. *Hindustan Times* 5 October 1986.
4. P. Tharyan. Unity in divesity : Example better than precept. *Hindustan Times* 18 October 1986 ; p. 9.
5. M.A. Ghani True secularism must take root. *Madhya Pradesh Chronicle* (Bhopal) 1 February 1987.

7

MAHATMA GANDHI AND HIS IMPACT

The second decade of the twentieth century saw the emergence of the new leadership, with Mahatma Gandhi taking over from men like Gokhale and Tilak.

It was Gokhale who, in a way, foresaw the potential of Mahatma Gandhi. The old moderate trading a path of constitutional evolution watched with admiration the fight which Mahatma Gandhi had with the racial regime of South Africa. There was something highly original, something individualistic, something native to the Indian mood and in the technology of non-violent resistance, *Satyagraha*.

Gokhale was quick to note how effective the technique would be, if only it could be adopted to Indian conditions, if only it could be exploited to wrest freedom for India. It was with the blessing of Gokhale that Mahatma Gandhi entered Indian politics. It did not take Gandhi long to get feel of the things. He took to politics with alacrity. And his training in South Africa stood him in good stead.

The evolution of Gandhi, who went to South Africa, intent on gaining a standing as a lawyer, from the ranks of the commoners to leadership makes fascinating reading. He did not have the vaguest idea of the racial discrimination practised by the South African regime.

Even though he had tasted some minor inconveniences during his student days in England, air around was more pure, less polluted by racial prejudices. Outwardly, at any rate, in England there were no laws or regulations which tilted the scales in favour of the whites.[1]

Gandhi had a taste of what was in store for him within a couple of days of arrival in South Africa. In order to familiarise himself with the courts and the procedures, he attended a magisterial trial. He entered the court, wearing the turban. The magistrate glared angrily at him and curtly told him to take the turban off. Gandhi considered it an affront to his dignity and walked out of the court.

Gokhale, who had toured South Africa in 1912, got a chance to measure the power of Gandhi's tactics. It was this which weighed with him when he asked Gandhi, who returned to India in 1915, to join the flight fight for freedom. The door wos held open for him by none else than one of the most popular leaders of the national movement. Gokhale was convinced that it was time to groom a successor on whom the mantle of leadership should fall. He was growing old. Tilak too was old. Other leaders who enjoyed public confidence were also past their prime.

Gandhi, when he returned to India, was just forty-five. He had the inner strengh to provide the necessary drive and initiative to the struggle for freedom. The choice, made by Gokhale, helped Gandhi to find his feet in Indian politics with ease. The fledgling had arrived.

The Mahatma toured the whole of India, studied the situation, made himself familiar with the scenario. He also met national leaders, discussed the tactics which would gain for Indians a larger say in the management of the affairs of the State, toyed with the idea of trying out his *Satyagraha* on native soil.[2]

Mahatma Gandhi dominated the Indian political scene for almost three decades from 1919 when he launched his non-co-operation movement to the day of his martyrdom on 30 January

1948. He vacated the Indian scene hardly within six months of the transfer of power on 15 August 1947. He was not only affectionately called 'Mahatma', but in his lifetime he was looked upon almost as a prophet, a saint, an apostle of non-violence who need be compared only to a Buddha or a Christ. The doctrines which he preached and, above all, practised in his daily life were called by a kind of overall blanket term "Gandhism". We are not concerned here so much with the ethical aspects of his teachings, how far they were or could be practically effective. Whether he remained a dreamer or a practicalist. We look upon him basically as the great leader, and a political leader at that, of the Indian national struggle and movement against British imperialist rule. If ever there was a man who lived as he preached and gave his life for the cause which he had upheld throughout his life, such a man was Mahatma Gandhi.

Our basic approach to Mahatma Gandhi then is that we must look upon him as the foremost political leader who strode across the Indian scene for more than three decades and helped to bring about, almost as it were out of the blue, a mass movement which in its breadth and sweep undoubtedly shook the mightly British empire.[3]

But he was not free of contradictions. And when we point out these contradictions, we do it from the basic standpoint of our class, the working-class, and other toiling masses, and we bring to bear there the cold scientific objectivity derived from our philosopy, that of Marxism-Leninism and materialist dialectics. Surely there is no room here for sentimentality of a somewhat subjective character nor is it to be supposed that we have any personal animosity to the great soul who roused the masses at a particular crucial and critical juncture of our national movement.

Gandhi is great, but greater no doubt are the masses whom be helped to rouse and bring into the national movement, against imperialism. And as the mass movement takes on its stride and masses and classes appear on the national scene with their own mass and class demands, Gandhi vacillated. This is the root of his contradiction, of his many inconsistencies as we will note presently. Basically they reflect and represent the vacillating role of the Indian national bourgeoisie which faces two contradictions and two crossfires respectively, that of imperialism and the people. It is necessary to see these positive and negative aspects of Gandhi (whether they constitute an 'ism' we will discuss later), this dual, vacillating role and it is this dialectical approach to the phenomena that was Gandhi which will help us to place the Mahatma in his proper perspective.

It was his philosophy that was accepted by the people of India in their struggle for freedom which forced the biggest and the mightiest empire in the world to withdraw from India and subsequently from other colonies like Sri Lanka, Burma and East Africa. Mahatma Gandhi's relevance did not end with India's independence. It only marked the beginning of the process. He not only insisted on pursuing the right goals but also using the right methods to achieve them ; for him "means were as important as the ends". This concept might ultimately save the future of the mother Earth that today faces the prospect of being blown out of existence because of the nuclear arsenal being manufactured by the world powers. There is no stopping a nuclear missile or a nuclear attack. The only check is the fear of retaliation. The way to end this threat to the world is to change the minds of the people who control our destinies. They need to be persuaded to divert their energies from manufacturing destructive weapons to investing their money in raising the standards of living of the people and making their life more worthwhile. Big and powerful people in great and industrialised countries have to be converted to the view that the world does not need nuclear weapons of mass destruction to save it from going over the brink, but the philosophy of universal friendship, love and *ahimsa* ; the non-violent moral force of mass protest rather than the weapons of hate for mass destruction. The struggle to fight for human dignity started by Mahatma in Transvaal in South Africa was later taken up by Martin Luther King in America in fighting for the honour and dignity for the Black Americans. Like the Mahatma, King also fell to the assassin's bullet, and like the Mahatma his spirit stalked the American continent and the Blacks won a place in the mainstream of the nation. Mahatma

Gandhi's philosphy will continue to be relevant and good for millenia to come, particularly if the world is to be saved from a nuclear catastrophe. The pressure of non-violent mass protest and the public opinion in the United States of America, the United Kingdom, West Germany, Japan and other developed countries is telling on their ruling elite who are truing to work for the mutual reduction of forces and controlling of the means of mass destruction. A number of European countries like Sweden, Norway and Denmark which are "nuclear threshold" countries have stopped the process of going nuclear because of the public agitation.[4]

Many today who read the writings of Mahatma Gandhi or books on him are drawn to him by some aspects of his life and philosophy, be it the concept of non-violence, soul-force, *satyagraha*, or the vision of moral man in a moral society.

But one who has glanced through the eighty odd Volumes of 'The Collected Works Of Mahatma Gandhi' discovers that, apart from his thought-provoking ideas, the human presence of the Mahatma, his candour and courage and child-like mirth, have an attraction of their own, exuding charm and warmth at once.

According to Venkataraman, Mahatma Gandhi was surely one of the most fascinating personalities to appear on the human stage in recent times. The recent film on him, excellent though it was, brought out only a few salient aspects of his extraordinary life and thought. The more one reads about him the clearer it becomes that we are dealing with a person at once remarkably simple and deeply complex ; a man whose philosophy was reflected in his actions and flowed from his experience. Whether it was religion or politics, social transformation or economic growth, individual growth or collective welfare Mahatma Gandhi had his own prescription which he only gave to society after he had practised it in his own life. His was a unique example of a practical philosopher, a man whose total approach to life revolved around certain clearly defined and expressed principles, whose life was his message.

Non-Violence, truth and moral integrity were the corner stones of his faith and actions. Mahatma Gandhi once said that he was prepared to compromise on anything except non-violence and truth. Non-violence as preached and practised by him was not a negative concept, but a positive and creative one. In practice this basic concept took the form of *Satyagraha* which was a unique weapon both for the individual as well as the collective to fight for truth, justice freedom and equality. Thus he not only believed in mass action but wanted to build up the individual also simultaneously with the society through the weapon of *Satyagraha* for social, economic moral and spiritual upliftment. Absence of external violence alone is not *Satyagraha*. A true *Stayagrahi* should not only abstain from violence in action but also his mind and thoughts should be free from it. The essence of *Satyagraha* is to invite or voluntarily accept self-suffering without causing mental or physical pain or suffering to anybody else in order to serve a just and reasonable cause. A true *Satyagraha* generates the forces of destruction of the evil and construction of the good in a same and simultaneous process.

For Mahatma Gandhi there was an integrated and organic relationship between precept and practice and in fact he emphasised more on practice than precept. His own life was an example of this great principle. A logical corollary of this was his belief that no distinction should be made between private and public life. What one preaches and practises in public must be reflected in his private life also. Again Gandhi himself was an example of this and he lived an open life, open for anybody to see.

Mahatma Gandhi was a strong believer and advocate of democracy, secularism and his own concept of socialism which for him meant non-exploitation and non-oppression of any kind. His concept of democracy meant respect for and tolerance of others views in true spirit of Indian culture and civilisation and strongly advocated decentralisation as a means to achieve political, economic and social democracy. Decentralisation is a guarantee against concentration of political and economic power, against bureaucratics and dictatorial trends and against the individual losing his identity in the midst of the crowd and the collective.

Some people cite the cases of Nariman, Khare and Subhas Bose as examples of Gandhi's intolerance of differences of views. But these differences were on fundamentals of Gandhi's faith on which he refused to compromise with anybody. There are other examples to show how Gandhi respected difference of views of the same did not go against his fundamentals. Although Pandit Nehru accepted Gandhi's leadership without question he did not agree with him on many matters. Both often had long arguments and yet remained unreconciled, whereas Patel, Rajendra Prasad and others followed Gandhi almost blindly. But in spite of this, Gandhi publicly named Nehru as his political heir and later in 1947 over-ruled the overwhelming majority of the Working Committee by insisting that Nehru must be chosen for the Prime Ministership of free India as against Patel, the nominess of the majority group of the Working Committee.

In the spring of 1944, Mahatma Gandhi, in prison then, had a protracted correspondence with the Viceroy Lord Wavell, on the Indian problem. In his letter of 17 February 1944 Lord Wavell had spoken of the conditions which must be fulfilled before India moved towards self-rule. These conditions included protection to British economic interests and satisfaction of the Princes and the minorities as to their future. Mahatma Gandhi, in his reply dated 9 March 1944 said :

"Without reasoning it out, I venture to give my paraphrase of your pronouncement. 'We, the British shall stand by the Indian soldier whom we have brought into being and trained for consolidating our rule and position in India, and who, by experience, we have found can effectively help us in our wars against other nations; we shall also stand by the rulers of the Indian States, many of whom are our creation and all of whom owe their present position to us, even when these rulers curb or actually crush the spirit of the people whom they rule, similarly shall be stand by the minorities whom too, we have encouraged and used against the vast majority when the latter have at all attempted to resist our rule. It makes no difference that the majority seeks to replace it by a rule of the will of the people of India taken as a whole. And in no case will we transfer power unless Hindus and Muslims come to us with an agreement among themselves'."

Mahatma Gandhi believed that his homeland, was destined to be a peace-loving power actively affirming such a political climate of international relations that would preclude the possibility of armed conflicts and wars. In November 1946, he announced that India's noble mission is one of establishing friendship and peace throughout the world. The weeks after the proclamation of independence, on August 31, 1947, Gandhi said again that it was she duty of free India to prefect the instrument of non-violence for resolving international disputes.

Gandhi's peace-making ideas made a strong impression on the overwhelming majority of leaders and activists of the Indian National Congress. They inspired Jawaharlal Nehru, too, though he did not accept Gandhi's grounds for the foreign-political orientation of independent India. Nehru approached problems of inter-state relations as a sober-minded politician and a talented and well-informed diplomat Credit goes to Nehru for awakening in the Indian National Congress interest in those problems and international solidarity. It is not by chance that in the Interim Government and then in the Government of independent India he was entrusted, besides the post of Prime Minister, with the post of Minister of External Affairs also.

In matters of international relations, the prevention of wars and the strengthening of peace, Nehru differed from Gandhi in that he deeply realised the social factors underlying international tension. Nehru was well aware of the need for a just settlement of disputes arising in relations between some states and in the entire community of nations. He believed that genuine stability in the international situation could not be ensured by just calling for non-violence, but by a whole set of social and political conditions, among which he mentioned the liberation of all nations still subject to colonial oppression. Nehru urged complete elimination of the colonial system of imperialism and, together with it, apartheid, racism and all forms of discrimination against individuals and whole ethnic groups, and advocated respect for the sovereignty of all states and non-interference in their internal affairs.

Mahatma Gandhi, gave top priority to building our national character which had been debased by centuries of slavery. But we have lost all we gained in 38 years in the rat race for material progress. The end now justifies the means. Honesty, we were taught, is the best policy. Today it has ceased to be so. Self is shamelessly placed before principles. Corruption and greed are rampant. Truth is at a heavy discount.

Mahatma Gandhi contemplated comprehensive social reform, not the mere political transfer of power. He had a double programme to achieve this end. One was to fight British imperialism through satyagraha. The other was to get the naiion to take up the work of national reconstruction. Most Congress leaders and party men accepted the first programme. But they had reservations about the second. This was considered to be the work of social reformers. Mahatma Gandhi gave top priority to *Khadi* and the spinning wheel ("*charkha*"). Yet, according to Acharya Kripalani, some of the top leaders often called the work on the "*charkha*" as "an old dame's work."

The Mahatma's *satyagraha* programme succeeded though not according to his desire. India won freedom. But the Congress leadership forgot the more comprehensive programme of social transformation, which was conceived in the Indian context. Wrongs were exposed by Gandhi in every field of activity and remedies were suggested. These remedies were spelt out in his constructive programme comprising 14 or 15 items aimed at economic and social reconstruction.

Mahatma Gandhi's doctrine of non-violence is applicable not only to the political battles but also to the battle for economic betterment. The great depression of 1929-33 and may smaller economic crises prove that it is the greed of some nations that is the root-cause of such maladies. A country or region has got the birth-right to forge ahead economically, but surely not at the cost of other countries or regions. But that is exactly the spirit of the modern world.

The spirit of cut-throat competition is everywhere. Even world bodies like the International Monetary Fund, the International Bank for Reconstruction and Development have failed miserably to bring about economic discipline to aching world.

Against this background, how meaningful were Gandhi's preachings. Gandhi wanted to prove that a country not only can prosper at others' cost, but also can transmit her prosperity to other countries too. In fact, the great upsurge for autarchy or nationalism frightened many western diplomats and political thinkers, and their apprehension was removed by Gandhi to a considerable extent. It is really a pity that India, that produced Gandhi, is now busy in regional squabbles instead of acting in a harmonious and well co-ordinated manner and thereby presenting a model to the whole world.

In the modern world, the value of human life seems to be rather insignificant in spite of the fact that much has been done to lengthen life-span and make life as comfortable as possible. The machnie has taken the place of primary importance in today's industrial world. Gandhi toiled for the superiority of humanity. He taught that all we do is to serve man, not to humiliate him. But what has happened today ? Human consideration has become the last consideration nowadays.

What is of utmost necessity today is to attempt to implement Gandhi teachings in practice with all seriousness and sincerity if the decaying economy of the country is to be saved. No doubt, a lot of abstract thinking has already been done on Gandhi's preachings. But what we need today is not any abstract thinking but practical implementation.

Today is too widely treated as an occasion for a ritual recapitulation of the continuing relevance of Mahatma Gandhi or Gandhism. And rituals can be red herrings. There is a whole school of "Gandhians", for example, who seek to project this relevance as an argument against India's growth to a state of self-reliance. Almost as though its proud identity as his country would be lost if the pathetic lot of those he identified with was changed : as though his premise of a sound socio-economic base for nation-building were the same as their status quoism. A truly Gandhian identification, on the contrary, will have to be with his spirit of struggle, of a struggle for change. Then, there are those who relate his relevance to one or the other of his several specific campaigns and thus, in effect, shorten it. To make matters of food, drink and clothing synonymous with his philosophy is something like making an eight-hour day the message of May Day. "My life is my message", said the Mahatma; and that life of epic heroism cannot be faithfully recalled in these limited terms. They do provide concrete images of a multifaceted personality and phenomenon; but concrete images shorn of their context run the risk of becoming caricatures.

All this, of course, does not make it any less fit an occasion to remind ourselves of Gandhi's relevance that has proved enduring beyond the ritual worshippers' comprehension. In fact, it is a fitter occasion than ever before, for his relevance is being recognised more widely than at any other time in the more than three decades since his martyrdom. The reasons for this rediscovery of the Mahatma are not far to seek. At the world level, it is the heightened threat of war and nuclear disaster that has inspired a new consciousness about what the apostle of non-violence uncompromisingly fought for : it is a new appreciation of the fact that what seemed a throwback to the past is actually a prescription for tommorrow and what wore a mantle of primitive simplicity promises a reign of civilized politics. In India, the revival of the memories of Gandhi and the Gahdhian age, and of interest in the phenomenon among the post-Independence generation, has come as a reminder of the values of the nation's freedom movement that underlay its vigour. It has come as a possible corrective to the corrosive cynicism, the legacy of the many failures and frustrations amid which the millions are continuing their often agonisingly slow march forward.

If that is the larger relevance, it has its immediate implications, too. With the practical-revolutionary spirit and humility of the "one-step-enough-for me" prophet, the patriotic Indian will today have to face the dire threat to the Mahatma's heritage. The saint's teaching demands more than archival homage, when recurring sectarian violence mocks at his supreme sacrifice. Religious in a fundamental sense, he was still never for what now passes for "religious fundamentlism." It is in a combat against the evil so sought to be elevated that his lifelong mission for man and "my Maker" culminated. This holiest of his crusades remains to be carried forward.

So we remainfully convinced about Mahatma Gandhi's relevance to our present situation. I think Nehru himself, after 15 years or so of his Prime Ministership, came to realise that after all, the path that Gandhi had shown was the right path to have been followed. It is very obvious that in the context of both socio-economic development and socio-economic change, Gandhi's is quite relevant. I believe Gandhi was the only top leader of the country on the morrow of Independence. No matter how powerful the State is, how good and honest the people are and how well-motivated the rulers of the country are, unless there is people's participation in all the processes of development, the country would not be able to march forward. In fact, Gandhi said that if in the first five years after Independence we failed to mobilise the entire people of the country for the task of nation building, the future would be dark. I think he spoke five years only because he knew that in five years, if this was done, there would be sufficient dynamism created and this dynamism would take the nation forward.

Mahatma Gandhi insisted that the means must correspond to the ends. He said : "Means and ends are convertible terms in my philosophy of life." They say, "Means are after all means." I would say, "Means are after all means." I would say, "Means are after all everthing." Today, foul means have a tendency of becoming a way of life. Creating a secure niche for oneself by hook or by crook is becoming the sole direction of an individual's effort.

Today is an age of conflict when almost every issue is sought to be resolved not through dispassionate examination and objective argument ; but through violence, students resort to violent methods for the redress of their grievances. Violence implies hatred and bitterness and it was against such hatred and bitterness that Mahatma Gandhi resolutely set his face. He advocated confrontation of evil, tryranny and injustice by the power of love.

Gandhi's philosophy is curative of the evils afflicting the social systems today. It is a possible answer to the global moral crisis as also to the human values and many other unresolved contradictions, such as between affluence and poverty, freedom and repression, technology and man.

There is nothing dogmatic about Venkataraman because he is a rationalist. He is of Gandhian vintage, is a strict vegetarian and a teetotaler. He believes in non-violence but like Mahatma Gandhi he holds that India must use every means to defend its integrity. In an speech at the unveiling of a statue of Sri Aurobindo he expressed the world's concern at the decay of values accompanied by a cancerous multiplication of materialist thoughtlessness, culminating with the threat of nuclear annihilation staring at our face which compels us to seek new moorings. "Our political struggle witnessed the initiative passing in due course from the hands of revolutionaries to the non-violent movement led by Mahatma Gandhi. But it should be realised that the war of India's freedom was won as a result of the part played by all the battles, violent as well as non-violent. We cannot understimate or belittle the roles of the different political schools, for each of them made their unique contribution," he said.[5]

Speaking at the Defence College in New Delhi a few months ago Venkataraman touched upon terrorism that stalkes the country today : "Day after day, come reports of deaths ; persons shot down only because they belong to a particular community. If terrorists think that they can compel a State to surrender to terrorism they are either living in a paradise of their own or are ignorant of history. State power is more potent than sporadic violence."

But will we so cynically give up Mahatma Gandhi ? Will we like a base Indian throw away this pearl ? Let us for once realize that Gandhi for us is not only an individual. Gandhi is a great deal more than Gandhi. He embodies the quint essence of our ancient culture. He became a political figure because when he lived amongst us our political emancipation was essential for the fulfilment of our moral destiny. He therefore made our politics essentially non-political, that is he gave our politics a moral and a spiritual dimension which changed the very character of our public life. He taught us that there was no worthy public life without private virtue. Rabindranath Tagore once said that 'the soul of the East has found a worthy symbol in Gandhi and that this great man is destined to play a prominent part in moulding the future of the world". So to renounce Gandhism will be to renounce our great role in history. And Gandhism is not really another 'ism', or political doctrine or school. It is the very breath of our true life if at all we must discover it from under the hard crust of political dirt that has accumulated around it during the last four decades.

Gautama Buddha was forgotton in the land of his birth. The Mahatma would seem to be facing the same threat. So far as the affairs of the nation are concerned they are hardly been conducted in the Gandhian style. People may wear the Gandhi cap, but that is all. It was left to Sir Richard Attenborrough to make a film on Mahatma Gandhi and revive his glory. Gandhian principles are not impracticable. But they are difficult to follow because the concept of duty, which is an integral part of Gandhian thought, has fallen from grace. In most cases people clamour for their rights without caring to remember that they have some duties to perform too.

REFERENCES

1. R.K. Murthi. Apprenticeship of Gandhi *Daily* (Bombay) 13 October, 1985 ; p. 15.
2. *Ibid.*
3. Dilip Bose. Mahatma Gandhi *Party Life* 7th February 1983; p. 15.
4. Som Nath Dhar. Relevance of Mahatma Gandhi today. *Indian & Foreign Review* 30 September, 1984 ; p. 4.
5. Promila Kalhan. *op. cit.*

8

NEHRU'S INFLUENCE

Venkataraman who had actively participated in the Quit India movement and had been detained for two years under the DIR got his first big break in 1950 when Kamaraj sent him to the provisional parliament. Here he came to the notice of India's first Prime Minister Jawaharlal Nehru who found him not only a keen debater and a painstaking parliamentarian, but one with a sound grasp of economic problems. Venkataraman, with his socialist background, found himself deeply influenced by Nehru's idealism, dedication to socialism and internationalism. In his own way he sought to strengthen Nehru's hands by forming a group in the Congress Parliamentary Party with the help of some other Members of Parliament like K. P. Tripathi of Assam. This brought him into conflict with T. T. Krishnamachari (TTK), a senior politician from the south, whom Nehru admired for his sharp intelligence and grasp of financial and industrial matters. One specific issue on which TTK and Venkataraman differed was that of automation of handlooms. Venkataraman was able to have his way and the government came out in favour of the handloom sector.

He also showed his progressive outlook when he succeeded in getting the scope of the amendment to the Compensation for Agricultural Property from the purview of the courts. Venkataraman mobilised enough support in the party for taking out compensation for urban and industrial property also from the purview of the courts, to the intense annoyance of TTK.

In spite of his being in tune with Jawaharlal Nehru's thinking and in spite of being a keen debater and active Member of Parliament—he was Secretary of the Congress Parliamentary Party in 1954—the Prime Minister rewarded Venkataraman with no ministerial office.

Though brought up in the Nehru tradition, probably in a state of forgetfulness he praised Nehru's arch opponent the famous industrialist J.R.D. Tata as a follower of Mahatma Gandhi's idea of trusteeship. Again as Finance Minister in 1980, he was misled into believing that the U.S. President Ronald Reagan's supplyside economy was the panacea of India's economic ills. These were permissible lapses in politics, for which he cannot be held responsible. No one gets over worked on unavoidable compulsions of a given situation.

In the bizarre politics of India Venkataraman emerged as a consensus candidate of the Congress conscience. The younger generation of India's rulers are being profited from his experience and also become conversant with the Indian reality. There is still some wisdom left in East.

Jawaharlal Nehru was one of the most charismatic figures of our times, second only to Mahatma Gandhi. Both these men assumed heroic dimensions in the context of Indian history India's freedom movement. No student of modern can be unaware of the remarkably close relationships that existed between these two very dissimilar men who had marked differences in background, valued and in the genesis and development of their political thought. Dr. Pillai, while commenting on their almost irreconciliable positions on matters relating to the policies of the Indian national movement also demonstrates how close they were in mutual affection and the fact that it was Nehru's great respect for Gandhi, his admiration of Gandhi's intuition, Gandhi's success in making the formerly elitist Indian National Congress a mass movement that led Nehru to defer to Gandhi by moderating some of his extreme positions on matters of national importance.

As for Nehru, his adherence to the socialist ideas is well known ; almost from the very start of his vigorous political activity in the 20's to the end of his life he remained a champion of socialism. Socialism, as envisioned by Nehru, had a social and economic orientation in a greater degree than a religious and moral one as was the case with Mahatma Gandhi. Way back in 1933, in one of his interviews, Nehru declared that the future prosperity of the Indian masses depended on a full reconstruction of the society along new lines.

After the gaining of indepedence, the leaders of the INC, primarily Nehru, continued to develop the concept of the primacy of the popular masses in social and political transformations. At the same time, more and]more attention was paid to the need to raise the cultural level of the masses and radically improve the conditions of their material life. A decisive means for achieving these aims they saw precisely in socialism, which Nehru understood as a social system ensuring social equality for all citizens of the country.

Taking the real correlation of forces in India into account, Nehru saw that it would hardly be possible for the country to proclaim socialism as the programme goal of the Indian National Congress as soon as it won independence. However, he invariably underlined that he was for socialism and hoped that India would build socialism.

Nehru's sincere devotion to socialist ideals exerted a thorugh influence on thc ideological foundation of the Indian National Congress. It was on his initiative and through his efforts that the INC session in Avadi in January 1955 proclaimed the building in India of a society of a socialist type as its programmatic aim.

After independence, Jawaharlal Nehru dominated the national scene. From a militant soldier of the Congress, he rose to be its topmost leader. With his largeness of vision, cosmopolitan culture, and his constructive and radical approach to the multifarious problems confronting the country, Nehru took India a long way towards progress and prosperity. He was a great democrat who helped to build democratic institutions. He taught India the temper of democracy. He was the greatest parliamentarian of his time, who upheld the dignity and decorum of Parliament. Secularism was a natural corollary of Nehru's democratic faith in the right of every individual to attain his full stature. Religious bigotry or communal fanaticism aroused his righteous indignation, and he was vehement in denouncing communal disputes. Indeed, he was never tired putes. Indeed, he was never tired of stressing the need for communal harmony as a prerequisite of national solidarity ; it was a recurrent theme in his numerous public speeches and writings. He was convinced that, for India with tremendous diversities, secularism was the only creed that could pull the country together. If India remained integrated and stood solidly behind him, it was because it was a secular country.[1]

Jawaharlal Nehru was a staunch believer in the socialistic pattern of society, but he was not an adherent of Marxist theories. His socialism was more Indian than Marxist ; it offered the best prospect of meeting the requirements of equality and social justice and the challenge of modern science and technology. Nehru's contribution to the economic development was his planning. He was convinced, that India could get ahead by the application of science and technology, by large-scale industrialisation, by the creation of a self-sustaining society. It was this conviction, which set in motion the process of integrated development and changed the face of India. The mighty river valley projects like Nangal, the giant steel mills like Bhilai, the heavy engineering and machine building plants, nuclear power stations, the oil refineries, the chain of national laboratories, the country-wide community development programme, the revived village panchayats were the products of his scientific attitude to life and planning. In the economic sphere, India achieved in two decades what other countries achieved in many a decade.

By 1960, almost a decade and a half after its original and rudimentary enunciation, the concept of non-alignment acquired a clarity and a specificity which, for instance, is evident from Jawaharlal Nehru's address at the first Non-Aligned Summit Conference held in Belgrade in 1961. He said :

> We call ourselves non-aligned countries. The word "non-aligned" may be differently interpreted, but basically it was coined and used with the meaning of being non-aligned with the great Power blocs of the world.
>
> "Non-aligned" has a negative meaning. But if we give it a positive connotation, it means notions which object to lining up for war purposes, to military blocks, to military alliances and the like. We keep away from such an approach and want to throw our weight in favour of peace.

He added :

> Some six, seven or eight years ago, non-alignment was a rare phenomenon. A few countries here and there asked about it and other countries rather made fun of it or, at any rate, did not take it seriously. "Non-alignment" ? What is this ? You must be on this side or that", that was the argument. That argument is dead today.
>
> The whole course of history of the last few years has shown a growing opinion spread in favour of the concept of non-alignment. Why ? Because it was in tune with the course of events ; it was in tune with the thinking of the vast numbers of people......because they hungered passionately for peace......

About a year before he died, Jawaharlal Nehru wrote an article in the journal *Foreign Affairs*, New York (April 1963), which includes probably one of his last reflections on the NAM and the UN. He wrote : "......'Non-alignment' has become a summary description of this policy of friendship towards all nations, uncompromised by adherence to any military pacts...... Essentially 'non-alignment' is freedom of action which is a part of independence......'non-alignment' is now an integral part of the international pattern and is widely conceded to be a comprehensible and legitimate policy, particularly for the emergent Afro-Asian states".

In this historical background it can be legitimately maintained that Non-Alignment as a concept of global politics, as a foreign policy premise and as a perspective of maximising national interests of the newly-liberated countries—is India's contribution to contemporary international relations. In an epoch of world history, when alignment with power-blocs and affiliation with ideological poles dominated international transactions, non-alignment emerged as an assertion of independence in foreign affairs, as a process of diffusion of 'bloc monoliths', as a symbol of defiance against big-power domination, and as a diplomatic innovation in the phase of politics of confrontation and cold war. But its main thrust was to shift focus from *status quo* to change, from arms race to development, from fragmentation in blocs to an emerging unified world of interdependence and co-existence imbued with the values of peace, equality, justice and humanism.[2]

There are lives which do not end with death. Jawaharlal Nehru's life was one such life. It is hard to think of anyone who responded so sensitively, creatively, and with such restraint and balance, and yet such a radical temper to the challenges of building new politics in the decolonised world as Jawaharlal Nehru did. This outstanding characteristic of his is to be understood in terms of historical constraints within which he worked and limitations of leadership of a very heterogenous movement—the Indian National Congress, as the liberation movement and also as a party which became the symbol of established national power, ceasing to be a movement without becoming a party in the conventional sense of the term.[3]

The Indian revolution of 1947 was an amazing phenomenon. Its impact has been felt by the large mass of people both in this continental polity of India and outside. This massive revolution of India's resurgence to new identity, a new identity and as a nation and as its symbol was largely possible through the effort of outstanding leaders. In this galxay of leadership, no one subsumed the finest elements of the ancient heritage and carried it forward into the contemporary age as are splendent synthesis of the past, the present and a vision of the future as much as Jawaharlal Nehru did. A remarkable aspect of Jawaharlal Nehru was this creative passion in his personality which all the time was attempting to reconcile radical ideals—which he had but was not able to translate into practice, was incapable of doing so since they were not posited in the structure—with the objective constraints of a situation complex as that of India.[4]

Jawaharlal's undying message is that no true leadership is possible without metaphysical commitment to human freedom and dignity, and any other national or internatioeal programme of action, howsoever grandiose, must be subordinate to this basic commitment. In fact, without this commitment which leads to total indentification with man in all his hunger, disease, want and insecurity, all agenda of action is meaningless. Creative initiative into future, into the possibilities of human destiny arise from the deep understanding of the emotional matrix which surround human existence. Jawaharlal's total identification with that intellectual and emotional matrix of man gave him that Asokan leadership.

Today we have more belligerence in man than anytime in history. Human selfishness has assumed more complex are more pernicious institutional forms. Ideological inflexibilities put human freedom in chains. Perversions of national ego commit worst crimes on human dignity. Men, women and children starve and die in one part of the world while large quantities of foo[illegible] are destroyed elsewhere. Whether it is world peace of I[illegible] national Economic Order, nowhere is there any concern for the universal man. And the most absurd thing of all is that all this is being done in the name of civilisation, human dignity and well being. We need today, as ever before, more Asokan leaders with metaphysical commitment to man, and man alone. Despite all the grandeur of human civilisation, it seems at times as if the journey towards the freedom and dignity of the universal man has hardly begun, and there are miles to go to fulfill the promises of Mahatma Gandhi and Jawaharlal Nehru whose memory ever helps to illumine the path to our goal.

It is difficult to speak about Jawaharlal Nehru. So much has been written on him and about him—not least by himself. It would be futile on my part to attempt to isolate some significant aspect of Nehru and subject it to a scholarly treatment. I felt, however, that there might be perhaps some point in recording the impressions of a person who had been reacting to Jawaharlal Nehru ever since he became conscious of the world around him, and who had the privilege to see him from far as well as near and to serve under him.[5]

The vast majority of us have no faces to show. We wear masks, Jawaharlal Nehru wore no mask. His face reflected every passing mood, feeling and emotion. Reading again through his autobiography I discovered the reason why his face was so sensitive. Contemplating the faces of Buddhist *bhikshus* (monks), Nehru reflects on the dilemma posed by his inner life and its outward manifestation. He observes.

> The dominant expression of almost all of them (*bhikshus*) was one of peace and calm, a strange detachment from the cares of the world. They did not have intellectual faces, as a rule, and there was no trace of the fierce conflicts of the mind on their countenances. Life seemed to be for them a smooth flowing river moving slowly to the great ocean. I looked at them with some envy, with just a faint yearning for a haven, but I knew well enough that my lot was a different one, cast in storms and tempests. There was to be no haven for me, for the tempests within me were as stormy as those outside. And if perchance I found myself in a safe harbour, protected from the fury of the winds, would I be contented or happy there?

Nehru spoke of secularism not to secure the votes of the non-Hindus. He preached socialism not because it attracted the poor to cast their votes in favour of the Congress. His secularism and socialism were based on well reasoned grounds because he knew no other way to either fight poverty and backwardness or to hold the country together. He thought big and acted big. A big country like India, he often said, could not be managed by small minded men. In the company of the great even small men become great. In the company of small and petty even great and noble souls are finally degraded.

In economic planning, and in all vital programmes of national welfare, Nehru acted as a true democrat and will be remembered in history as one of the best democrats of the century. He was open to conviction, and prepared to modify a previous stand, or, at any rate, not to adopt too ritid a posture. His willingness to set aside his scheme of co-operative farming in the teeth of opposition is an example of his flexibility and accommodation. Never ruthless in his methods, he believed in winning opponents over rather than in fighting them. In the formulation of all major policies, and, in particular, those concerning economic or industrial planning, he was keen on achieving a national consensus by consultation with the various political parties. Jawaharlal Nehru bestrode India like a colossus. He represented its spirit. He was the dynamic, living image of our national ethos, who despended its historical vitality and latent strength. As a leader of a great country, with people of multifarious castes and creeds, languages and other diversities, India presented a gigantic challenge. With enormous patience and great persuasive powers, Nehru showed to the people, that both democracy and socialism were inevitable in the conditions prevailing in the country, and that both could go together. It was his effort to reconcile the democratic process with the socialist process, and it was in the pursuit of this endeavour that he gave the right direction to the country. In dedication and in the unwearied pursuit of his ideas, there are few parallels to Nehru. It is Jawaharalal's rich heritage that needs to be cherished. That Nehruism still evokes intense sympathy and respect, and attracts many an intellectual, explains how comprehensive and potent is his world outlook.[6]

"In a democratic country like India, we cannot think of any social objective which does not touch the vast masses of the people". This profound statement unfolds the life's purpose of the great son of India who laboured for the economic emancipation of his countrymen after freeing them from political serfdom. This declaration was made by Jawaharlal Nehru before a galaxy of industrialists and economists, both as a challenge and as an inspiration. Nehru had the vision of the kind of socialism that suited the Indian environment on an enduring basis. An early votary of British Fabian socialism, Nehru's ideas were influenced by Sydney and Beatrice

Webb, Harold Laski and Bernard Shaw. In 1907 Nehru got initiated to the subject of socialism through a lecture by Bernard Shaw at Cambridge. However, it was Nehru's short visit to the Soviet Union in 1927 that transformed him in a sense. Nehru then became a staunch advocate of socialism which he regarded as the only alternative for India.[7]

In his book, "Soviet Russia" published in 1928, Nehru spoke of the "Dynamic forces released by the Revolution of 1917". Viewing the conditions confronting Russia and India, he noted, "Both have to face poverty and illiteracy. If Russia finds a satisfactory solution for these, our work in India is made easier."

At home, Nehru intended to create a society in which every individual had an equal opportunity to develop and progress. There was a robust sense of history and a deep commitment to a scientific secular outlook in him. To Nehru, planning basically implied the extension of the domain of rationality from the individual to the area of social decision-making. An admirer of the Russian experiment, Nehru distilled his own brand of socialism with a deliberate attempt to effect a compromise between extreme totalitarianism and a system that would ensure freedom for the individual to develop, his personality in his own way. And in this task, Nehru shone and emerged as a heroic blender of opposites. With malice towards none and charity for all shades of ideas, he drew the best from differing political ideologies with great circumspection that was no characteristic of his own.

Socialism attracted Nehru not merely in the humanitarian sense but, more than that, in its welfare ethos. His socialism included nationalisation of the primary means of production, distribution and exchange. And yet, unfortunately, one of the abiding ironies of the Nehru phenomenon has been that his economic and socialist ideas were not easily grasped and correctly interpreted even as they were not that inscrutable, In the dithering economic situation that was yet to form its shape after the country's freedom from foreign rule, unwittingly our economists and socialists distorted his views by drawing an invidious cleavage between the philosophies of Mahatma Gandhi and Nehru on vital economic issues. However, what

Nehru did by unfolding his socialist ideas was nothing but taking the Gandhian ideology to its logical conclusion in the social milieu of India. The disciple of Gandhi did it because he believed in its strength and viability, and not because he was a blind follower.[8]

Nehru's feeling for socialism for the country can be gauged from his presidential address at the All India Congress Committee Session in Lahore as early as 29 December 1929—much before independence of the country. Nehru said: "I must frankly confess that I am a socialist and a republican, and am no believer in kings and princes, or in the order which produces the modern kings of industry, who have greater power over the lives and fortunes of men than even the kings of the old feudal aristocracy. I recognise that in the present circumstances of the country it may not be possible to adopt a full socialist programme. But we must realise that the philosophy of socialism has gradually permeated the entire structure of society the world over; and almost the only points in dispute are the pace and methods of advance to its full realisation. India will have to go that way, too, if she seeks to end her poverty and inequality, though she may evolve her own methods and may adopt the ideal to the genius of her race."

On the issue of poverty and inequality, Rousseau propounded the basis of inequality among men by pointing out that the progress of science degarded the morals of men. Proudhon declared property as robbery and found it as the fountainhead of inequality. Mahatma Gandhi branded the property-owner a thief who are without work. And when Nehru thought of the equalisation of wealth, he meant its equalisation through plenty. His view tended to suggest at times that he would prefer inequality without poverty to equality with poverty.

Nehru never disagreed with Mahatma Gandhi on the question of heavy industry vs. small-scale industry and yet, he is mistakenly drawn into this controversy by those who did not have an understanding of the resilience of the growth process itself. As times passed many thought that modern technology and science, together with the pressures of social justice and democracy, blunted the sharper edges of conflict between heavy and small-scale industries. But that was not to be. Nehru allowed both to grow as complementary to each other. He appointed the Karve Committee and placed adequate emphasis on small and village industries in the 2nd Plan.

Nehru's simultaneous emphasis on heavy industries was the theme of an effort towards a self-generating economy, to make India capable of producing what it sought from outside and free it ultimately from the psychological and practical burdens of foreign dependency. With fast developments in science and technology in the developed world. Nehru would have betrayed conservatism and lack of foresight had he not tried to modernise India's heavy industry sector.[9]

That the use of modern-science and technology was unavoidable was the central focus of Nehru thought. The mighty industrial structure of today's India has not only raised our status in the eyes of the world but has also triggered off our development process at a much faster speed. It is a living testimony to the wisdom of the man who said : "I do not think it is possible for India to be really independent unless she is technically advanced country". The present level of the country's industrialisation is sufficient evidence of the inspiration drawn from these words of Nehru.

Socialists of all brands, from Utopian to Scientific, agree that socialism is a means for social reconstruction. Nehru starts from the same fundamental and as he proceeds, he find his own way of working it out. Through years of thought, Nehru evolved his own ideas about socialism and gave it a practical shape for initiating the process of structural changes. Writing to his daughter Indira in 1933, Nehru said : "Socialism, I have told you, is of many kinds. There is general agreement, however, that it aims at the control by the state of the means of production, that is, land and mines and factories and the like, and means os distribution, like railways, etc., and also banks and similar institutions. The idea is that the individuals should not be allowed to exploit any of these methods or institutions or the labour of others to their own personal advantage." *Glimpses of World History. Vol. II, pp. 851-52*).

As 'scientific socialism' became the refrain of Nehru's frequent utterances, propaganda pamphlets, dubbing him "a high priest of Communism" came into circulation. And the Intelligence Bureau of the then British Government issues a note to all provincial governments in 1937. The note called Nehru "a self-inspired Communist and anally of all that mass revolution means." But then, it was a tribute to Nehru to have been recognised as a leftist pillar who would destroy the British empire through a mass movement based on an ideology, not sentiments or hatred.

Truth must triumph, said Mahatma Gandhi. That mankind must survive and co-operate was the clarion call of Nehru to the whole world. This international statesman gave as much wisdom to the world as he did at home on the virtues of social transformation. His greatest contribution is the conviction that "India will pull itself up by work and sacrifice, it consents to do so, but never, never under the knout". And thus, Nehru proved that he understood the "seamy side of life" although no less a person than his father, Motilal Nehru, was sceptical in his life-time about this aspect of Jawahar's personality.[10]

Nehru, the socialist, craved to establish a society where the suffering people are fully covered by various social security measures. Nehru, the economist, would like to fulfil this dream only as a by-product of development, not as its prerequisite. A down-to-earth social reformer, Nehru embodied in himself humanity personified for whom no cause was dearer to his heart than wiping out the tears from the face of every citizen of India.

Jawaharlal Nehru faced worse problems than the one in Punjab during his Prime Ministership. In 1950, there was an exodus of Hindus from East Bengal. The trouble in two Bengals led to the resignation of S.P. Mookerjee from the Union Cabinet in April that year. Then there was the China problem in 1962.

As regards internal problems, the linguistic issue of 1956 and famines, droughts and floods had been the bane of the country. There had never been a year without one or another crisis in India.

Venkataraman would like the present generation to read books written by Jawaharlal Nehru. "There give the responses of a sensitive mind who was totally committed to his country but had an international perspective. Only by knowing Nehru's thoughts and actions can we deal properly and correctly with the problems of the country and the world."

Jawaharlal was a dreamer of an wonderful world in which peace would prevail, nations would discard arms to settle their disputes and co-operate on a global plane to lift the overwhelming majority of humanity out of the abysmal poverty, disease and ignorance, and function as sovereign states irrespective of their size, wealth or population. He believed that despite differences in race or colour, all human beings belonged to only one species. He loved humanity and, above all, the people of India from whom he received immesne affection and love.

He proudly claimed : "I have received so much love and affection from the Indian people that nothing that I can do can repay even a small fraction of it, and indeed there can be no repayment of so precious a thing as affection."

Nehru's love for India reflected not in the words he uttered, though to hear him was always like listening to a poet or a *rishi*. People loved him because he meant what he said and what he said he sought to implement in real life. The entire period he presided over the destiny of our nation as Prime Minister is packed with creativity and the foundation stones of modern temples to which foreign guests are invited to pay visit. He knew the fundamental principles of nation building and acted accordingly. He generalised and conceptualised the experience of the capitalist and socialist societies in the five year plans he helped to formulate and put into effect.

An intensely spiritual man, Jawaharlal Nehru was secular in thought. He might have visited temples and mosques, *gurudwaras* (Sikh shrines) and catherdrals to see their architectural beauty, treating them as a stage in human yearning for great and noble deeds. In the archives of the Press Information Bureau there may not be any picture of Nehru worshipping at any shrine or lying prostrate before idols or dead bodies lying in marbled graves. No minister during his days dared to perform *puja* in his office or ask the Minister for Housing to allot him a house selected by his astrologer. He respected all faiths but stuck to his own. If the Constitution of Indian could not be as secular as the constitution of the United States or as socialistic oriented as he wanted it to be, it was mainly due to the crowd of politians with whom he had to work. He was not a voluntarist, imposing his views on others against their will either in government policies or in the organisation largely controlled by people whose preoccupation with power he intensely hated.

This is not to say that he did not lead or put his foot firmly down where matters of principle were involved. Many of his colleagues parted company with him but he rarely gave consent to any one's expulsion. Compared to him Gandhi was a disciplinarian who on occasions coerced his followers into accepting some thing that did not want by his own novel way of "self-purification" and penance. He hated mediocrity, listened to the lowest with great attention, honoured men of science and literature. His personality was an open book, open to all to look into it. Secrecy was a sign of cowardicy or something that one feared to admit in public.

What seems most striking now about Nehru is the contemporary relevance of the issues that weighed heavily on his mind in the closing years of his life. He was a legend in his life-time. Nehru spent his formative years in Edwardian England. Then he spent years to grapple with the questions of war, peace and Nazi outrages in the years between the two World wars. It was largely his initiative that forget an astonishing linkage between India's struggle for her own freedom and all-sided renovation and the central questions of his time which were then deciding the destiny not only of one particular people or nation but of humankind.

Nehru is the author of non-alignment—the global credo now of all nations which cherish the sovereign right to take autonomous decisions on international questions. He was the pathfinder of newly freed former colonies of the West. But the road of assertive independence he enjoined on the former colonies has now become a global movement, a valid policy for all nations keen on defending their independence and desire for peace. Nehru spoke of non-alignment in 1946, even before the British withdrawal from India. Fifteen years later, in Belgrade, when the government leaders of non-aligned countries made a modest beginning of the movement, imperialism had combined with the nuclear threat to constitute a grave crisis. It was Nehru again in that assemblage of government leaders who warned in 1961 of the calamity thermonuclear weapons meant for the mankind.

Imperialism, he knew, was doomed, no matter what rearguard battles the West might offer to shield it and the mutation old-fashioned colonialism might undergo. In 1961, world Africa was still in bondage ; and many countries around the were waging their separate battles for national independence. The movement of the unaligned was in the forefront of that struggle. But Nehru comprehended the fundamentally altered world situation thermonuclear weaponry had created. With the clarity of a true seer, Nehru wanted the movement of the non-aligned to take notice of the lenghening shadows atomic weapons were casting on the future of homo sapiens as a species on the only planet on which it is known to exist. His concerns then often attracted mocking disbelief in the West and also in those Indian circles whose mental bondage had not terminated with the end of British rule in India. Now when humanity is menaced by a capacity for overkill which had not materialised in Nehru's time and the US threatens to militarize space, Nehru posthumously regains contemporary relevance for our current concern about humankind's capacity for survival.

As regards Nehru's love for his countrymen, let us recall what he felt of the people of his great nation : "I have received so much love and affection from the Indian people that nothing that I can do repay even a small fraction of it, and indeed there can be more payment of so precious a thing as affection."

As we look at the world today, threatened with extinction through nuclear warfare, beset with serious conflicts between States, big or small, and unable to eradicate the poverty of hundreds upon millions, the vision of Jawaharlal Nehru—for a new moral and material ordering of the world community ; for sanity and tolerance in relations between States and within States ; for an end to exploitation in all its forms ; and last but not the least, for an awakening of the creative capacities of the common man—acquires a new relevance for our times. This vision needs to be restated over and over again in its essentials. Jawaharlal Nehru's outlook was shaped by the aspirations of the people of India in the course of their epic struggle for freedom. It combined all that was noble and true in the culture of India—as expressed by Mahatma Gandhi—with the compassion and humanism of the 20th century. Within India, Jawaharlal Nehru sought to transform a civilisation of antiquity into a modern industrial state, secular in outlook, democratic in its political character, and permeated with the vision of a new social order. Beyond the frontiers of India, Jawaharlal Nehru sought to promote peace between nations, big or small, and impart a new voice to the newly-liberated countries of Asia, Africa and Latin America.[11]

In its essentials, the vision of Jawaharlal Nehru continues to inspire the internal development of India, just as it also shapes our foreign policy ; and beyond India, this vision influences the attitude of the non-aligned and peace-loving peoples as a whole.

A great achievement of Nehru's theoretical concepts in the sphere of international politics was the concept of non-alignment, and he was the first to put it into effect. A major distinctive feature of this concept and, accordingly, of the policy of non-alignment is its anti-imperialist orientation, opposition to any aggressive militaryblocs, advocacy of the principles of peaceful coexistence of states with different social systems and active championing of peace. The putting forward of the policy of non-alignment as a line pivotal to the foreign policy of the Republic of India, know as the Nehru line, brought it high prestige and the status of a leader among all the newly—independent of states of the socialist community and the support of all champions of peace and progress.

Therefore, in the complex and multiform ideological heritage of Gandhi and Nehru there is a series of substantial elements that have predetermined the progressive features of the ideology and practical activities of the Indian National Congress. The past decades have fully confirmed the lasting value of the ideological heritage of Gandhi and Nehru, which was passed on from one generation of the INC politicians to another and have enabled the party to remain the most authoritative and influential force in the political arena of India today.

Today India finds herself in a position of carrying forward the major aspect of Nehru's policy in other forms ; we insist on opposting the non-proliferation treaty and its discriminatory provisions ; we also insist on continuing to oppose atmospheric tests in the first instance and all tests later. Our own single peaceful nuclear explosion was an underground one with no threat of radiation to any one either in our country or in the neighbouring states. We believe that only a comprehensive test ban treaty together with the outlawing of nuclear weapons and the graduated reduction of the stockpiles would lead to acceptable conditions in which the world community can survive and flourish.

Apart from these global strategic issues and specific disputes and conflicts in which India was involved, there was the equally important pervasive problem of economic development for the newly independent countries. Nehru's total world vision encompassed the evolution of a socially just society within India ; for this purpose he devised in a certain pragmatic manner 'a mixed economy' in which the public sector was given a dominant role while the private sector was encouraged to be active within certain limits. This was the original vision. In actual practice, as we all know, things have not exactly turned out to be as he hoped for. We do have a substantial though much criticised public sector, but there is a much more active, even turbulent private sector more powerful and influential than had been scheduled either in the pre-Independence programming of the Congress Planning Committee under Nehru's chairmanship or in the successive Five-Year Plans.produced by the Goverment after independence.

As far as external relations were concerned, however, this decision to evolve a mixed economy at home led to inevitable policy consequences. The political and strategic decision to refrain from too much nearness to the major powers was complemented by an equally clear willingness to cooperate responsively with all nations in economic matters. From the very beginning, India has believed in international economic cooperation in the giving and receiving of credits and in the exchange of technical skills. The post-war economic system. the post-war monetary institutions etc, were found by our country to be extremely useful props to our own development efforts ; more than that, we developed in the first decad after independence, a certain expertise as an aid-giver and an aid-recipient in strictly limited circumstances and with comparatively small funds in the Colombo Plan.

As a freedom-fighter, Venkataraman is proud of what India has done with-its freedom. "If you compare India with the other countries to have achieved independence after the Second World war, you will find that it is head and shoulders above them all."

"India", he says, "is going through the pangs of development." And, he holds that it is faced with many of its current problems because "we have deviated from Nehru's path."

Elaborating, he says : "If we try to follow the American model, where the Devil takes the hindmost, or the Communist method where rigour is demanded, it may not suit the Indian genius, Nehru's doctrine of democratic socialism, of the mixed economy, is in tune with the people's thinking".

REFERENCES

1. Manmohan mehra. Legacy of Jowaharlal Nehru. *Hindustan Times* 13 June 1986 ; p. 9.
2. Rasheeduddin Khan. Peace and security in nuclear age *Secular Democracy* (New Delhi) November 1986 : p. 54.
3. Rasheduddin Khan Nehru—Makear of national consensus *Patriot* 26 Junary 1987.
4. *Ibid.*
5. P.K. Haksar Relevence of Jawahrlal Neeru *Mainsthream* 24 May 1987 ; p 23.
6. Monmohan Mehra. *op. cit.*
7. Navin Chandra Joshi soeialism Nehru wanted for India *Patriot* 14 November 1986 ; p. 4.
8. *Ibid.*
9. *Ibid.*
10. *Ibid.*
11. R. N. Haksar National declaration on Nehru's Vision of peace and Security in nuclear age *Secular Democracy* November 1986 ; p. 3

9

THE SECRET OF SUCCESS OF KAMARAJ

History has few parallels, if any, in which a person with no advantages of birth, status, wealth and education rose to high positions of trust and responsibility as Kamaraj has done. The late Prime Minister (Jawaharlal Nehru), once remarked that there is something positively great in Kamaraj that enabled him to overcome all the handicaps and march forward in the service of the people. Many a politician in India and abroad has asked me about the secret of success of Kamaraj and I have no doubt the mystery will ever remain. He has been an enigma even to his closest associates and has never shared some of his innermost thoughts with any. Gifted with an insight into human nature, he can easily size up men and situations with uncanny precision. No facade, no artifice is beyond his piercing intellect though he looks apparently convinced. He is truly India's Man of Destiny.[1]

"Kamaraj built up slowly and step by step his hold on the masses by understanding their problems and trying to find solutions for them. His broad sympathy for the people and his anxiety to serve them, very soon made him the idol of the masses. He developed inordinate patience to hear all the grievances and to console and comfort almost everyone who came to seek his assistance.

"He has another deep philosophy and that is the people are right." He has never allowed any laws, rules, regulations, or other social inhibitions to stand in the way of doing the right by the masses. Often times during the course of administration many came and represented against the tyranny of some executive orders, rules and regulations. On all those occasions, he had been advised by officialism that the requirements of rules, laws and regulations were compiled with and that the consequences or the situations were either inevitable or irremediable. On those occasions when Kamaraj felt that the grievances were genuine or that the hardships should be remedied, he never hesitated to have the rules changed or the regulations modified, in order to see that justice was rendered.

He toured widely throughout the State only for the purpose of keeping his eyes and ears wide open and collecting all the details and information that were available. Sitting in the Secretariat and dealing with the files one normally gets the impression that everything is sound and satisfactory with the administration. It is only when one goes and meets people in different walks of life, in different situations, who are affected differently by the administrative measures that one gets a correct picture of the numerous shortcomings in otherwise perfectly valid administrative measures. His wide knowledge of all the details and his quick and receptive mind gave him a mastery over the State's entire administration. It looked as if he was all the time checking with the masses the correctness of the administrative measures taken by the Government. I know of very few administrators who brought to bear this new approach to administration.

The world has seen men of humble beginnings going up the ladder of life. But it always happens that when they reach the height of social status or political power, they forget the surroundings and environs from which they have grown. But in the case of Kamaraj whatever positions he achieved he retained the basic love of the common man and of the less fortunate section of society. He firmly believes that the real progress of the country lies in uplifting the masses and he has devised two basic programmes. It was his dream that every boy and girl in Tamil Nadu should be enabled to study up to the School Final without any fees and with mid-day meals, if possible. He gave the highest priority to education since he believed that once people got some basic knowledge they would somehow manage to earn a living. In the years before he became the Chief Minister of Madras he used to speak at all the rural meetings urging people somehow to educate their children. He used to insist that it was only by educating the children that the future of this great country could be ensured.

"His second programme was rapid industrialisation of the State with a view to increasing the employment opportunities and to provide the wherewithal to the largest number of people in the shortest possible time. Until Kamaraj took charge of the administration, Madras was primarily an agricultural State. He launched on a programme of rapid industrialisation and took a bold decision about financing the ventures. Realising that capital in Madras was both poor and shy, he enabled the Madras Industrial Investment Corporation to supply the deficiency by a bold and imaginative policy of participating in the share capital of private enterprise. It is this decision which has enabled the State to march forward during the decade of his administration from a primarily agricultural State to one of the highly industrialised States in India. On one occasion, when it was suggested to him that an investment of a crore of rupees would have to be made, a lesser man would have shrunk from the proposition but he said that if the project was worthwhile it should be encouraged and then he added characteristically that big achievements could not come without big decisions.

"He firmly believed in the dispersal of industries throughout the country and took keen interest on the location of even small individual projects. In everyone of the functions inaugurating new industries, he never failed to draw attention to the 'employment potential' of the industry and its impact on raising the standard of life of the people of the area.

"Kamaraj has the genius of growing bigger than the job confronts him. Though elected President of the Tamil Nadu Congress Committee with a bare majority, he became its unquestioned leader within a short-time. Similarly, though many doubted his ability to carry on the administration of a highly intellectual and political State like Madras, he proved bigger than the task before him. When he was elected President of the Indian National Congress some people doubted whether he could translate his success in the provincial field to an all-India field comprising different elements, speaking different languages and having different outlook and approach to national problems. But the way in which he handled the critical situation on the demise of our beloved Prime Minister Jawaharlal Nehru showed that there is no task which is too big for him. He has no complexes—either inferiority or superiority. He retains his genuine self whatever be the strata of society he has to deal with. He never feels himself superior when he talks to the masses, the poor and illiterate in the fields and farms. Likewise, he does not feel inferior in the presence of statesmen, scholars or foreign dignitaries and other personages. His genuis for conveying the most complicated concepts of economics into the simple, intelligible language of the masses, his conversational style of speaking at public meetings and his vast knowledge of things gathered mainly by discussions with intellectuals have greatly contributed to his unique command over the mind of the masses. His transparent sincerity and unquestioned integrity have a great mass appeal.

"Disclosing the Kamaraj Plan before formulating it to the Working Committee, he said, that in this country the *sanyasi* was more respected than the king and that the man who sacrificed was more admired than the man who possessed all the wealth of the world. It is his desire to live the life of a political *sanyasi* that has given him the lead over all our leaders today.

"The time for evaluating Kamaraj's services to this country has not yet come. In fact, he is in the midst of making history and the country expects him to give the lead for another quarter of a century. The chronicles of a nation are bound up with the lives and work its leaders and the name of Kamaraj will be immortalised in the pages of our national history".

For long, Kamaraj has been a patron-saint of Congressmen of all shades in Tamil Nadu. He played a key role on the national scene too. His admirers have often echoed, in all seriousness, the famous words of Moliere's character Mascarille that "people of quality know everything without ever having learnt anything". Kamaraj did not have any formal education worth mentioning.

The Congress (I) in Tamil Nadu continues to swear by Kamaraj. Yet, there is also an effort now to project. Prime Minister Rajiv Gandhi as a saviour-successor to Kamaraj in this State. Indira Gandhi could never assume such a mantle mainly because of her proclivity to change sides in Tamil Nadu politics.

As against Rajaji, the freedom struggle also produced in the south another Gandhian who was a pragmatic socialist. It was Kumaraswamy Kamaraj who openly used to say that he did not believe in Gandhian economics. He believed in large-scale industry, modernisation and technological advance. But he believed the spartan simplicity propagated by Gandhi was essential if the Congress was to be an instrument of meaningful social change. He used to say : "Gandhi was not fool. He knew that poverty and unemployment could not be done away with for a hundred years. So he called upon public workers to be meek and humble so that the people would know that they too shared their poverty. This would give them more endurance in the struggle for better living". So as Nehru did in the all India sphere, Kamaraj outshone Rajaji as a Gandhian committed to bring about basic institutional changes. And he did a lot to remember him by.

It was, however, Kamaraj who, possibly sensing that his protege was not getting what he deserved and realising his own need to have him by his side when he formed the government in Tamil Nadu in 1954, wanted Venkataraman back. Kamaraj had been diffident about taking over the Chief Ministership of the State owing to his lack of administrative experience and the handicap of not knowing English, but Venkataraman had assured him of his help. Even though he had been elected to the Lok Sabha in 1957. Kamaraj pressed him to join state politics and made him Minister of Industry, Labour, Power and several other departments. He was elected a member of the State Council and was for the next ten years leader of the House and a senior minister of the cabinet. It was as Industry Minister that Venkataraman established his reputation as a "go-getter". Thanks to the contacts he had made in Delhi and the backing of his Chief Minister, he was able to implement a massive progrrmme of industrialisation, particularly in the medium and small-scale sector. For the *Brahmin* community in the South, this came as a boon. With employment in services barred to them owing to the strident non-*Brabmin* movement, it provided the community an outlet to utilise its talents.

In 1967, the Congress suffered a rout in Tamil Nadu. Venkataraman, who became out of job, was made a member of the Planning Commission, incharge of industry, labour, transport and communications. He remained a member of the Planning Commission till 1971. This was a crucial period for Kamaraj who had been instrumental in making Indira Gandhi Prime Minister twice, in 1966 and 1967. From 1968 onwards differences between Kamaraj and Indira Gandhi started simmering and the two parted company in 1969 on the presidential candidate issues. Indira Gandhi split the Congress Party and Kamaraj found himself in the opposite camp. It said that Venkataraman distanced himself from his mentor and went out of active politics as he did not want to get himself involved in the political warfare going on at the time. When his Planning Commission membership ended in 1971, he kept away from the Lok Sabha elections and became politically inactive. He took up the editorship of *Swarajya*, founded by C.Rajagopalachari, and concentrated on his *Labour Law Journal* and the UN tribunal work. In 1975, Kamaraj came out openly against the Emergency, Venkataraman's reactions were lukewarm and some of Kamaraj's friends thought that perhaps he was trying to mend his bridges with Indira Gandhi. One explanation could possibly be that after Kamaraj's death Venkataraman came to feel that the Congress movement in the south could sustain itself against the regional forces only through close ties with Indira Gandhi. This was the advice purported to have been given to him by his *guru* (religious master) Shankaracharya of Kanchi. In 1977, Venkataraman contested for the Lok Sabha on the Congress ticket and was elected. In 1978, when Indira Gandhi split the party, he did not initially join her and for some time remained an unattached member. But after Indira Gandhi was expelled from the Lok Sabha and deprived of her membership, he was terribly distressed and returned to the Congress (I) fold. He was returned to the Lok Sabha in 1980 as a Congress (I) nominee.

When Indira Gandhi formed her government in 1980, she included Venkataraman in the ministry as there were few members in her party matching his political skill, administrative experience and parliamentary stability. As Finance Minister it was his ingenuity no less than the massive majority of the party in Parliament that played an important part in geting the controversial 5.6 billion dollar IMF loan through a critical House. Indira Gandhi chose him to bail out the government, whenever she was in a tight corner particularly during the Antulay exposure and the notorious Kuo Oil deal debates. It, therefore, came somewhat as a surprise when he was quickly shifted from the key portfolio of Finance to the prestigious but light charge of Defence. Indira Gandhi's critics said that Venkataraman was too straightforward a person to be a convenient Finance Minister and had been replaced by a pliant acolyte, Pranab Mukherjee.

The period from 1934 to 1954, a period of complete two decades was a period of intensive work by Kamaraj at the Tamil Nadu Congress Committee (T.N.C.C.). This was also a period of florescence of that work and hence a period of satisfaction to Kamaraj who loved constructive work. This period laid the foundations in Kamaraj's life and established him as a leader of masses.

In 1932, the British Government, in pursuance of its repressive policy, had dissolved the Central Assembly as it was then known. In 1934, the Congress Party having withdrawn the Civil Disobedience Movement, was concentrating with full force, on the Council Entry Programme. The 1934 elections were, therefore, a prestige issue between the British and their Indian collaborators and the Congress Party, in opposition. In Madras, the struggle for national honour was fought by Kamaraj who was, by then, a known and a stubborn provincial figure. Kamaraj was thumping up and down Tamil Nadu with fiery determination to inflict heavy blows on the anti-nationalist forces. The result was a thumping success for the Congress in Tamil Nadu leading to a deservedly elevated pace for Kamarajin the Tamil Nadu Congress. Before I plunge into the internal politics of the Tamil Nadu Congress and the intense and, at times, bitter rivalry between C. R. and Stayamurthi backed by Kamaraj, it would add to our comprehension to know first the relationship between Satyamurthi and Kamaraj.[2]

Assessments of this relationship vary. At one extreme, I have the assessment that Satyamurthi was the *guru* (master) and Kamaraj the *chela* (disciple) ; then there is the other extreme that Kamaraj was just a broomstick for Satyamurthi ; and somewhere half-way is the appraisal that Satyamurthi needed the mass organiser Kamaraj and Kamaraj needed the leader Satyamurthi, so as to be able to climb up the social and political ladder.

Tamil Nadu politics at that time was dominated by stalwarts like Srinivasa Ayyangar and C. Rajagopalachari, both incidentally *Brahmins* by caste though not so much by any religious conviction. The shadow of *Brahmin* and non-*Brahmin* controversy was a dark reality in Madras politics and not just a pale shadow. It dominated the Madras scene for decades and however, secular and non-communal Madras Congressmen may loftily claim themselves to be, the reality at bottom was an intense caste and communal struggle, with its muddy under-currents in one ugly shape or another. That feeling, if not dominant now, still persists in subdued and sophisticated forms. Even within the Madras Congress, there were two distinct groups. There was the Leader Group of intellectuals, lawyers, professionals or generally the intelligentsia and as distinct from this group was the Worker Group of illiterates and semi-literates, without much education or social status. In between these two groups, stood Satyamurthi, a lawyer, with talents but with indifferent earnings ; who for years continued to be given a monthly stipend by a well meaning and a scrupulous patron. Satyamurthi loved the finer things of life and made no secret of his appreciation of beauty in its cultivated forms. So much for the somewhat elusive side of Satyamurthi's life. On the public side, Satyamurthi was one of the great orators of his day and a great parliamentarian of refinement who could, at the same time, hit hard. If Satyamurthi then was not at the top of Tamil Nadu politics, he had abiding aspirations to climb up and climb fast and it is precisely the up-climb that presented formidable difficulties to Satyamurthi Satyamarthi was a *Brahmin* while the rising democratic force and the strength of the masses came from the non-*Brahmin.* Inspite of education and attainments, to be a Brahmin needed for the political aspirant the cloak and cover of the non-*Brahmin* vintage. And Satyamurthi found one in Kamaraj Nadar, a non-*Brahmin* of the Nadar hue which had smarted under age-old caste and communal discriminations and under social and religions ostracism. There was fire, fury, passion and a spirit of revolt amongst Nadars and other such rising non-Brahmin classes. That was precisely what Satyamurthi, the intellectual *Brahmin*, needed. And further, Kamaraj had, by then, given ample proof of his organising talent and that is precisely what the arm-chair intellectual Satyamurthi needed to complement his political activity. The Satyamurthi-Kamaraj alliance was, therefore, a marriage of convenience, though in fairness it should be said that in course of time and with hand to hand wading through of political storms and crises, mutual regard and respect grew between the two.[3]

Kamaraj, by then just a step up the provincial ladder, also needed someone to push him forward and bring him in the limelight. Kamaraj lacked what practically all leaders in those days were expected to have education, social status, refinement and finesse. Satyamurthi had these graces in varying degreed. And therefore, in the resulting analysis, it would be factually correct to say that Satyamurthi needed Kamaraj just as much as Kamaraj needed Satyamurthi. The '*guru-chela*' (master-disciple) label of relationship does not fit in ; however, reverentially even Kamaraj may have occasionally and politically put it. Kamaraj was by temperament too dominating to be a broom-stick in the hands of Satyamurthi ; the organising power, throughout, lay in his hands and he knew how to use it to good and at times devastating purpose. Instead of the '*guru-chela*' trade mark. it would be more to the point to say,that Kamaraj "adopted" Satyamurthi as his leader and Satyamurthi found in Kamaraj an able and indefatigable worker and this, in the context of Tamil Nadu politics, proved also a bridge between the Leader-group and the Worker-group.

Another-cementing factor between the two was their common dislike of C.R., at that time head and shoulders above them both. We shall analyse the role of C.R. in the rise of Kamaraj but at this stage, we wish to assess the equation between Satyamurthi and Kamaraj and to them both C.R. was a common hate-target.

The Congress, on the all India plane, had stopped the Civil Disobedience movement earlier launched by it. The new Government of India Act was in the offing ; the Congress wanted to take advantage of the avenues of fruitful activity, and decided to embark on the Council Entry programme with all vigour. The 1934 elections became, therefore, a test and a trial of strength as between the Congress and the British rulers of the day and their hei.chmen in India. In Tamil Nadu, the persons who organised the elections on the provincial scale were Kamaraj and Satyamurthi ; their success was phenomenal and an example of how deep political furrows could be with a sustained application of work.

1936 brought to the fore caste feelings ; the same festering sore of *Brahmin*-non *Brahminism* in Tamil Nadu politics. The Contestants for the Presidential throne of the provincial Congress were Satyamurthi (*Brahmin*) and Muthurangam Mudaliar (non-*Brahmin*). C.R., with his tactically inopportune support, had united his otherwise divided opponents. Satyamurthi, no doubt, won with C.R's open support but the non-

Brahmins, as a group, felt enraged and in the process got united. The cards were badly played. C.R., was no doubt possessed of much ancient wisdom but greater political wisdom would have been to let the warring groups contest ; let the cocks fight and thin out their feathers.

As far as Kamaraj was concerned, Satyamurthi made him the General Secretary of the Tamil Nadu Congress Committee and in that capacity, Kamaraj was able later to take Nehru round on a triumphal tour of Tamil Nadu. The aristrocrat Nehru was deeply impressed with the organising talent of the rustic Kamaraj and in the years to come, Nehru's opinion of Kamaraj turned into one of respect for this simple selfless man. Nehru recalled the words of introduction which Satyamurthi had used for Kamaraj at the Lucknow Congress and after his Tamil Nadu tour, he was himself convinced that Satyamurthi had under-rated the latent talents of this unsophisticated Tamilian, swarthy to all appearances but of great talent. 1937 saw the revenge for 36. Muthurangam Mudaliar stood again for the Presidential election. C.R. for or C.R. against, Muthurangam made a better alignment of his non-*Brahmin* array this time. C.R. was not to be out-witted either ; he was ready with his manoeuvre. It may work or it may not work, that was irrelevant. Omandur Ramaswami Reddiar, another non-*Brahmin* to match the Mudaliar, wanted to oppose him and the Satyamurthi-Kamaraj group was supporting Ramaswami Reddiar. C.R. had better ieda ; he got on direct to Reddiar over the heads of Satyamurthi and Kamaraj and persuaded him to realise that wisdom was preferable to valour and he should not contest the elections.[4]

The most important thing that attracted Venkataraman's special attention to Kamaraj from among the leaders of India was that he was completely different from them.

Venkataraman found Kamaraj very simple in appearance and habits. Of course, there were many more such leaders. He could be approached for help by anybody, be it men of high rank or of the poorest lot at any time and without obstacles. Apart from his simplicity, his skill in dealing with people who approached him with intricate problems and questions, had always remained admirable.

If one raised a problem or put a question with Kamaraj, he neither gave ones a ready answer nor would he reject the question but dealt that in his characteristic manner. His ways of dealing with pressmen were wonderful. He was putting across the same question or problem back to the man who raised it and made the questioner think along with him.

Famous Tamil Nadu film actor Sivaji Ganesan found Kamaraj image in late Indira Gandhi. He said : "My body is for the Congress, my life is for Madam Gandhi. They are inseparable. I will be loyal to Indira Gandhi. I have found the Kamaraj image in her. So long as she remains, I will be loyal to her. Even after that I will be loyal to Indira Gandhi. Nothing can be predicted, but at present I am totally loyal to her".[5]

Prime Minister Indira Gandhi's open appeal to the followers of the late Kamaraj to join her party and C. Subramaniam's four-day mission to the state to press the suit had indeed raised expectations of an immediate decision. Probably, the timing of the move was a little too hurried. A party which suddenly finds itself orphaned is hardly in a position to make up its mind on such a vital question. For the time being, the TNCC (O) has naturally preferred to rely on the departed leader's famous "wait and see" policy. This will also enable the party leaders to gauge the feelings of the rank and file.

The TNCC (O) President, P. Ramachandran, took care not to commit himself on the likey response to the Prime Minister's invitation. But the executive pointedly stated that pending a final decision in December that year (1975) the party was still bound by the resolutions passed by it in February and July 1975. The first resolution ruled out association with any party connected with the DMK or the ADMK and their allies. The second related to the party's well-known stand on the emergency and censorship.

If the Congress was averse to any proposal to unite the two parties other than a merger on its own terms even when Kamaraj was alive, it was unlikely to be more accommodating then that he was not on the scene. But it was not as if the

Congress (O) had entirely lost its bargaining strength. Kamaraj had left behind a fairly sound organisation at the grassroots level which was superior to what the other Congress had at that time. It took time to overcome that deficiency even if some Congress (O) members were brought in by the bandwagon force. The Congress had also to take into account the DMK's efforts to woo Kamaraj's men to its own fold. In any case, a take-it-or-leave-it approach would not pay in that peculiar situation in Tamil Nadu.

Kamaraj, used to insist that his cabinet colleagues did something for the service of the people ; however small that something be. His successor Bhaktavatsalam, going back over the years of his administrative association with Kamaraj, says that single fact was responsible for the contentment of the people in the Madras State because they, the people, were genuinely anxious to do its bit for the people. In that sense of the matter, Kamaraj had truly mastered Thiruvallur's maxim.

> "The king who gives not facile audience (to those who approach him), and does not examine and pass judgment (on their complaints) will perish in disgrace."

With that basic approach, Kamaraj and his cabinet colleagues, unlike other old type administrators, were accessible, approachable and attentive to public complaints and grivances. As a Chief Minister, Kamaraj personally kept up his mass contact, which had paid him such rich dividends as a political organiser.

In providing stable and sound administration, Kamaraj had been firmly of the view that the number of ministers should be as small as possible, consistent with efficiency. Competent observers had remarked that considering the population density and the area, the Madras Cabinet under Kamaraj, was really small. Kamaraj thought that the main consideration of distributing and broad-basing political favours could never succeed and all the members of a legislative assembly or even of the ruling party could never be satisfied ; it was, therefore, not wisdom to whet political appetites unnecessarily by making a start in that direction. A smaller cabinet meant greater homogeneity and concentration of ability and that was more important that a collection of well-meaning but at times even ill-meaning ineffectuals. The first principle in the pursuit of achieving stability in administration that Kamaraj had consistently pursued and with obvious success had been that of a small well-knit cabinet.[6]

Kamaraj's second guiding principle had been to choose his colleagues to be with utmost care and selection, allocate to each such duties as would be justified by the past background, physical and tempermental, of the person concerned. Kamaraj was known to be a shrewd judge of men but that shrewdness was itself based on a study of men and not on any arbitrary emotional reactions, likes, or dislikes. Venkataraman, the then Industries Minister of Madras was a case in point. Venkataraman has a very knowledgeable background of labour and industrial relations and along with his other qualities, he deservedly attracted Kamaraj's attention, now eminently justified. Madras, from a backward industrial State, has risen today to occupy the third place in the industrial map of India. Kamaraj's own knowledge of industry is not as profound as his knowledge of agriculture but making good use of Venkataraman and men like him, he was able to make Madras the best administered State in India. Kamaraj thoughtfully put into practice every bit of what he learnt from the following maxims of Thiruvallur:

> Let (a king) choose no one without previous consideration ; after he has made his choice, let him unhesitatingly select for each such duties as are appropriate.
>
> Let the choice (of a king) fall upon him who largely possesses these four things ; love, knowledge, a clear mind and freedom from covetousness.
>
> Let (a king) act, after having considered the great (whom he is to employ), the deed (he desires to do), and the time which is suitable to it.
>
> After having considered, "this man can accomplish this by these means", let (the king) leave with him the discharge of that duty.

> Prosperity will leave (the king) who doubts the friendship of the man who steadily labours in the discharge of his duties.
>
> The minister is one who can make an excellent choice of means, time, manner of execution, and the difficult undertaking (itself).
>
> The minister is one who in addition to the aforesaid five things excels in the possession of firmness, protection of subjects, clearness by learning and perseverance.

It would be incorrect to say that Kamaraj, as Chief Minister of Madras, never interfered in the work of his cabinet colleagues. It would, however, be correct to say that he interfered when complaints reached him and when he was *prima facie* satisfied that something had gone amiss and called for his intervention. Even then, his approach was not that of a dictator wielding the rod but that of a big brother, an adviser or more accurately, a friend, philosopher and a guide. That has been the main reason for the success Kamaraj has had with his colleagues. After his intervention, no trace of hurt feelings or offense was left with his colleagues. What his colleagues all along felt was the impact of advice ; deserving, superior and worth listening to. The process they had gone through was that of self-criticism and introspection but certainly not of a wounded ago. It was also noted of Kamaraj that while his criticism was frank and candid, it was always within the four walls of his room. He could be relied upon to give due public protection to his colleagues if the occasion arose. His colleagues could count on him and thus themselves drew the line between a bonafide mistake and a malevolent intet to which no quarter would be given. Having established these healthy working relations with his, colleagues which he described to the author as "fellowship", Kamaraj let them work uninterruptedly and to the best of their inherent talents and abilities. The results were invariably satisfactory and upto his expectations. It is also remarkable that the leader of the House during Kamaraj's tenure as Chief Minister was usually some trusted colleague of his and Kamaraj spared himself even the trouble of having to defend his government on the floor of the house.

This step of putting up someone other than the Chief Minister was partly tactical ; criticism especially the sensational and irresponsible one, loses its edge if the target is not the executive head of the State but a lesser being. His step was exceptional but this calculated manoeuvre, inspite of its innovation, was sound. There was hardly an instance of such a performance in any other State of India and that too, for so persistent a period. This translated in practice, another maxim of Kamaraj that the acts of an administrator should speak for him but his tongue need not wag ; that an administrator should act and not so much speak. The reverse is the position in most of the States and elsewhere.

Kamaraj appeared inscrutable but was intensely human. Of Mahatma Gandhi, it was said that he was a naked *fakir* (beggar). Kamaraj is just as much of a '*fakir*' in physical and spiritual terms as was the Great Mahatma and may be, by the time the had unrolled the full pattern of his life and work and risen to still greater heights, history might well come to record that in practical terms, the manifold accomplishments of Kamaraj were far greater than that of Gandhi and that was no disparagement, far Gandhi achieved much.

There is, however, a world of difference between Gandhi and Kamaraj. While Gandhi was an idealist and a dreamer in many of his pet ways, Kamaraj had not pet dreams and no illusions to hug. He was a realist to the core and did not believe in day-dreaming and was naturally impatient with those who vaguely talked of vague things and theories, however beautiful, but not true. There was, therefore, an atmosphere of 'No Nonsense' in Kamaraj's commanding presence. There might, at times, appeared an air of impatience about him but it was not the impatience of a haughty, arrogant or a vain-glorious man with little substance in him ; for Kamaraj symbolised the solid mass of substance in him and the nation. There was a marked quality about Kamaraj; he was an intense listener who imbibed all new points with an open receptivity. That, in fact, was his greatest asset as also the quality of an intensely active and vigorous mind. He had the capacity to listen to different viewpoints and to imbibe and absorb, in depth, the minute and kaleidoscopic angles of any problem facing him in his day-to-day national tasks. That was also the quality of a true democrat who was charged with the duty to present the common denominator in national life. Kamaraj thus saw the various facets of national life but in seeing the nation as a whole, the interpreted the nation to the nation. Kamaraj, therefore, symbolised the national will. He saw all, heard all and were little but when he did speak, the words spoke the measured words of an intellectual giant. It was this inscrutable giant and leader of men whose thoughts and actions were fully unraveled by Venkataraman.

After nine years as Chief Minister of the Madras State, Kamaraj was getting restive. He was always a man of the masses but he started feeling, that inspite of all the mass contact he had been strenuously keeping, he was getting out of touch with the public. That was a strange feeling to have for a man who had been a mass leader, in the true sense, all his life. But the feeling was, genuine. However, much Kamaraj may have toured in the country side but as a Chief Minister, shackles of office and office hours and the dull routine of having to keep up formal public engagements and to put up with the long winded and unrealistic speech craft of the speech-makers, were increasingly convincing him that he was not fully in tune with the masses and their aspirations. He saw unreality or a definite out-of-step performance not only in the State Governments but what was worse and what was more harmful, even at the Centre. Nehru, thought Kamaraj, had rendered great services to the nation but inspite of his great respect for Nehru, Kamaraj could not help feeling sad that the Nehru Government was fast losing grip on reality ; the reality that was the sad plight of India, especially after the 1962 Chinese invasion of Indian territories on the north and north-east. Our performance had been deplorable and the preceding years of sloth and stagnation had taken a heavy toll of our national self-respect at the hands of the Communist Chinese, who having come to power two years after India, had given an excellent performance of their might in the difficult Himalayan terrain. The all-India 1962 performance, the economic stagnation, coupled with the difficulty Kamaraj had himself been experiencing in his home State, made him feel that something drastic was called for if India was to be saved. He had also seen that in his own State, the D.M.K., with its secessionist propaganda, had gained ground and he frankly acknowledged to himself that much against his personal wishes and predilections, he had not been able to spend as much time with the masses as he would have loved and liked to spend and the result, therefore, was an erosion on his hold on the masses.

Keen observer Kamaraj had been throughout his life, he felt that only a drastic remedy could do. He saw how afflicted Nehru was after the Indian debacle at the hands of the Chinese but in countrast, he noticed at the same time, the striking mass enthusiasm in the length and breadth of India. He saw the inertia at the top and he saw the revolutionary upsurge at the bottom. Analysing the situation, Kamaraj argued to himself that the base of the Indian nation—the heart of the Indian people was sound but sadly enough, it was the top that was in decadence and disarrary. As a loyal party man, he was not able to say publicly all that he burningly felt but he poured out his thoughts to Nehru in no unambiguous terms. Nehru long familiar with the depth and sincerity of Kamaraj's feelings being himself also conscious of the rut in which the country had got into and being equally conscious of the failures of some of his colleagues, readily agreed with Kamaraj's diagnosis of the national malaise and subsequently actually encouraged Kamaraj to express his views more publicly. Kamaraj, therefore, started by placing his views before the Congress Working Committee, the policy body of the Congress Party. The Congress Working Committee also agreed, as it paid to be heroic and especially as no one except Nehru and Kamaraj had calculated clearly and seriously the consequences. And so the yes men said 'yes', 'yes' to Nehru, but fondly hoped that like the brave and airy party resolutions on Democratic Socialism, this brave posture would also end up on a beautiful smoke screen and that too with a fragrance of Congress high-mindedness and an aroma of virtuosity of the non-believer.[7]

Equally sad it is to say that to Nehru also, Kamaraj's idea of renunciation of office and selfless work with the masses, presented a well dressed and a neat opportunity to get rid of troublesome colleagues like S.K. Patil, contenders for leadership like Morarji Desai, controversial persons like Jagjivan Ram and generally those who were not hundred per-cent Nehru Men. Nehru, knowing fully that the party would not think of relieving him, offered gallantly but calculatingly his own resignation. The noble example having been set, practically all the Congress faithfuls in high places and in the discharge of high ideals, vied with each other and placed their resignations in the hands of the patriarch Nehru. And with all the 52 cards neatly placed before him, Nehru played his hand deftly and proceeded to weed out the unwanted. This was the first unfortunated blow to the Kamaraj Plan and with that initial mis-direction, the Kamaraj Plan virtually died still-born. There was a sense of shock to those who had been weeded out and a sense of sceptic dismay in the public. It was generally felt that the Kamaraj Plan, though morally conceived, had been politically executed and there was little of that idealism that had prompted the framer of the Plan while presenting it to the nation. Sharks and publicly despised Congress Chief Ministers like Partap Singh Kairon in Punjab and others were left in office while Central Ministers like Morarji Desai, S.K. Patil, Jagjivan Ram, etc. were asked to cool their heels in the verandahs of their rented home. There was no organisational work for them to do except to sulk, fret and fume. Patil was the most outspoken of all and publicly stated :

> "The administration has not only deteriorated during the past month. It has come to a full stop, and therefore nobody knows when he will have to go." And commented from London, the *New Statesman* :
>
> "But under the Kamaraj Plan, Patil, with his dynamism and his proved skill as party boss, is among the three or four who are leaving the Central Cabinet."

While this was the emerging sorrowful state, Nehru in order to add stature to the grandiose plan, chose Kamaraj to head the Congress Party organisation as its President and so the party and its High Command proceeded faithfully to elect Kamaraj as its President and that is how Kamaraj, though mildly reluctant, found himself transformed, from his last assignment as the Chief Minister of a State, to the exalted position of the Congress President. Nehru had, however, not meant it to be anything as exalted. In his time as Prime Minister, he had humbled Purushottam Dass Tandon and Acharya J.B. Kriplani, who, while Presidents, had hugged some exalted ideas about the role of the Congress Presidency. Nehru had his own ideas about the all pervasive role of the Indian Prime Minister and knowing that Kamaraj had been a faithful and a loyal worker, he had not meant him for a different cast. Nehru wanted a Congress President in the type and style of the meek Gandhians who would keep a raised eye on the Nehru eye-brow. Destiny, however, has its own ways. It has been seen time and again that in Kamaraj's life those who are, or happen to be on his destined onward path suddenly die and be thus removed altogether by the hand of fate. There is no mysticism about it but that has been a seen pattern in his life. Nehru's death in 1964 removed the only person in India who would not have let Kamaraj come into his own as a Congress President. Subsequently, the people were to see a similar spectacle. Lal Bahadur Shastri, by all accounts was virtually pitchforked as the Prime Minister of India by Kamaraj but later, Shastri's office grew on him and he started posing problems in personal relations to Kamaraj. But again, after a short lived tenure of 19 months, said it was that the cruel hand of fate removed Shastri also. It would, however, be highly unfair to say that Kamaraj has ever willed such grave happenings and eve if he willed, it won't do the deed, but time and again such things have strangely happened and destiny seems to clear for Kamaraj the path to ·tread and march uninterruptedly on. That fact is starkedly noticeable in his life ; obstructions or likely obstructions seem to disappear without his having done a thing about it. Few have that luck of nature's gift in the lap. The man of destiny is for all to see.

REFERENCES

1. R. Venkataraman. Kamaraj's unique career. Hindu (Madras) 15 July 1964.
2. R. P. Kapur. *Kamaraj : The Iron Man* New Delhi, 1966
3. *Ibid.*
4. *Ibid.*
5. See Sunday Observer (New Delhi) 18 March 1984
6. See also R. P. Kapur *op. cit.* p. 109.
7. *Ibid.*

R. Venkataraman with Giani Zail Singh at former's Birthday, New Delhi.

R. Venkataraman and K.C. Pant at the Delhi University Convocation.

R. Venkataraman at Tagore's anniversary celebrations.

R. Venkataraman at Nehru's Samadhi at Shantivan, New Delhi.

R. Venkataraman at Dargah Hazarat Nizamuddin, New Delhi.

R. Venkataraman with PLO Chief Yasser Arafat.

R. Venkataraman with Princes Anne of England.

R. Venkatarman with K. Kamaraj.

10

HIS ECONOMIC PHILOSOPHY

Venkataraman's views on economic matters are well-defined. He had this to say to the Indian Chamber of Commerce in Calcutta : "It is incumbent upon business leaders and managers to do some soul-searching and self-introspection in their work-styles—styles of living and styles of problem solving. In our situation, the State must play an active part in the management of the nation's economy and it can do so best through the totality of planning. Planning does not necessarily mean controls, planning means having a vision of the future, having a well thought out approach for development of key sectors, a well articulated policy towards acquiring and developing technologies."

Venkataraman has had a very distinguished record in Tamil Nadu—he brought that state to the third position on the industrial map of the country. He could be legitimately called the father of Madra's industrial progress. He had also experience in a number of world-bodies and had earned the admiration of U.N. Secretary-General Kurt Waldheim.

Ever since the government of India laid emphasis on rural development, the tempo of integrated rural development has increased in Tamil Nadu. The State Government has taken upon itself the responsibility to make rural development as a mission. And efforts are well on way to show spectacular results.

The programme is a multi-faceted one. It aims at distributing all surplous land available to the landless labourer; it aims at putting up agro-based industries wherever possible, in rural areas so that these industries could give the poor villagers additional income. The programme also gives encouragement to setting up of village poultries, piggeries, and small fisheries wherever possible. These efforts have shown some success.

The District Industries Centres Programme has also caught up in Tamil Nadu. As many as 14 centres have already been set up. The places are Chingleput, Dharmapuri, Kanyakumari, Pudukottai, Ramanathapuram, Salem, South Arcot, Tirunelveli, Coimbatore, Madras, Madurai, North Arcot, Tiruchirapalli and Thanjavur. These centres are reported to be doing well, not only by identifying new rural entrepreneurs but also by encouraging them to undertake new lines of production. Cash assistance and bank loans are being given to them in right earnest to start new ventures. The assistance varies from Rs. 750 to Rs. 5,000 depending on the nature of the business.

Their output, mainly handicrafts, metalware, handloom, silk, wood-carvings, etc., are being marketed effectively by the State Handicrafts Board. This gives the producers not only a reasonable price but also prevents them from being cheated by unscrupulous middlemen. Marketing of their produce also helps the village artisans with assured and stable marketing facilities which many of them could ill-afford either singly or even collectively. Noteworthy progress has already taken place in the handloom sector where Tamil Nadu holds the pride of place in India. Kancheepuram silk weaving industry is too well-known to make any mention. On the handicrafts alone as many as 47,000 persons have been trained in different skills. There has been rapid improvement in recent years on the handloom sector. With the introduction of DIC's there is scope for a rapid increase in employment and income for the villagers. The question of co-ordinating the activities of the well-established decentralized sectors like handloom and sericulture on the one hand, and DIC's on the other, is being pursued vigorously. Such a co-ordination will avoid duplication of work. It will also ensure that existing field level agencies will be provided with sufficient professional knowledge.

Under the new Handloom Development Programme, it was anticipated that the base of handloom production would move up to 3,700 million metres of cloth by the need of the Sixth Five Year Plan.

This base production was being consciously expanded through activisation and enlargement of the existing looms.

Since the ultimate destiny of the handloom weaver lied in his association with the co-operative movement, steps had already been initiated by the Government of Tamil Nadu to form a large number of new co-operative societies of about 30,000.

Handloom exports have picked up considerably. From a total value of about 15 crores a decade ago, export earnings from handloom cloth had already touched the figure of Rs. 285 crores in 1978-79.

Handloom has also entered the modern age. In Kancheepuram, Arni and other places known for their handloom silk product, a successful attempt has been made to produce on commercial scale polyester-blended fabrics. These fabrics have proved to be very popular. But the price is a bit high on account of the high cost of imported polyester. The demand of the handloom sector in Tamil Nadu is to get the price of imported polyester reduced from Rs. 150 per kg. to at least Rs. 50 per kg. if not more.

A word about the employment scheme. On an average, creation of one extra job in the organised mill sector will required an investment of Rs. 50,000. But in the handloom sector the investment will be only Rs. 1,000 for an additional job opportunities generated by the handloom sector alone in Tamil Nadu during 1980 would be around, 50,000.

The recent announcement by the Government of India to reserve further expansion of the match industry to handmade matches in the cottage industry sector has been welcomed by Tamil Nadu. It is well-known that Sivakasi produces the bulk of the handmade matches in India. The total output of matches is worth about Rs. 16 crores annually.

At the dawn of independence, Tamil Nadu was a part of the composite State of Madras. Its potential was larger, especially in water and mineral resources. But, the available natural resources were not harnessed for industrial production adequately prior to independence. The exports were more in the form of primary products, and the few industries that were set up were agro-based—such as cotton textiles, sugar, rice-mills and oil-crushing, leather and tobacco. In the first few years after independence, the government promoted *khadi*, handlooms, and village industries. It was not till the commencement of the First Plan that the real emphasis was placed on major industrial development, especially in starting new units for engineering and chemical production. The Andhra partition in 1953, and the state reorganisation in 1956, reduced the size of the state. This was followed by the concentrated attention of government to transform the agricultural economy into an industrial one, utilising the resources available in the compact state. It was soon recognised that the natural resources available in Tamil Nadu were also far less, especially in major minerals and in water. The limited experiences in the earlier decades, the thirties and the forties, had shown the indispensable need for power for industrial expansion. Thus the state realised early (i) the need for a survey of mineral resources, to assess the potential of the state ; (ii) to conserve water and optimise water management ; and (iii) utilising thereby every available source of water-supply for hydro-electric generation as well, before irrigational use. Steps to implement schemes in all these directions based on techno-economic surveys were launched. The state policy adopted in the decades 1951—1970 was to increase hydro-electric generation. But the sources were subject to the vagaries of the monsoon, and the firm availability of power was in jeopardy. Thermal generation alone could help meet the deficit. The Neyveli Thermal Plant, utilising the lignite mineral available in the State (besides Salem magnesite and iron-ore), and increasing the thermal content in the grid by setting up coal-based thermal stations were taken up. The need for import of power (from Karnataka and Kerala) persisted at the higher prices demanded. To meet this recurring deficit, efforts were launched to set up a Nuclear thermal station as well, even in 1964-65 though the plant started supplying the grid only from 1984.[1]

Table 10.1 sets out the rapid progress achieved in power development from a low total installed capacity of 156 MW.

TABLE 10.1

Period	Installed capacity	Peak-demand	Gross Generation and purchase	Per capita consumption
1	2 (MW)	3 (MW)	4 (MU)	5
Pre-plan (31.3.1951)				
I Plan (1951-56)	156	110	630	12
II Plan (1956-61)	256	172	1053	21
III Plan (1961-66)	571	381	2214	60
IV Plan (1969-74)	2254	1326	7105	127
V Plan (1974-79)	2719	1710	10414	175
VI Plan (1980-85)	3344	2154	13731	220
				For 1984-85.

The thermal content was only 18.67 per cent in 1960-61 and it has risen steadily to 52.10 per cent in 1984-85, and Nuclear power fed was 7 per cent in 1984-85. Strikingly, peakload demand had always outstripped availability. In the Seventh Plan too this deficit will continue and it is estimated at 1060 MW in 1988-89, and in 1989-90 at 977, and in terms of energy at 3336 MU and 3600 MU respectively. The number of industrial consumers in the state is 1,84,752 and they accounted for the following percentage of the total consumption: 1960-61: 53; 1970-71: 50.10; 1980-81: 48.97; 1983-84: 47; 1984-85: 51. Despite significant improvements in plant-load factor of the thermal stations, the supply of power in future will still fall short of demand; with hardly any potential for new hydro-electric generation, it is necessary to add to the thermal content in the grid, despite its higher cost.

Progress achieved in industrialisation of the State during 1951-66 was striking, in the traditional textiles and sugar industries. The increased intake of technical and engineering institutions and the opening of new polytechnics were facilities added. Also financing and development institutions were organised from 1949 onwards, to help entrepreneurs. Several new enterprises sprang up in the State during the period. Conscious promotional efforts by Government such as guaranteeing the finances, arranging for infrastructural facilities, and even for technical collaboration, were availed of by a large number of industrialists in the state.

Central projects were also implemented, like the Avadi Defence Factory, integral Coach Factory at Perambur, the BHEL, and the Small Arms Project at Tiruchirapalli and the Photo-films Plant at Ootacamund. A refinery at Manali also paved the way for further downstream production and petro-chemical units. By 1966 spining mills rose from 59 (in 1951) to 158. The number of spindles doubles and so too for weaving. Yarn supply increased to handloom weaving, an important labour-intensive industry in the State. Sugar mills rose from three with production of 40, 656 tonnes (in 1951-52) to 13 with production rising five and a half times, to 2,26,828 tonnes in 1965-66. The cement industry had five units with a total capacity of 1.8 million tonnes. Electro-chemical units, fertilizers, and automobile and machine-building industries (in all 24) and two tyre units were also set up during the period. Even though the area had extended only from 30, 339 hectares to 33, 153 hectares, the increase in tea production was from 25,225 thousand kg. to 47,041 thousand kg. during 1951-65. Coffee production rose from 3,470 million tonnes (in 1950-51) to 7910 million tonnes in 1965-66. Rubber plantations spread

TABLE 10.2

Year	No. of Units	No. of workers employed	Productive capital	Total input value	Total output value	Output Input	Value added	Total Employees
1	2	3	4	5	6	7	8	9
					(Rs. in lakh)			
1962	4307	279490	25514	29142	42063	144	11456	312186
1970	5766	446820	107058	99827	136234	136	30648	558429
1980-81	10182	656762	346221	532370	676852	127	126642	822918
1982-83	11778	688716	402973	726584	924883		174922	861902

from 3348 hectares in 1953 to 7820 hectares in 1965-66 and production rose from 1380 million tonnes to 3195 million tonnes. During the subsequent period 1967-85, industrial expansion and production had continued, but the rate of growth had somewhat slowed down. On a closer analysis it can be said that Tamil Nadu shared this trait with all-India trends during the period after the mid-sixties. In industrial licensing and letters of intent issued and the registration of joint stock companies there was almost completed correspondence between all-India trends and experience in Tamil Nadu. Production had a mixed trend, largely plagued by power-cuts of varying intensity, and labour disputes resulting in a higher proportion of the man-days lost. Nevertheless, the trend in select economic indicators were positive as Tables 10.2 and 10.3 will show.[2]

TABLE 10.3

Small-scale Industries Basic Data

Particulars	1977-78	1982-83
1	2	3
Number of units registered	18789	46378
Productive capital (Rs. in lakh)	15054	32718
Installed capacity (Value in lakh of Rupees)	65264	121285
Value of production (Rs. in lakh)	33620	64075
Number of workers employed	118452	142919

(*Source* : Tamil Nadu—An Economic Appraisal—annual publications from 1970 to 1984-85).

Tamil Nadu finds itself in such a position that any meaningful improvements in standard of living and opportunities for employment can be secured only through the diversification of economic activity on the basis of rapid and balanced industrial expansion. It is in this context that much emphasis has been placed on the industries sector and it is the government's resolve that no worthwhile scheme should suffer for want of encouragement and support. Several steps have been taken and are being taken to create an environment conducive for progress.[3]

The following deserves a mention :

Single Window Clearance

A High Power Committee under the Chairmanship of the Commissioner and Secretary to government, industries department has been set up which acts as a single window agency for large and medium industries. This Committee meets once in a month to expedite issue of clearance and provision of infrastructrual facilities require by entrepreneurs.

New Areas of Assistance

The volume and range of development in the state calls for a greater sophistication in the emerging units. In other words, the need has arisen for intermediate technology based and high value added units. In order to encourage investment in such fields. The State Industries Promotion Corporation of Tamil Nadu has taken up the following two areas :

(*a*) *Leasing activity* :

The Corporation will provide finance for acquiring balancing equipment and generator. As a measure of further assistance, it will buy and provide the equipment generator on convenient lease terms.

(*b*) *Assistance for Non-resident Indians* :

The Corporation will assist non-resident Indian entrepreneurs by obtaining industrial Licences on their behalf. It will also offer such entrepreneurs a Portfolio Investment Scheme whereby the non-resident Indians can invest with SIPCOT and then these investments will be converted into equity in the assisted companies subsequently. A separate International Cell has been opened in the Corporation for such purposes with a view to encourage investment by non-resident Indians. So far 10 non-resident Indians have implemented their projects in the state at a total project cost of Rs. 666.10 lakhs. Another set of nine non-resident Indian projects are in the implementation stage involving a total investment of Rs. 1169.00 lakhs.

The Electronics Corporation of Tamil Nadu has prepared a Fiver Year Perspective Plan for the development of the Industry in the state, involving an outlay of over Rs. 200 crores. Tele-communication, professional electronics, consumer electronics and component manufacture will be the principal sectors of development. With a view to encourage such industries in the small-scale sector, the infrastructural support is intended to the be strengthened. Accent is on strengthening creation of new industrial areas, establishment of raw material depots, Testing and Product Development Centres etc.

It may also be relevant to point out here that electronic Industries (alongwhith drugs, automobile ancillaries and solar-energy equipment units) are entitled to a special 10 per cent capital investment subsidy in all areas other than such areas where either the Central/State Capital Subsidy Scheme is in operation. The subsidy will be equivalent to 10 per cent of the value of the fixed assets to be created or Rs. 20,000 per every regularly employed worker whichever is less subject to a maximum of Rs. 10 lakhs.

With Venkataraman's advice still intact and Tamil Nadu's government relations with the Centre very cordial, the State can look forward for a quantum leap into the 21st century as regards industrial development.

Venkataraman had attempted in his talks to give his audiences a broad sweep of the economic resurgence generated through the method of democratic planning adopted in the country. India is yet a young nation : "Our experience in planned economic development is limited to a short period of eighteen years. By any standards, the problems we have inherited are immense, and the effort involved is stupendous. We are attempting to telescope within decades the developmen spread over centuries in other countries. We have had our share of failures but even allowing this, our achievements are impressive. The economy is more dynamic, diversified and strong. In a sense, we are now in the intermediate stage of development no longer an under-developed country nor at the same time falling in the category of developed countries where the process of further growth can be left, more or less, to the normal economic forces without special efforts by Government. If the momentum of development is kept up with some further effort, the economy may be expected to reach a point in the next decade or so when the savings in the economy voluntarily generated may be adequate to keep up a reasonable rate of growth. On the other hand, if this effort is not forthcoming, the economy may slip back and there is a grave danger that it may not be possible to retain even the levels already reached. I have every confidence that with a pragmatic approach to industrial planning we shall not only sustain the progress achieved but march forward towards a better life.

In his talk on "the Role of Planning in Industrial Development", delivered on September 10, 1969, under the auspices of the University of Madras,[4] Venkataraman said : "Soon after Independence, we adopted planning as a means to accelerate economic development. Since then we have completed three Five Year Plans, followed by three Annual Plans. We have thus behind us the experiecne of 18 years of planning. It would seem opportune at this stage to look back and assess to what extent planning has helped industrial development of the country and what role it has played and might play in future. Has planning fulfilled the objectives with which it was initiated? What were the problems which arose? How were they surmounted?

Before proceeding to deal with the achievements and shortfalls in Indian planning with particular reference to industrial development and the perspectives in relation to the future, I would like briefly to touch upon the significance of planning and the historical context in which planning as a means to influence and accelerate development has come to be evolved in recent times.

One of the most outstanding and in many respects, unparalleled events in recent world history has been the negotiated transfer of political power by the colonial rulers and the emergence of independent and sovereign nations in Asia and Africa after the Second World War. In the great movement for independence which culminated in the redrawing of the political landscape of these two large continents, India under the enlightened leadership of Mahatma Gandhi and his colleagues played a unique and leading role. It would be no exaggeration to say that the success of the political struggle leading to the withdrawal of the British from the Indian sub-continent set the pattern and paved the way for the rapid disappearance of the colonial empires in other parts of the world.

To the newly independent countries, political freedom was only first and initial step in the arduous path towards the ultimate objective of improving the cconomic and social status of their large mass of people, steeped in ignorance and poverty, and of uniting and welding them into progressive and prosperous nations. Economic development thus became the prime concern of the Governments in the post-independence era in most under-developed countries. Activisation of the stagnant economies was by no means an easy task. In several ways, it presented more complex and formidable problems than even those which had to be surmounted in achieving political freedom. With the attainment of independence great expectations had been aroused.

The growing expectations in regard to minimum essentials of life such as adequacy of food, education and health facilities and employment opportunities had to be met. All of these involve massive outlays of capital and resources—in agriculture, industry, social services and so on. Capital was, however, the most scarce resource, the under-developed economies being unable to raise the necessary savings to sustain the order of capital investment necessary to meet the minimum requirements of the people. To raise adequate capital in order to sustain reasonable levels of investment for bringing about even a modest rate of growth in national incomes thus became a challenge to most developing countries. More so, in a situation in which the rise in population outs deeply into even the existing meagre living standards through the multiplication of additional numbers to be fed and to be looked after.

Difficult though the problem is, the harnessing of capital

alone does not bring about economic growth. The socio-political environment and institutional arrangements have an equally vital bearing on the nature and pace of development. Development invariably implies change—change in approach, attitudes, values and hierarchy. The resistance to change in the tradition—bound societies is indeed one of the major factors inhabiting rapid growth in the under-developed countries. As an instance, it takes years to educate farmers in the use of new methods of agriculture ; to use fertilizers to change the cropping pattern or to accept better seeds. Similarly, the inculcation of enterprise and enterpreneurship to venture into industrial operations in a community which is at best familiar with trading activities requires considerable reorientation of the traditional attitudes. In a variety of other matters such as the mode of savings, banking habits, approach to work, economic wants and aspirations, a new outlook has to be brought about ; in short, the very pattern of life will have to be altered to become development-oriented. At the same time, the trend and movement in this direction will have to be sustained by the creation of new institutions and the modification or abolition of the old ones. Abolition of Zamindari, land reforms, establishment of agricultural and industrial credit institutions, expansion of banking facilities, etc., are examples of the kind of institutional reforms designed to bettress the development efforts.

Another important factor which sets the pace of development is the extent of availability of skills, knowledge and technology. These are not acquired in a short time and have to be fostered by a carefully planned long-term programme of action. Scientific, technical and training institutions have to be established and expanded.

There are thus several facets to the process of developmental growth of an under-developed economy. It has to be viewed essentially as a co-ordinated efforts in several directions, each supporting the other and assisting in the onward march to national wealth and prosperity. It is evident that left to normal forces and individual effort, not only would the development be tardy and spasmodic, but it would also be wanting in the integrated and balanced growth required in different directions for the orderly progress of the economy. To the new developing countries lacking in capital and skill the development of these scarce resources in a planned manner to achieve optimum results is. therefore, a matter of vital importance. It is this realisation that led to the broad acceptance in many new countries of the concept of economic planning as a means of accelerated development. Beginning with the Soviet Union, economic planning in one form on the other has gradually come to be adopted not only in most of the developing countries but also in many advanced countries.

In any programme of planned economic development, industrialisation occupies a central and pivotal position. Industrialisation and economic development have become so integrated with each other that the economic progress of a nation is often assessed in terms of the measure of its success in transforming its agricultural economy into a modern industrial economy. This emphasis on industrialisation stems from a variety of considerations. Increased production and productivity are the hall-mark of national wealth and prosperity. While undoubtedly scope exists for increasing agricultural production and productivity in many of the developing countries, there are severe limitations by way of land resources and technology in maintaining a sustained and rapid growth rate on a continuing basis in the agricultural field. Furthermore, improvement in agricultural productivity will throw up surplus man-power on the farms for whom employment has to be found. Productive improvement in agriculture is itself dependent on an industrial base capable of supplying inputs like fertilisers, pesticides and farm equipment. Thus, nations aspiring for accelerated and continuing growth cannot rest on the modest gains that could be expected from farm incomes alone, but have to seek massive additions to national wealth from an expanding industrial sector. Thanks to modern technology, output and productivity in modern industries are continuously being improved upon, making it possible to maintain a steady growth in production and income. The known natural resources are sufficiently large and new resources are continuously being discovered. So there is no danger in the foreseeable future of industrial growth being impeded by shortage of basic raw materials or energy inputs. Industrialisation thus provides the key to rising income, employment, wealth and prosperity.

The beginings of modern industrial development can be traced to the middle of the 18th century which ushered in an era of technological transformation with the invention of steam power. This paved the way for use of machines for industrial production, transformed the means of transport with the introduction of railways and steam ships and brought about organised systems of commerce, banking and insurance. The most notable impact of the "Industrial Revolution" was the replacement of the domestic system of industrial production by the factory system. The factory system in turn brought about a change in the distribution of wealth. Many self-employed artisans and craftsmen were thrown out of their occupations and started working as wage earners in the new factories that sprang up. Capital came to occupy a commanding position in industrial organisation. Those who could afford began to multiply it as a result of the introduction of the process of large-scale production. A new class of capitalists emerged who got a lion's share in the gains of production. Society was divided into two distinct classes, namely, capitalists and wage earners. During the next hundred years or so, many new industries were set up. Industrial production increased manifold in the Western world. Planning was unknown and there was virtually complete freedom to the capitalists. Government did not actively interfere in the matter of location of industries, in the form of organisation or in the conditions of work. The *laissez faire* philosophy—let things—alone—prevailed.

Essentially, the rate of growth depends on the rate of capital formation which in turn is determined by the amount of resources used for investment. The less you consume, the more capital you are able to accumulate. The more you accumulate the more it helps you to increase it further. Whatever might have been its social and political consequences, the laissez faire theory which allowed the capitalist class to accumulate capital, at the expense of the working class, helped in the rapid progress of industrial development in the western countries during this period. The nations which got the advantage of earlier development also came to occupy commanding political positions and to dominate the less developed parts of the world. The colonial expansion of these nations into countries of Asia and Africa helped them in fostering their interests. Their commercial and financial policies were formulated to the advantage of the metropolitan countries. They bought the raw materials and primary goods from the colonies at cheap rates, converted them into manufactured goods and sold their manufactured goods in these colonies. Through political domination they manoeuvred the economic policies of the colonies in such a fashion that while on one hand their industrial development was stifled, on the other they became captive markets of the imperial powers. This enabled them to acquire increasingly greater control over the economies of the colonies.

In the words of the great patriot, Dadabhai Naoroji, it was a process of draining out the wealth of the colonies that was started by the ruling nations of Europe. The colonies were prevented from getting any benefit from the technological innovations made in the Western world and after some time it became an unequal struggle between the old and new technologies. Therefore, even when some of the discriminatory policies were relaxed on account of political pressures and other considerations, the economies of the colonies which were stagnating continued to be dependent on the metropolitan countries. This dependence was further accentuated by policy measures. It is well-known that further accentuated by policy measures. It is well-known that even the development of railways which were built in India by the British companies at heavy costs was oriented either to maintain the British rule in India or to serve the British dominated export industries. The freight rates were so devised as to help the movement of raw-materials towards the ports and help the British industries in competition with the industries in the interior. The colonial policies were thus designed to suppress indigenous manufacturing industries and promote the interests of industrial ventures in the metropolitan countries. Gunnar Myrdal, well-known Swedish economist, in his "The Asian Drama" has remarked that if, in spite of such policies followed by the colonial governments, some industrialisation has taken place in the colonies, it is really a thing to be wondered at.

Favourable historical factors helped the European countries to make rapid advances in industrialisation. At home, the *laissez faire* philosophy of the capitalist system uninhibited by considerations of social justice and equitable distribution of wealth enabled the accumulation of capital and its reinvestment leading to greater industrial production. Abroad, the colonial rulers through their economic and political power ensured a ready market for their industrial output and amassed further capital for their industrial programmes. The world came to be divided into two broad groups : the developed and the under-developed ; the rich and the poor nations, with a wide gulf between the two.

The social tensions that developed in the *laissez faire* era with the newly rich capitalists commanding the bulk of the national wealth and the mass of the people labouring under extreme conditions of poverty and distress, eventually led to the evolution of the concept of the Welfare State. The State assumed the responsibility for ensuring the welfare of all its citizens and for safeguarding social justice, fair wages, reasonable working conditions and employment. In order to fulfil these obligations the State had to intervene in economic matters. Labour laws were enacted ; social security schemes were introduced. Taxation assumed a deeper significance than mere collection of revenues, Fiscal and monetary policies were designed to correct aberrations in the economy and to achieve the broader socio-economic objectives. Apart from indirectly influencing the course of the economy in this manner, the State also assumed in some cases direct ownership of productive enterprise such as public utilities.

The recognition of an active public policy or, in other words, the role of the State in economic development laid the foundation for economic planning which has now been widely recognised and adopted. Recent developments in macro-economic theory and its practical application in national accounting, input-output analysis and production techniques have further strengthened the need for some measure of planned action for achieving higher rates of growth. The desire for quick economic recovery for reconstructing the war affected economies in a number of Western European countries led to the formulation of plans on a national scale. The relative importance of the public sector increased. All these developments paved the way for accepting planning as an essential instrument for rapid industrialisation and economic growth. Apart from the socialist countries, even countries which had for centuries remained wedded to the system of private enterprise and of free onwership of capital have come to appreciate the need for planned development. Countries like France, the Netherlands, West Germany, Norway and Sweden have accepted planning as a matter of public policy.

To day the importance of planning and the contribution it can make to economic growth is not only well-recognised but has come to be accepted as a necessary means. The degree of detailed planning and emphasis differs. This is not because of much divergence in the ultimate objectives, but because of certain values that are attached to the means for achieving these objectives. Broadly speaking, economic planning as practised by different countries can be categorised into two types : Central planning as adopted in the socialist countries and indirect and indicative planning as adopted in the free market countries. In one system, total planning right from the top to the bottom is considered an absolute imperative for ensuring the twin objectives of growth and social justice. In the other, planning is regarded merely as a means for guiding the way to a quicker growth. The major difference in the approach to planning in socialist economies and those of the free-market economies is that in the socialist countries the means of production and trade are, to a significant degree, the means of production and trade are, to a significant degree, controlled and operated by the State. In the other economies, the targets and objectives of the economic plan are sought to be achieved largely through fiscal, monetary and other regulatory mechanisms. In these market economies, the right of the individual to the ownership of capital and means of production and his freedom of economic activity are still largely respected. The distinction has been drawn by calling planning in the former as "direct planning" i.e. "where the Central authority responsible for the Plan has powers of disposition over the preponderant share of national resources, it can, therefore, assume the functions of both owner and entrepreneur and planning then becomes the explicit technique for economic management." The other approach is called "indirect planning" : "where such powers are diffused among members of the community in individual or corporate entities and the State is restricted (outside the limited area of its own direct activity as investor, consumer or banker) mainly to measures influencing the use of these rights". However, these means are not completely exclusive to these two systems. Some elements of direct planning are applied in the market economies and the socialist economies also use indirect methods of planning. It is true, however, that the differences in the approaches are fundamental. In fact, even within these two broad systems, one finds quite a significant degree of difference in approach among the various economies.

The differences betwecn Eastern and Western planning systems from a difference in the form of economic organisation and the range of instruments of intervention and control with which the planners can operate. For instance, in the East European countries the State has full authority to regulate the total wage bill, the price level, the rate of savings and the greater part of national investment and foreign trade. The treatment of these variables becomes a matter of secondary importance. On the other hand, in the market economies planning is mainly concerned with the regulation and treatment of these major variables, viz., the savings, investment consumption, the volume and directions of trade, etc., so as to achieve the overall objective. Thus in the former, the control on the "commanding heights" of the economy permits a reasonable degree of swift and effective corrective action while in the latter case, as only indirect means are adopted to achieve the objectives, they are constantly exposed to recurring imbalances. It is not that imbalances do not occur in centrally planned economies, only they are more manageable. The experiences during the last few years in some of these countries show how difficult and complicated it is to achieve appropriate balances. As a result, the need for certain degree of flexibility, particularly at the lower levels, has been felt. The role of profit and the price mechanism has been increasingly recognised. In the case of market economies, since ultimately a great deal is determined by the market forces, the process of regulation to achieve the ultimate objective becomes considerably more difficult.

I have dealt with some of the broad distinctive characteristics of the approach and the objectives of planning under the two systems : the so-called centrally planned and the market economies. The process and objective of planning vary not only among these two broad groups, but even among countries within these groups. Among the centrally planned economies, Yugoslavia, for instance, marks a distinct departure from the approach that has been followed in other East European countries. Although the basic premises such as the public ownership of means of production, the existence of central machinery for economic administration and State monopoly of foreign trade exist as in other centrally planned economies, yet Yugoslavia has been trying to combine central planning with extensive use of the market mechanism. Unlike the Soviet Union, the plan is not the main tool of economic management nor does it seek to regulate economic activity in such great detail as in the Soviet Union. The plan stipulates only a few basic objectives formulated in rather aggregate terms, aimed at providing conditions appropriate for stable growth and for bringing about the structural changes which are held to contribute to the overall stability and efficiency of the economy. The Yugoslav plan is not mandatory for the management of individual economic units nor does it seek to force the latter by means of decrees and instructions from above to adhere latter by means to the decisions of the planning authorities. To a good extent reliance is placed on indirect regulatory mechanisms to influence the decisions of the decentralised units. Thus, unlike other centrally planned economies, the public enterprises enjoy a fairly large degree of autonomy and the activities and policies of the individual enterprises are left to be determined to a considerable degree by the operation of market forces. The profit motive is considered a necessary stimulation for improving efficiency and day to-day operations of the individual enterprises. Departures of this nature towards decentralisation are discernible in some of the other centrally planned economies like Hungary and Czechoslovakia.

Among the market economies there are varied approaches as well as objectives. Though essentially all these economies have certain common objectives such as of maintaining full employment, higher rates of growth of national incomes, and all of them mainly rely on indirect means of achieving these objectives, yet there are variations in the immediate objectives as well as in the methods of achieving these objectives. These again are due to the various stages of economic development, the structure of their economies and due to the variations in the priorities. Even the degree of importance to planning as such differs. In France, for example, planning has gone substantially farther, as compared to a number of other West European countries. While no attempt is made on total and obligatory plans of operation for the private sector, yet it tries to influence the individual investment decisions through a system of consultations with the representatives of industry both at the stage of plan preparation as well as implementation. It is a sort of co-operative planning between Government, the public sector and the private sector and largely depends on the voluntary nature of the observance of the plan targets by the private sector. It has, therefore, been generally described as a system of "indicative planning".

Although time does not permit us to dwell upon the variety of planning approaches as adopted by various countries, few words may be said about the interesting example of Japan. The approach to planning in Japan has been to indicate the desirable directions of change and to help doing things which it may be difficult for private enterprise to carry out such as the construction of roads, reinforcement of railways and provision of public utilities designed to assist in fostering economic growth. The Japanese approach believes in minimum of direct activity by Government and in providing considerable freedom to private enterprise. However, the State through certain regulations or through other promotional measures helps as well as directs the course of industrial development. Another interesting features that characterises Japanese planning is its reliance on the flexibility in its approach. The Japanese plans, which have come to be called "revolving plans", are made every two or three years. Though long-range plans are also formulated, these are not regarded as rigid and are continuously revised in the light of the movement of the economic forces.

I have broadly touched upon the historical background of the industrial growth in Western countries, the significance of industrialisation to the developing nations, the emergence of economic planning as a tool for accelerated development and the distinctive features of the approach and methods of planning adopted in market economies on the one hand and socialist economies on the other. With this introduction, I shall now deal with the planning techniques adopted in India which in many respects are different from those I have so far described.

The role of planning in bringing about a transformation of the fabric of social and economic life and to tackel the problems of mass poverty was recognised even before the advent of independence. To the Indian National Congress, freedom was not merely the wresting of political power from an alien ruler but was the means to bring about social and economic transformation. Thus as early as in 1931, The Indian National Congress at the Karachi session resolved that "in order to end the exploitation of masses, political freedom must include real economic freedom for the starving million". In the years that followed, Mahatma Gandhi and Jawaharlal Nehru gave content and shape to the socio-economic philosophy of the National Congress. Based on the principles of democracy and equality, its objective was to evolve an egalitarian society in which there was the largest measure of freedom and equality of opportunity for the citizens. It was realised that only through a system of comprehensive planning that the desired social changes and rapid development could be achieved. This led to the appointment of a National Congress towards the end of 1938. The work of the National Planning Committee was unfortunately interrupted when the leaders were interned during the 1942 Movement. The planning idea, however, caught on. Several plans were prepared in the pre-independence period such as the Bombay Plan of 1944 prepared by a group of industrialists and economists. About the same time, even the then Government thought it necessary to set up at Department of Planning and Development.

The adoption of national planning as part of official policy, however, had to wait till the advent of freedom. One of the first tasks our Government undertook, on achieving freedom, was the establishment of the Planning Commission. The Commission, set up in 1950, was given the primary task of "formulating a Plan for the most effective and balanced utilisation of the country's resources, defining the stages in which the Plan should be carried out and proposing the allocation of resources for the due completion of each stage." The Commission was also charged with the responsibility of determining conditions to be established for the successful execution of the Plan, determining the nature of the machinery necessary for successful implementation and periodically appraising the progress achieved and recommending the adjustments of policies and measures as necessary. The Planning Commission is an advisory body, but the great importance attached to the Commission and its advice was fully recognised in the association of the Prime Minister as Chairman of the Planning Commission.

The social and political values accepted by the people decide the objectives and methods of planning adopted in any country. The Indian Constitution has embodied the social and political philosophy as adopted by our people. The objectives of the Indian Plans are derived from the Indian Constitution which has also a considerable bearing on the method of Indian Planning. To these aspects I shall now refer to in some details.

India is a political] democracy. The planning techniques have, therefore, to be consistent with democratic principles. Individual freedom is cherished; freedom of speech, enterprise and ownership is respected. A large share of the economic activities is carried out in the private sector and individual and corporate decisions influence, to a considerable extent, the pace and direction of the economy. In so far as economic decisions are so widely decentralised, total planning of the economy is not within the control of Government. Detailed planning can be achieved only with respect to programmes in the public sector; for the rest Government at best can influence, through appropriate policies, the economic activities in the private sector, but certainly cannot ensure the absolute fulfilment of the tasks and targets expected from or earmarked for the private sector in the Plan. As the fulfilment of a large part of the Plan is dependent on the private sector, it also becomes necessary that the broad objectives and programmes in the Plan are accepted by the nation as a whole. In other words, planning has to be democratic with the widest possible consultation and has to achieve the largest measure of agreement among the different strata of the community.

Secondly, India has a federal constitution. Under the Constitution, States have considerable freedom in certain economic spheres and in the allocation of their resources. Planning at the State level is the responsibility of the State Government concerned. It becomes the task of the Planning Commission to integrate the programmes of different States with chose of the Central Government in a coherent and balanced manner with a view to achieving broad national objectives and to ensure the distribution of total resources; both Central and State, in a manner that will enable the fulfilment of the national Plan in its totality. This requires a considerable degree of understanding of the special and specific requirements of each State and adjustments in relative priorities to meet local needs without sacrificing the broader national priorities and objectives. As the ultimate sanction of the Plan rests on the general acceptance of the Plan by the Central and State Governments, the careful balancing of the claims and needs of all the States is a pre-condition to the success of the Plan. The formulation of a practical and effective plan is thus more than an academic exercise of technocrats and economists, involving as it does the complex and intricate task of piecing together the programmes at various levels and reaching agreed conclusions on the sharing of responsibilities and benefits of the Plan between the Central and State Governments, local bodies and the organised and decentralised private sector.

The broad objectives of Indian planning and its social premises stem from the Directive Principles of State policy a set forth in the Constitution. The more important of these Directive Principles are that the State shall strive to promote the welfare of the people and secure a social order in which social, economic and political justice will prevail. The State shall in particular direct its policies towards securing adequate means of livelihood for the citizens, men and women equally. It has also been specifically mentioned that the ownership and control of the material resources of the community should be so distributed as to subserve the common good and that the operation of the economic system should not result in the concentration of wealth and means of production to the common detriment.

These principles or values have been summed in the phrase "socialist pattern of society". As explained in the Second Plan Report, essentially, this means that the basic criterion for determining the lines of advance must not be private profit, but social gain and the pattern of development and the structure of socio-economic relations should be so planned that they result not only in appreciable increases in national income and employment, but also in greater equality in incomes and wealth. The benefits of economic development must accrue more and more to the relatively less privileged classes of society. There should be a progressive reduction of the concentration conditions, the State has to take on heavy responsibilities as the principal agency on behalf of the community as a whole. The public sector has to expand rapidly. It has not only to initiate developments which the private sector is either unwilling or unable to undertake; it has to play the dominant role in establishing the entire pattern of investments in the economy, whether it makes the investments directly or whether these are made by the private sector. Economic advance has to proceed on democratic and egalitarian lines.

These considerations mark out as something distinct the course adopted in India in her economic development. There is no parallel to it in the Western world or in the East European countries.

In the Western nations, rapid development took place in a period when the concepts of social welfare were still to be evolved. Economic development preceded political and social reform : before the concepts of democracy and equality became pervasive, the Western world had already a thriving economy. In India, on the other hand, this process has been reversed. It has already a working democracy committed to the furtherance of social and economic justice. Economic development has, therefore, to proceed simultaneously with measures for reduction of inequalities and wider diffusion of incomes. This makes the task more complex and difficult.

What India is attempting to do in economic development is also different from the method adopted in East European countries. In those countries, all economic activities are controlled and regulated by the State and ownership rests entirely with the State. There is no private enterprise ; production is nationalised. The State, having a complete command over the factors of production, is able to decide fully the production targets, allocation of resources, foreign trade, deployment of labour, wages and prices. Planning is total and the State can decide the direction and pace of economic development. Within the political democracy in which India operates, this relatively easy course in not open to her.

These differences in the economic conditions and the socio-political objectives between India on the one hand and the East and West European countries on the other are reflected in Indian planning, which represents for the first time an attempt by a developing country in democratic planning. In this respect Indian planning has certain distinguishing characteristics. In Western nations, planning is a later development as applied to an already developed economy. Economic planning in the Western countries has been a consequence of the economic changes related to the emergence of a more advanced industrial society. Having attained already a dynamic and sophisticated economy, the Western countries largely depend, in their planning, on the operation of market forces influenced indirectly through monetary and fiscal measures. On the other hand, as

I earlier said, planning in the Eastern countries is all comprehensive and total in its concept. In adopting a planning technique which is different from the indicative and indirect planning in the West European countries and the centralised planning in the Socialist countries, we have chosen, consistent with our socio-political objectives, a distinctly different course which some economists have chosen to call "a third world of planning" In doing so, we have attempted to adopt a method which can bring about rapid economic growth without sacrificing the democratic freedoms of the people. This method is obviously a more difficult one.

The method of indirectly influencing the course of the economy through monetary and fiscal policies, which may be appropriate to an already developed economy, would not suffice for Indian conditions where the necessary dynamism has to be still infused. The State has thus to play a crucial role to activise the economy and to bring about the impulses of growth. As early as in the First Plan the policy was, therefore, enunciated that the State must not only assume the responsibility for providing the infrastructure facilities, but also undertake direct promotional work. The need for the intervention of the State in the industrial field was recognised and the development of basic and strategic industries was earmarked to the public sector. At the same time, large-scale nationalisation was eschewed ; it was clear that the task before the country was so large that the initiative of both public and private sectors would be necessary to secure maximum growth. A complementary role was assigned to the private sector and a large field of operation was left open for private sector activities. The concept of mixed economy was evolved, envisaging the operation of both public and private sectors on the basis of equal treatment. Over the greater part of activities including not only the organised industry but also agriculture, small industry, trade and construction, individual effort and private initiative were regarded as necessary and desirable.

The concept of a mixed economy was given concrete shape and policy direction at the commencement of the Second Five Year Plan by the announcement of the Industrial Policy Resolution of April 1956. This Policy Resolution continues to provide the framework of industrial policy even now. The basic consideration underlying the Industrial Policy Resolution was to venture into new fields and to provide the country with the foundations of economic development by strengthening the basic industrial structure of the country. This implied long-term programme and substantial investment by the State not only for the development of basic and heavy industries such as iron and steel, machine building, fertilizers and chemicals, but also providing the essential services such as water supply, power, transport and communications, besides undertaking direct promotional work of providing finance, marketing facilities, technical advice and other assistance to foster industrial development.

The Industrial Policy Resolution splet out the role expected to be played by the pubiic and private sectors. As the Resolution puts it, "the need for planned and rapid development requires that all industries of basic and strategic importance or in the nature of public utility services should be in the public sector. Other industries which are essential and require investment on a scale which only the State, in the present circumstances, could provide, have also to be in the public sector. The State has, therefore, to assume direct responsibility for the future development of industries over a wide are". Two schedules were drawn up : Schedule 'A' enumerating 17 industries, the future development of which will be the exclusive responsibility of the State and Schedule 'B' containing a list of 12 industries which will be progressively State-owned and in which the State will, therefore, generally take the initiative in establishing new industries, but in which private enterprise will also be expected to supplement the efforts of the State. All the remaining industries were in general left to the initiative and enterprise of the private sector. This classification is, however, not rigid. The Resolution has left open considerable flexibility so as to permit the entry of the private sector wherever necessary in the fields which are generally allotted to the public sector, and vice versa.

The basic soundness of this policy has been demonstrated by the progress made in the industrial field in the last few years. The structural transformation that has been achieved would not have been possible but for the initiative taken by the State, especially in the field of basic and heavy industries. The State is also instrumental in creating the necessary "infra-structure" which is to so vital for rapid growth. It is this heavy investment in economic and social overheads, combined with the vigorous growth of basic and heavy industries in the public sector, that has forced the pace of industrialisation and created the necessary environment for stimulating industrial production in the private sector.

Within the broad framework of the Policy Resolution, the Industries (Development and Regulation) Act provides the main instrument through which the development of industries in the private sector is regulated. The industrial licensing system was designed to canalise investments in the desired directions in accordance with Plan priorities and targets, to protect the small-scale sector, to prevent concentration of economic power and to bring about progressively economic and technological improvements in the development of industries in the private sector. The Development Councils which were set up under the Act were expected to give particular attention to technical and economic studies and to such factors as economies of scale, cost of production, operational efficiency, import substitution and export development.

The need for a measure of control in a planned economy, particularly in a developing country, needs no emphasis. These controls are necessary to direct scarce resources in the desired directions. This is one of the fundamental objectives of the Industries (D & R) Act. The other more important regulations are those pertaining to foreign exchange control and price and distribution controls. In the initial stages of development, the need for imports of capital equipment and raw-materials is large. As exports are confined primarliy to traditional commodities and the value of volume of such exports cannot be increased substantially, developing countries face an imbalance in their external payments.

As exports cannot finance adequately the large volume of imports needed, it becomes necessary to allocate foreign exchange on priority considerations. Price and distribution controls are intended to protect the vulnerable sections of the community from sudden or persistent shortages in particular commodities and to prevent undue profits being made by the trader of producer. These controls are, however, kept periodically under review so that when these become unnecessary they are eliminated. Thus, for example, in recent times price and distribution controls over a number of commodities have been partially or completely removed with the improvement in their supplies.

Until now, I have dealt with some of the distinct characteristics of Indian planning and its objectives. In my next lecture I shall touch on some of the achievements and failures in the field of industrial development and the future policy measures required for healthy and orderly growth.

From the foregoing analysis, it would appear that the mixed economy which we have developed during the last eighteen years of planning is perhaps best suited to the genius of our people. Any attempt to hustle this society towards total planning with totalitarian control over the means of production or to revert to a state of unregulated laissez faire can be contemplated only at the cost of democracy on the one hand and social justice on the other. Wisdom lies in steering a middle path, however unpopular it may appear to be.

In his second lecture on September 11, 1962, Venkataraman proposed to give his listeners a panoramic view of some of the significant changes in the economy since the advent of the planning process with special reference to industrial development. He followed this up with a general exposition on the approach and programmes for industrial development during the Fourth Five Year Plan period.[5]

"At the beginning of the First Five Year Plan, in 1950-51, the Indian economic scene presented a typical, characteristic picture of a stagnant economy. Traditional agriculture and languishing rural industries provided the main occupation for the mass of the people which eked out a bare living. With the exception of few agriculture-based industries like cotton and jute textiles and sugar, modern industry virtually did not exist. For almost all industrial products, the country was dependent on imports ; imports of even consumer goods were quite large. The climate for development of industries did not exist. Installed capacity of electricity was as low as 2.5 million K.W. Electrification had not proceeded beyond some of the big cities and a few towns. Long term institutional finance was unknown. With the exception of a few managing agencies there was virtually no enterprise or initiative for the development of new industries. The technical skills for the development of modern industries were conspicuous by their absence. The educational pattern was oriented largely to provide the administrative personnel, rather than geared to technical and scientific subjects. No more than 6 per cent of the children of the school-going ages reached the high school stage. There was virtually no machine-building capacity.

The production of steel, a key element in industrial growth, was no more than a million tonnes.

During the last eighteen years of planning, the economy has been taken out of the traditional rut and a sense of dynamism infused in it. The rate of investment and national income have been substantially stepped up. Structural changes conducive to growth and development have been brought about. The strength and potential of the economy have been considerably raised, not only in terms of higher levels of capacity and production already achieved but more importantly, by way of developing the necessary human resources and talent. Institutional changes helpful to greater effort and initiative on a wider scale have been successfully introduced. Greater dispersal and decentralisation of economic effort and benefits has been achieved. The people are better fed, better clothed, better educated and better looked after than ever before.

Let me highlight some of our achievement in greater detail. Talking in aggregate terms, India's net national income increased by about 80 per cent from Rs. 9,650 crores to Rs. 17,300 crores (at 1960-61 prices) between 1950-51 and 1967-68. The national income is estimated to have risen further by 3 per cent in 1968-69. The rate of growth in the First Plan was 3.4 per cent and in the Second Plan 4 per cent : in the first four years of the Third Plan, a growth rate of 4.2 per cent was maintained. In the subsequent two years, 1965-66 and 1966-67, there was a drop in national income on account of a sharp decline in agricultural production. The national income recovered in 1967-68 to approximately the same level as in 1964-65. Thus, over a fairly long period, we have been able to achieve a growth rate of about 4 per cent in our national income. Though this is not large enough, it has to be compared with the growth rate of barely 1 per cent in the-Plan period. In spite of its various short-comings, the planning process has stimulated economic growth and increased national income at rates substantially higher than witnessed before in the Indian economy. However, in spite of this relatively good performance, the pcr capita income has improved only marginally and at an annual rate of less than 2 per cent because of the accelerated pace of population growth

It is this aspect which has given special significance to the high priority and urgency attached to family planning and population control.

Coming more specifically to the different sectors of the economy, there is room for satisfaction with our performance. The production of food-grains increased from 51 million tonnes in 1950-51 to 89 million tonnes in 1964-65 and further to 95 tonnes in 1967-68. There has been an equally remarkable growth in the production of other agricultural commodities; oil seeds production increased from 5.2 million tonnes to 8.2 million tonnes, cotton from 2.9 million bales to 5.6 million bales and jute from 3.5 million bales to 6.4 million bales and sugar cane from 6.9 million tonnes to 10 million tonnes between 1950-51 and 1967-68. Taking the overall agricultural production, the increase has been of the order of 70 per cent.

In the industrial field, the progress has been equally remarkable. Industrial production nearly trebeld over the three Plan periods. Production of finished steel went up from 1 million tonnes, to 4 million tonnes, aluminium from 4,000 tonnes to 96,300 tonnes, coal from 33 million tonnes to 68.5 million tonnes, cement from 2.7 to 11.5 million tonnes, petroleum products from 0.2 million tonnes to 14.4 million tonnes, nitrogenous fertilizers from 9,000 tonnes to 3,67,000 tonnes, machine tools from Rs. 0.3 crores to Rs. 23.5 crores and automobiles from 16,500 to 67,000 between 1950-51 and

1967-68. These are merely illustrative and indicative of the substantial increase in the volume of output over a wide range of industries. The production of many new sophisticated industrial products was taken up for the first time. The industrial structure was expanded and diversified. Not only are all the consumer goods produced locally but a substantial proportion of the requirements of the producer and capital goods are not from domestic production. Our dependence on imports for basic commodities like steel and alloy steels, non-ferrous metals, petroleum product, construction materials, heavy chemicals, and drugs and pharmaceuticals has substantially diminished. Furthermore, a considerable march has been made in the production of capital goods. For the growth in transport, power, irrigation and industrial and mining sectors, we can now increasingly rely on the availability of capital equipment from within the country. The heavy electrical projects at Bhopal, Hardwar and Ramachandrapuram along with the capacity in the private sector can meet the bulk of the requirements of capital equipment for power generation, transmission and distribution. Locomotives, wagons, trucks, motor cars, ships and aeroplanes are now produced in the country. Industrial equipment ranging from those required for textile, cement and other traditional industries to those for steel and fertilizers are available from domestic sources. More than the gross increase in industrial production, this diversification has given considerable strength to the economy.

To highlight some of the other achievements, I may refer to the increase in the installed capacity of electricity from 2.5 million K.W. to 13.13 million K.W., the three-fold increase in the intake of school students from 23.5 million to 71.8 million and six-fold increase in the intake of engineering and technology graduates from 4,000 to 25,000 per annum during the period 1950-51 to 1967-68. Against 40 per cent, the percentage of children going to school is now 80 per cent. As against 4,000 villages electrified in 1950-51, the number of villages electrified in 1967-68 was 62,237. With the extension of health facilities, the expectation of life at birth has now increased from 35 years to 52 years.

Apart from these physical achievements, there are other directions in which significant progress has been registered during this period. I had occasion to refer in my earlier talk to the traditional attitudes inhibiting the process of economic development. To some extent we have made advances in breaking the barriers of tradition and in bringing a larger section of people into the stream of the development process. The most heartening feature in this regard is the success achieved in inducing the traditional farmer to the use of modern methods of cultivation. The success of the "green revolution" lies not merely in our ability to provide the necessary inputs by way of fertilizers, pesticides and better seeds, but in securing the acceptance by the farmer of their use to increase production and to earn larger incomes. The fact that it has been possible to increase our agricultural production so substantially and the hopes we entertain in maintaining a 5 per cent growth rate in agriculture during the Fourth Plan are indications of the healthy transformation in the attitudes among the large farming community. Similar attitudinal changes have been witnessed in the industrial field also. Although there are indications pointing to concentration of industries in the large houses during the Plan periods, there is no denying the fact that a new class of entrepreneurs has also come into being. There has been phenomenal growth in the development of small-scale industries, largely owned by middle-class entrepreneurs who a few years ago would not have ventured into this kind of productive activity. The entrepreneurial spirit has been infused over a wider field. Industrial management has become more scientific and less family oriented. Sophisticated technology in a variety of fields has been acquired and absorbed. Industrial research and consultancy services have considerably expanded. There is greater quality consciousness and cost consciousness within the industry. This is evident from the fact that in a variety of non-traditional goods we are today in a position to compete successfully in the international market with developed countries.

I would not like to explain in some detail the transformation in the industrial scene and the extent to which the objectives of the Industrial Policy Resolution have been attained over the years. Among the salient objectives of the industrial policy are the development of a diversified industrial structure, the diffusion of industries with a view to reducing regional imbalance and the promotion of a healthy and viable growth of small-scale industries. Industrial licensing has been one of the main instruments for achieving these objectives. It is legitimate to ask whether industrial licensing has served the purpose for which it was intended and what has, in fact, been the record of its performance.

The industrial licensing has to a considerable extent helped in diversifying the industrial structure and directing investments in newer industries, cannot be denied. This is evident from the structural transformation that has already been witnessed in the industrial sector. On the eve of independence the structure was simple and totally unbalanced. The overall contribution of industry to the national income was low. The relative backwardness of industrial development may be judged from the fact that its contribution to national income was a mere 5 to 6 per cent and the total labour force engaged in this sector was about 2.4 million or less than 2 per cent of the total working population in the sector. The more serious dimension of backwardness was that except for the production of simple consumer goods like textiles, sugar, paper and some other consumer durables like bicycles, fans and sewing machines, very few key and heavy industries existed. The qualitative change in the direction of industrialisation after the advent of planning is evident from the remarkable progress made in some of the growth promoting sector, as may be seen from the following table :

These aggregates, besides indicating the large strides taken since the beginning of 1950 also underline the structural changes that have occurred during the period. While the percentage increase in value added in respect of consumer goods was only 87 per cent, it was as 593 per cent for intermediate goods and 922 per cent for machinery items. The growth sectors have expanded much more rapidly than the traditional industries.

The diversification in industrial structure in these years is also reflected in the employment position invarious sectors.

TABLE 10.4

Value Added in Manufacturing Industry

(Rs. million at 1960-61 prices)

Industries	1950-51	1965-66	Pereentage Increase
Consumer goods	2,607	4,876	87%
Intermediate goods	895	6,202	593%
Machinery	309	3,159	922%
Others	31	103	232%
Total	3,842	14,340	

For example, while the labour employed in traditional industries like textiles and sugar (organised sector) increased from 1.12 to 1.26 million and 95,000 to 1,31,000 i.e., by 13 per cent and 38 per cent respectively in 1966 as compared to 1951, the percentage increase in labour force in newer fields like basic metal industry and machinery (other than electric) industry was of the order of 159 per cent and 222 per cent respectively. The employment increased from 1,02,000 to 2,64,000 in basic metal industry and from 1,07,000 to 3,45,000 in machinery industry (other than electric). The increase in labour force in electric machinery industry was as high as 400 per cent for the corresponding period.

In directing industrial investments in accordance with the Plan strategy and programmes, the industrial licencing system has significantly contributed to the emergence of this diversified structure in the private sector.

Industrial licensing has also played a useful role in the remarkable growth of small-scale industries over the last decade. One of the serious difficulties withrespect to assessing the growth in the small-scale sector is the paucity of reliable data on the actual production, investments and employment in this area.

So wide-spread and so numerous are the units in the small-scale sector that a complete enumeration of them will always present difficulty. We have, therefore, to be guided, by and large, by the small-scale industries which are registered with the State Directorates of Industries. Generally, it is only such of those small-scale industries which have to secure some facility or the other like imported raw materials which register themselves with the Directorate of Industries. The number of units registered with the State Directorates of Industries, therefore, does not present the total number of small-scale industries in the country. Nevertheless this would provide some indication of the progress of the small-scale industries over the years.

Maharashtra and Tamil Nadu have kept up the lead in the growth rate of small-scale units during this period, though in terms of absolute numbers Punjab and Uttar Pradesh have also a prominent position. Some of the relatively backward States like Rajasthan, Kerala, Madhya Pradesh and Assam have also very many more small-scale units now than before.

This growth in small-scale industries has been achieved through a variety a variety of measures. In certain industries which are particularly suitable for development in the small-scale sector, a policy of reservation or common programme was adopted. In other words, no large-scale units were allowed to come up in such industries or their entry was restricted so as to provide adequate room for the simulataneous growth of small-scale industries. This policy was generally enforced through the mechanism of licensing. In addition, other positive support by way of price preference in the purchase of products from small-scale industries, fiscal incentives and technical guidance and marketing assistance was also provided. That this policy has generally had a beneficial effect on the wide-spread development of small-scale industries is evident from the statistics given above. In several small-scale industries, competive ability has improved to a point where they are in a position to stand on their own without special reservations in their favour. The main thrust of policy is to make them increasingly viable and technologically efficient so that they become an integral part of the total industrial structure, capable of making their contribution on their own strength.

Looking now at the changes in the regional picture of industrial growth, it must be admitted that while a small measure of dispersal has been brought about during the Plan periods, the positton is not altogether satisfactory. There is a variety of indicators by which the spread of industrial development in various States can be judged such as the number of factories, the productive capital employed, the number of persous employed and electricity consumed.

A qualitative analysis of the situation would indicate that although the setting up of industrial units in the various States was largely on consideration of locational advantages, dispersal of industries was, however, possible in respect of light engineering, textile and food industries. Bihar, Madhya Pradesh, Maharashtra, Orissa and West Bengal have attracted large industries which are raw-material-oriented. Medium and small industries have largely contributed to the industrial progress in States like Gujarat, Mysore, Punjab, Tamil Nadu and Utter Pradesh. Both large and small industries seem to have contributed to the progress in Maharashtra.

A conclusion that emerges from the above analysis is that licensing as an instrument for bringing about regional dispersal of industries has many limitations. It is only to the extent that sufficient number of entrepreneurs are forthcoming for the location of industries in backward areas can the Licensing Commmittee have a choice to prefer them in place of others to be located in the more developed States. Experience has shown that it is only through the adoption of positive measures that better regional dispersal can be effectively achieved. Thus, certain States like Gujarat and Tamil Nadu have significantly improved their position in the industrial land-scape of India between 1955 and 1965. On the other hand, in spite of massive public sector investments in some big projects in States like Madhya Pradesh and Orissa, the general run of industrial development in these States has remained backward. The explanation lies in the fact that the mere establishment of a few large giant projects does not contribute to general industrial development. It is only through the development of a large number of medium and small-scale industries that the spread effect of industrialisation can be secured.

In this context, the role of the State Governments in the development of industries needs to be emphasised. Apart from the industries declared by Parliament by law to be necessary for the purpose of defence or for the prosecution of war and those, the control of which is declared by Parliament to be expedient in the public interest, all other industries belong to the State List. The States have a great scope to the growth and dispersal of small-scale industries. It is only by a positive and helpful approach that the States can attract, foster and develop industries in their area. Provisions of infra-structure facilities like power, communications, land and water, financial assistance through the State Finance and Industrial Development Corporations, removing obstacles and cutting out the red-tape are some of the positive steps necessary for industrial growth. Labour policy in States is also a major factor in the continuance and growth of industries. Friendly guidance from the State Ministers and offlcials will go a long way to develop local entrepreneurship. In short, States have a much greater role to play in industrial development than it superficially appears.

The effectiveness of the licensing system and its administration have been matters of scrutiny and anaylsis by a number of committees and economists in recent times. The Swaminathan Committee looked into the procedures in licensing and suggested a number of changes to streamline the procedures. Prof. Hazari made a rapid analysis of the working of the licensing system over the more recent years and came to the conclusion that it had led to concentration in the large industrial hiouses. More recently, the Industrial Licensing Policy Inqury Committee has studied the same aspect in some further detail. While there is no doubt that the licensing system as administered has suffered from a variety of deficiencies, the fact remains that in the initial stages of our development it has made a valuable contribution in channeling investment activities in appropriate directions, in assisting the growth of small-scale industries and to some extent in influencing the growth of industries in backward areas. In fact, it is doubtful whether it would have been possible to implement the

Industrial Policy Resolution without an instrument like industrial licensing.

Considerable though our achievements have been, a number of shortcomings have also come to light. I shall refer to only the more important.

Let us take first the question of our external economic relations. Our economic development in the last several years has been assisted to a considerable extent by the inflow of foreign aid. The total amount of aid received up to the end of 1968-69 is estimated at about Rs. 8,500 crores. This aid helped us to secure equipment and materials which we could not finance from our own foreign exchange earnings. It also helped us in augmenting the total pool of resources available for plan financing. However, foreign aid has not been an unmixed blessing. We now find that we have a very large external burden which has to be serviced from our export earnings. The total debt service payments during the Fourth Plan are estimated at Rs. 2,280 crores. Our total export earnings during the Fourth Plan are estimated at Rs. 8,300 crores. Thus, about a third of our export earnings will have to be set apart merely for debt service payments. This is too large a burden for any economy to carry. Indeed, even the maintenance of the economy has become now critically dependent on fresh inflow of foreign aid. It is thus clear that we have to reorient our policy in regard to foreign aid and should aim to achieve a measure of self-reliance in our external payment situation as early as possible. This is one direction in which the Fourth Plan has marked out a new approach. The Plan has been formulated in a manner that would enable the quantum of net foreign aid to be brought down by about half by the end of the Plan and to be virtually eliminated by the end of the Fifth Plan.

One of the objectives of the Plan is to prevent concentration of wealth and to reduce disparity in incomes. The policy framework for achieving this objective was, however, not adequately spelt out. The interaction of the complex system of controls on private investment seems to have indirectly provided an advantage to the relatively more organised and strong industrial groups to the detriment of the weaker ones. Indications are that not only has there been no diminution in the concentration of wealth, but actually there appears to have been a trend in the opposite direction. Even in the matter of agricultural incomes it would appear that it is the more properious and well-to-do farmers who have generally benefited from the various services and financial aid provided by Government. The small farmer and the landless labourer do not seem to have improved their lot. Thus, one of the primary objectives laid down in the Plan namely reduction of inequalities in income and wealth and a mere even distribution of economic power, has not been achieved. It is, therefore, necessary to take corrective action. The Fourth Plan has indicated the direction in which such action should be taken. One of the means by which the large industrial houses were able to increase their concentration was the substantial support they were able to secure from the financial institutions. An important recommendation in the Fourth Plan is that in future the contribution of the large industrial houses should be proportionately higher in order to be eligible for assistance from financial institutions. It is also proposed that in industries in which sufficient development has already taken place, large industrial houses should not be permitted to expand production ; these fields should be left primarily for new entrants. A variety of other policy measures have also been indicated in the Fourth Plan to assist the marginal farmer and the landless labourer and the new entrepreneur.

The industrial licensing system and the strict control on imports also led to certain aberrations in the industrial structure. Pre-determined targets laid down in the Plans formed the basis for industrial licensing. As the administrative machinery was not geared to review these targets in accordance with the changing economic situation, this led to the creation in some cases of considerably larger capacities than necessary and in other lower than what was needed. The result was an imbalance in the industrial structure with surplus capacities in certain industries and shortages in others. The targets were taken as sacrosanct. The private industry relinquished even its normal responsibility of assessing the market situation and carrying out market surveys. There was too great dependence on Plan targets and Government estimates. Furthermore, at the beginning of the Plan when the targets were announced, there was a rush of applications for industrial licensing. The entire Plan targets were fully covered by industrial licensing right at the beginning. There was no proper phasing. This led to sudden pressures on the financial institutions for rupee funds and on foreign exchange resources. Such of those as succeeded in obtaining licences blocked the entry of new entrepreneurs. Assured of freedom from competition an account of strict import controls., no consideration was given to capital costs or cost of production. All this resulted in maldistribution of scarce resources and in the growth of a high cost industrial structure. While production levels were stepped up, these were secured at a heavy cost to the economy. This situation has to be corrected, so that while industrial capacity is increased and the competitive ability of Indian industry is also enhanced.

I have referred to the imbalance in the industrial structure leading to under-utilisation of capacities in certain industries, and shortages in others. In order to ensure that industrial development in increasingly in conformity with market requirements, the Draft Fourth Plan proposes to allow in some respects a greater degree of freedom for the operations of the private sector. The new Plan strategy calls for considerable modification in the existing regulations pertaining to industrial licensing. With the diversified industrial structure already built-up and the availability of a substantial part of the capital equipment and raw materials from domestic sources, it is no longer necessary to exercise detailed control on all industries as hitherto. It is, therefore, proposed that except where significant foreign exchange outlays are involved either by way of import of capital equipment or import of raw materials and components, there need be no industrial licensing. In other words, entrepreneurs who are capable of utilising indigenous equipment, raw materials and technology can be given the freedom to set up enterprises without obtaining industrial licences. The only safeguard envisaged is that with respect identified small-scale industries it would still be necessary to maintain the licensing system with a view to giving the small-scale industries the required protection from undue competition from large-scale industries.

As a logical corollary to this policy, the Planning Commission has suggested that rigid targets need not be laid down for a variety of industries in which the judgement of the private entrepreneurs about markets should form the basic criterion of the capacity that might be created. In the past, the targets laid down by the Planning Commission provided the basis for licensing. Within the targets, licences were given. The entrepreneurs did little or no market studies on their own. In actual practice, some of these targets turned out to be too high or too low. Furthermore, such of those who were able to secure licences in advance foreclosed the possibilities of new entrants and obtained protected markets. All this led to considerable disequilibrium in the economy and erosion of cost consciousness and efficiency. We expect that the new policy will provide conditions in which efficiency would be rewarded and would lead to the emergence of a competitive economy.

The elimination of detailed administrative controls and industrial licensing for a number of industries which are largely based on domestic resources will then make it possible to devote special and particular attention to the development of high priority industries which are critical for import substitution and future growth potential. For these high priority industries, the Planning Commission will continue to lay down definite targets and will take the steps to ensure that the targets are, in fact, realised. Industrial licensing would carry with it priority consideration for the allocation of rupee funds, foreign exchange, scarce materials, electric power and other requirements. These industries would be periodically reviewed and actively assisted. Licences in these industries would be revoked promptly if action is not taken for implementation, so that disinterested parties are replaced by promising new ones.

An examination of the recommendations of the Industrial Licensing Policy Inquiry Committee (the Dutt Committee) becomes relevant at this stage. There is broad agreement between the Planning Commission and the Industrial Licensing Policy Inquiry Committee regarding the target setting, licensing and assurance of credit and foreign exchange to the 'key' or the 'core' sector of the Plan. Likewise, there is agreement on the need for reservation of certain areas for the development of the small-scale sector.

For the middle area, the Industrial Licensing Policy Inquiry Committee have proposed that while in the main the development should be let free subject to market forces and fiscal and financial devices, it should be subjected to industrial licensing for the limited purpose of preventing the dominating influence of large industrial houses. Thus, for this middle area, the licensing system will operate essentially as a negative instrument preventing establishment of units by the larger industrial houses and foreign concerns and leaving the area free for development by others. With this background, the Dutt Committee have recommended that the entire list of delicensed industries should be reviewed.

Thus, while the Planning Commission is of the view that effective and detailed planning should be limited to the 'key' sector and that planning in respect of the 'middle' sector should only be indicative and that its regulation should be through the mechanism of fiscal and financial instruments, the Industrial Licensing Policy Inquiry Committee desires to bring the entire industrial development under a comprehensive licensing system.

It is open to question whether merely for the purpose of preventing the entry of large industrial houses in certain industries, the entire complex of industrial licensing system should be retained for those industries if, for other reasons, it is not considered necessary to keep them within the licensing area. As the 'core' area is a limited one, the largest number of applications are likely to be from the so-called 'middle' area. By maintaining all these industries within the licensing system, there would be no reduction in the administrative work-load. With the best of simplification in procedure, the procedural hurdles which an entrepreneur has to pass through will remain. This would certainly be a serious impediment to the free entry of new entrepreneurs and to the emergence of a competitive environment in these industries. It should be possible to devise some other simpler course to prevent the domination of large industrial houses in this middle area. The essence of planning lies in its selectivity. If virtually all industries have to be retained in the licensing system either as core industries or banned industries or middle sector industries, detailed attention to the strategic industries would not be possible. Comprehensive planning has to be limited to vital sectors. There is considerable advantage if leaving the rest of the field freed for normal market operations within the broad frame work of indicative targets.

The Industrial Licensing Policy Inquiry Committee has recommended that a detailed plan for industry covering a period of ten if not fifteen years should be drawn up. Such a plan should take note of the available technologies, decide the optimum one in our conditions, determine the total number and phasing of projects and their locational distribution. I doubt if such a detailed exericse will at all be possible except in the 'core' sector. When technological innovations sweep rapidly over the world, a plan drawn up for a period of 10-15 years, based on the limited knowledge of technology available at the time of the preparation of the Plan, is bound to leave us far behind in the competitive world. Such an effort may lead to setting up of unrealistic targets and repetition of the past mistaker in planning. Morever, the uncertainty regarding resources, both internal and external, renders such long-range planning difficult if not impossible. But I agree that so far as the 'core' sector is concerned, every effort should be made to draw up comprehensive plan covering the period till the project goes into production.

The role of larger industrial houses in future industrial development has been raised in the Report of the Industrial Licensing Policy Inquiry Committee. According to this Committee, larger industrial houses should concentrate their resources on the development of heavy investment industries which would mainly belong to the 'core' sector, and the applications from concerns belonging to larger industrial houses as well as those from foreign concerns should be automatically rejected in the case of industries in the 'middle' area. The Planning Commission has a less rigid approach to this question. It postulates that big industrial houses should not, as a general rule, be allowed to enter in relatively common industries such as production of consumer goods and that they should have full scope in technologically challenging fields. The financial institutions should not divert an undue proportion of the available resources to the larger industrial houses where own contribution to the project should be proportionately larger compared to medium-scale or new entrepreneurs.

India has accepted the goal of a rapid increase in the standards of living of the people through measures which also promote equality and justice. It is the aim of planning that it should bring about greater equality in income and wealth and that there should be a progressive reduction of concentration of incomes and economic power. Whether a total exclusion of larger industrial houses from a vast field of middle sector is necessary for achieving this objective is not clear.

The Industrial Licensing Policy Inquiry Committee has further recommended that establishment and expansion of luxury industries should be banned for a sufficiently long period of five years. Though, at first sight this may seem innocuous, the translation of this policy into practice bristles with difficulties. Firstly, there is no acceptable definition of luxuries. Air conditioning, which may be called a luxury, is an indispensable necessity for precision grinding. A blanket ban may cause more difficulties than it solves. Secondly, banned items will become scarce and a prices spiral and blackmarketing will appear. The remedy suggested, namely, imposition of excise duties to mop up the unconscionable profits will result in further pushing up the prices. Lastly. we should try and utilise all available resources and move towards a philosophy of plenty. As formulated by the Planning Commission, if indigenous equipment and raw materials can produce luxury articles, the banning of such production will result in under-utilisation of capacity. The problem today is not the absence of capacity which prevailed a decade but how to find fuller utilisation of capacity built up in the country.

In short, while the Planning Commission is more concerned with development of industries and the economy, the Industrial Licensing Policy Inquiry Committee confines its attention to the concentration of economic power and the steps necessary to correct it.

I had earlier made a reference to the policies proposed in the Fourth Plan to prevent undue concentration in large industrial houses. An equally important aspect is the need for more balanced development of all regions and areas in the country. In a vast country like ours, there is bound to be some disparity in the levels of income and growth in different regions. These are partly of historical origin, but certain economic factors have also tended to perpetuate these disparities. While a number of steps have been taken during the last three Plan periods towards greater dispersal of industries in the country, there is no denying the fact that the areas which were already developed have made greater progress than the areas which were relatively backward. The large investments in some of the industrial projects in the public sector in relatively backward regions and measures to influence the location of private industries in backward regions through the industrial licensing system have not materially altered the picture. The fact is that the natural endowments are not equally distributed and when it comes to relatively large investments, broad techno-economic considerations become paramount in the locational decisions of industrial units. This being the case, a uniform industrial development all over the country is not feasible. However, some of the disabilities which act as deterrent factors in the location of industries in the backward regions are capable of being eliminated. If measures in this direction are taken and certain positive incentives are provided for the location of industries in backward regions, a some-what wider dispersal will be feasible. Industries can be attracted to backward regions only if all the required infrastructure facilities are made available. Some steps have been taken in this direticon by the State Governments through the programme of establishment of industrial areas. However, a great deal more needs to be done. It is necessary to identify the areas to which special attention has to be given. These areas are to be delineated and apart from providing the necessary infra-structure facilities, certain incentives may have also to be offered. Two Working groups set up by the Planning Commission have been detailed consideration to these aspects. One of them has identified the criteria for selecting industrially backward areas and the other one has recommended the various incentives and measures to promote the growth of industries in backward regions. These reports are now under consideration by a Standing Committee of the National Development Council. We expect that based on the decisions to be taken on these reports, it would be possible to move in the direction of greater dispersal of industries.

Both from the point of view of dispersal of industries and also prevention of economic concentration, the emergence of a modern small-scale sector has an important place in the strategy of industrial development. In the Indian context, it has several other merits. Small-scale sector is relatively more labour intensive and therefore, provides a large employment potential which is an important consideration. It requires generally lower capital per unit of production ; with a give capital it is, therefore, possible to achieve a higher level of output in the small-scale sector. The Fourth Plan, therefore, gives considerable importance to its development. The emphasis is primarily on the modern small-scale industries with reasonably high level of productivity. These are industries where in the economies of scale are not particularly important and which are, therefore, capable of being dispersed in small units without the disadvantage of lower levels of technology or productivity. Many of these industries have been identified and have been earmarked exclusively for the development of the small-scale sector. In respect of other industries, co-ordinated development of large and small-scale sector will be encouraged through the promotion of ancillaries as feeder industries to larger units. Increasingly, the direction of development would be to improve the levels of technology in the small scale sector so that they are able to stand in competition with the large-scale sector without subsidies or other protective instruments. In the interim period, protection would be given to the extent necessary by reservation of capacities in favour of small-scale sector either exclusively or partially, but this will be progressively reduced and ultimately eliminated.

I had referred to the strategic role of the public sector in forcing the pace of industrial development and its impact on the industrial structure. The public sector in organised industries has expanded considerably since the Second plan. There are over 80 Central Government industrial and commercial enterprises representing an investment of the order of Rs. 3,500 crores. The investment in Hindustan Steel alone was over Rs. 1,000 crores at the end of 1967-68. Including the investment in Bokaro steel, the total investment in the steel sector was of the order of Rs. 1,200 crores. The other more important fields in which large ago, investments have been made are engineering—Rs. 830 crores, chemicals—Rs. 350 crores, petroleum—Rs. 380 crores and minerals and metals—Rs. 270 crores. These are large investments and were expected not only to contribute to the total national production but also to larger resources by way of profits. The performance of the public sector enterprises is, therefore, a matter of vital concern to the economy. The fact that the financial performance of public sector undertakings on the whole has not hitherto been altogether satisfactory has focussed considerable public attention on these enterprises. Criticism has been voiced that the public sector as a whole is inefficient and that there should be no further expansion in the public sector. But the performance of the public sector has not been wholly bad. There are a number of public sector projects which are giving good returns. During 1967-68, 31 of the public enterprises showed a net profit of over Rs. 48 crores. The losses incurred were mainly those of Hindustan Steel Limited and four engineering enterprises—Heavy Engineering Corporation, Bharat Heavy Electricals, Heavy Electricals India and Mining and Allied Machinery Corporation.

In judging the performance of the undertakings, it cannot be forgotten that public sector has entered into the more difficult fields in which normally private enterprise would have been reluctant to go into. These have been taken in the public sector because of their critical importance to the economy and to growth. They have saved substantial amounts of foreign exchange through their production and lessened the burden of our foreign exchange requirements. Several of them have made significant contribution to our export effort. The industries are of a highly capital intensive nature with long gestation periods not ordinarily expected to yield large returns in the short run. Besides, when reference is made to the public sector, the total investments of all categories are clubbed together. A substantial part of the investments in the public sector is in projects which are still in the construction stage. These projects cannot be expected to provide returns. The fact that the public sector enterprises had to provide large overheads by way of townships and other social amenities is also often overlooked. A dispassionate consideration of the performance of the public sector projects should legitimately take into account the total national contribution they have made to the economy, rather than judge them merely on the commercial returns.

Nor can it be assumed that private sector enterprises are always profitable. In his statement to the 20th Annual General Meeting on September 26, 1968, the Chairman of the Industrial Finance Corporation detailed the working of concerns assisted by IFC as follows :

> "Loans were outstanding as on 30 June, 1968, either wholly or in part, from 261 concerns of which 29 had not yet got into production. Of the 208 concerns which were in production at the end of the year as against 217 concerns in the previous year, 135 incurred losses in the year under review or could make only marginal profits, as compared to 133 in the previous year. The number of concerns which were able to declare equity dividend during the year was 73 as compared to 84 last year......"

In my view, the profitability of an enterprise does not depend on the sector to which it belongs but on good management and sound policies. Verbal warfare between the public and the private sector is a meaningless waste of time. In a country like ours where private savings are inadequate and the need for accelerated economic development is urgent, the public sector must be recognised as one of the tools in the armoury and kept in proper shape and trim to discharge the role assigned to it.

There is not doubt that considerable room exists to improve the efficiency of the public sector and to see that it makes maximum contribution to our national resources. It is in this spirit that a number of suggestions have been made in the Draft Fourth Plan to improve the working of the public sector enterprises. Greater autonomy and freedom of management, inventory control, better personnel policies and strengthening of the marketing organisations are some of the directions in which greater attention would need to be paid during the Fourth Plan. It may also be necessary to review the capital structure of some of the public sector enterprises and to distinguish the capital resources employed for production purposes from those which are in the nature of social amenities or township. The expenditure on the latter will have to be recognised as part of the social responsibilities of the Government and not strictly a charge on the enterprise as such. In order to provide the incentive for greater efficiency and larger resources generation, the Planning Commission have recommended that except in special circumstances further expansion of existing public sector enterprises should be based largely from their own resources. This is also expected to prevent the tendency to super-impose expansions even before the original construction programme is completed.

The question of operational autonomy for the management of public enterprises with minimum of interference from Government in their day-to-day operations raises an important issue whether autonomous public sector companies are accountable to Parliament and, if so, to what extent. With large public funds, invested in these undertakings, Parliament certainly has a responsibility to see that these funds are properly employed and the undertakings are operated efficiently. At the same time, it should be ensured that this accountability to Parliament does not weaken the initiative and performance of the management. Therefore, a balance has to be struck between the two desired objectives. As early as 1959, the Krishna Menon Committee had made a number of recommendations intended to reconcile the accountability of public undertakings to Parliament on the one hand with their autonomy for ensuring efficiency on the other. While Parliament must oversee and review the performance of public undertakings with a view to promoting and safe-guarding public interest, the manner of achieving this purpose should be such as not to weaken initiative in the management and thus affect its efficiency. Parliament should be primarily concerned with the efficiency of the overall operations of the enterprise rather than the day-to-day details. From this point of review, it is necessary to develop healthy conventions which are consistent with the special needs of public enterprises.

I had referred to the objective of achieving a substantial reduction in foreign aid during the Fourth Plan. A clear strategy for achieving greater self-reliance in every direction including industrial development is called for. In other words, a larger proportion of the equipment and raw materials required for our growing industries would have to be met from domestic sources. With our diversified industrial structure, this is now largely possible. In order that the maximum utilisation is made of domestic talent and engineering facilities, our approach to foreign collaboration and foreign investment will now have to be more selective. Foreign investment and foreign collaboration should be allowed only for the purpose of supplementing the domestic effort and should not be allowed to come in the way of improving our own capabilities. In the past, in the absence of adequate capabilities within the country, foreign collaboration was permitted rather liberally. Instances are not lacking where in spite of the availability of basic know-how and engineering facilities, foreign collaboration was allowed.

In future, it would be necessary to see that foreign collaboration is not permitted in all those fields in which domestic expertise is sufficient to meet the needs. Thus, for example, in the large range of consumer goods industries it would not be necessary to seek foreign collaboration any longer. Considerable amount of research is carried out in the national laboratories and elsewhere and where the achievements have been satisfactorily demonstrated to be of practical and commercial value, we should encourage them by refusing foreign collaboration arrangements in these areas. Similarly, we should also encourage our design and engineering organisations by appointing them as consultants as far as possible. As a rule, foreign consultants should not be engaged except when it is clearly proved that in any particular field domestic consultancy services are not adequate. Even where foreign consultants are appointed, it would be desirable to appoint an Indian consultancy agency as the primary consultant. This would enable the Indian consultancy agencies to acquire experience and expertise which would later be of great value. The Indian consultants, being more familiar with Indian conditions, are in a better position to formulate the designs in a manner that would enable the maximum utilisation of the demestic fabricating capacity and thereby reduce the need for imported capital equipment.

Self-reliance can be achieved only by a determined endeavour to meet our import requirements from our own export earnings. Economic development is invariably accompanied by a growing requirement for imported materials and commodities. In order that these increasing requirements are financed from our own export earnings, exports will have to grow *pari passu* with imports. In the context of the Fourth Plan and also in the years to come, we will have continuously to increase our exports and take measures to this effect.

The Fourth Plan envisages a step up of 7 per cent per annum in exports. As traditional exports cannot be expected to grow at this rate, the additional export effort has to be primarily concentrated on what are known as non-traditional exports. These are largely the outputs, from the modern industrial sector. The possibilities of increasing our exports substantially in commodities like steel, engineering goods, capital equipment and a variety of other manufactured products has been adequately demonstrated recently. The market for our engineering industries primarily lies in the developing countries through some of the simpler items are also being exported to developed countries. Trade with developing countries would require provision of technical and financial assistance along with engineering goods. Very often turnkey projects are sought and consultancy services becomes paramount for the sale of machinery and equipment. As we are now in a position to take up integrated exports including consultancy services, these possibilities would need to be fully exploited.

Venkataraman on December 28, 1975 called upon economists to formulate time-bound targets for the elimination of poverty and completion of work on the design and content of anti-poverty programmes.

Venkataraman who was inaugurating the 68th All India Economic Conference in Ahmadabad observed that even though economic progress was substantial since independence, we have not overcome the basic problem of mass poverty.

Planning has been instrumental in putting the country's economy on the path of sustained progress despite severe odds.

Recalling his past experience as Finance Minister Venkataraman felt that the problem nexus between efficient use of rcsources, self-reliance and poverty eradication was not simple. "We need to reflect deeply and debate dispassionately to make economy function and perform better," he pointed out.

The growth in productivity, was confined to agriculture sector, where it was also limited to cereals. Productivity should be diversified to meet basic needs of people and decrease economic defendence on imports and external assistance, he said.

With regard to industrial growth, Venkataraman was of the view that with expansion of resources and infrastructure in the country, it was no longer necessary to retain the shackles of controls which had built in undue rigidities and delays.

In this connection, he described as "significant" the series of measures announced by the Centre under the new economic policy. He expressed the hope that the industry would take the opportunity to modernise and expand production.

Real India is rural India. The vast majority of its population lives in its many villages. Yet all the time there has been pampering of the urban areas at the cost of the rural areas—which have been denied a square deal. Time has come, nay it is overdue, to rectify the imbalance.

The working population of the country is about 34 per cent. Only 10 per cent is in the organised sector. Cultivators and agricultural workers form the bulk of the traditional workers. Reliable data is available only for the organised sector. Most of the Acts passed by Government for the welfare of the workers related to the workers in this sector. A rural labour inquiry was conducted between 1963-65 through the National Sample Survey. Data were collected on consumption expenditure, income, employment, unemployment earnings and indebtedness of rural households. The field work of the second rural labour inquiry was completed in 1975. The Labour Bureau brought out a summary of the Rural Labour Enquiry 1974-75 which contains provisional results of on an all India basis in respect of selected economic indicators. In 1978 Government convened a conference on rural unorganised labour to consider the problems of agricultural labourers. A central standing committee was constituted to advise government on measures needed to ameliorate the economic condition of unorganised rural labour. The problem of bonded labour is very much there though it has been abolished by law in 1976.

There is an ILO convention which requires ratifying countries to facilitate the establishment on a voluntary basis of strong and independent organisation of rural workers. India has ratified the ILO Convention which makes it obligatory to abide by its provisions. The present Commission is a first step in the direction of translating into practice the provisions of the Convention. Organised labour not only insists on getting its rights but also holds society to ransom on occasions because of its strength. Rural labour does not even know its rights. Even if knows them it is weak and has no strength to fight for them. Some sort of independent organisation to fight for them is needed. There is the Minimum Wages Act. But it is honoured more in the breach than in observance. Wherefore the Naxalites find it congenial soil to cultivate the workers in many tribal areas. Even what little the law gives them, they do not get ; not to speak of better wages. Some sort of independent organisation of rural workers must be set up to ensure that they get bare justice.

Rajiv Gandhi's reiteration that his Government is committed to Mahatma Gandhi's ideal of wiping out every tear from every eye has to be appreciated in the context of new anti-poverty programmes undertaken in a big way. These programmes have been given top-most priority in the Seventh Plan. The setting up of a human resource development ministry in the major reshuffle at the Centre is part of the process which aims at bettering the lot of the common man. Some slef-styled votaries of the Mahatma, who only pay lip sympathy to him, have of late been carrying a motivated campaign that the Congress Party has deviated from the path of Mahatma Gandhi. In the process they forget that it was the Mahatma who had chosen Jawaharlal Nehru, to lead the battle for freedom at a crucial juncture. The Mahatma was aware of the fact that Nehru different with him on certain issues. What Rajiv Gandhi said at Jaipur in October, 1985 on 'Gandhi Jayanti' celebrations is similar to what Nehru had said. The point the Prime Minister emphasised was that there should be fusion of tradition and technology for a complete development of the country. Nehru undertook the task of setting up a public sector and described the new projects as modern temples. The projects undertaken thereafter have put India on the industrial map of the world. Our scientists and technocrats have won recognition all over the world and stand out for their acumen.

Instead of appreciating the progress made, some vested interests and narrow-minded politicians have all along tried to belittle what Nehru did. It appears that a similar attempt is being made to find fault with Rajiv Gandhi's stress on technology. There is no denying that rural India needs more attention and whatever is done the new policy-makers would not forget the significance of the uplift of the rural masses. Rajiv Gandhi during his visit to the interior parts of different states got a first-hand account of the plight of the neglected and weaker sections. The imbalance in planning priorities because of bureaucratic functioning and neglect by the ministries in certain states has posed certain problems. But there is a marked change in the atmosphere.

Venkataraman, basically an economist in active politics, looks back with pride at the striking progress the country has made in the last four decades. His own contribution in this progress, first as minister and confident of the then Chief Minister of Tamil Nadu, K. Kamaraj, and subsequently as a senior minister heading various important economic ministeries at the Centre, has been significant.

As Venkataraman puts it, one need not compare India's progress, with western countries which have had nearly 200 years of industrial revolution. But compared to other countries, which became independent after World War-II, India's achievement has been phenomenal. India could not participate in the industrial revolution because of the colonial rule, but it had more than made up for it in the last forty years, for which the nation should be really proud.

Among the country's problems, Venkataraman attaches the highest priority to the population explosion—"the single biggest factor against the success of our economic programmes", all the more so far the population growth rate being "higher below the poverty line".

REFERENCES

1. R. Thirumalai. Infras Infrastructure, holds key. *Economic Times* 13 September 1986 ; p. 8.

2. *Ibid.*

3. V. Madhusudan. Multipronged approach to industrial development *Industrial Times* 21 July 1986 ; p. 13.

4. R. Venkataraman. *Role of Planning in industrial development.* New Delhi, 1969.

5. *Ibid.*

11

LITERATE THE MASSES

What would happen if the whole world became literate? Answer: not so very much, for the world is by and large structured in such a way that it is capable of absorbing the impact. But if the whole world consisted of literate, autonomous, critical, constructive people, capable of translating ideas into action, individually or collectively, the world would change.

All over the world, children troop to school. The great globe swings round out of the dark into the sun; there is always morning somewhere; and forever in this shifting region of the morning light, one sees the little ones in companies and groups, couples and bright solitary figures, for they all seem to have a soft heavenly light about them. One sees them in country lanes and rustic villages; on lonely moorlands, on the hillsides, in the woods, on the stepping-stones that cross the brook in the glen, along the sea-cliffs and on the water-ribbed sands; trespassing on the railway lines, making shortcuts through the corn, sitting in the ferry-boats; in the crowded streets of smoky cities, in small rocky islands, in places far inland where the sea is known only as a strange tradition. The morning-side of the planet is alive with them: one hears their footsteps everywhere. And as the vast continents sweep "eastering out of the high shadow which reaches beyond the moon", and as new nations with their cities and villages, their fields, woods, mountains and seashores, rise up into the morning-side, one sees fresh troops of these school-going children of the dawn. The wonderful vision expresses the natural eager joy of children to grow and to learn.[1]

Venkataraman is a man in whose many-sided activities grown a devotion to and a deep knowledge in all the educational problems of the country.

"Education" means to bring up. The word "Education" is derived from the Latin verb 'educase' which means' 'to rear'. In fact education is process which helped in shaping, forming and moulding the behaviour of an individual. It transmits cultural values from generation to generation. It also assist in the development of human personality. The purposive aspect of human personality is developed through a acurse of education. According to Plato "the function of education is not to put knowledge into the self but to bring forth the best tallents which are latent in the soul".

The advent of nation-state is a recent phenomenon. It is five to six centuries old when in the western part of the globe there occurred a distinct structural transformation from a monarchical-feudal society to a democratic-industrial nation based on the concept of citizenship. While in the earlier social formations the primordial loyalties centred around caste, estate, language, region, religion and race were fundamental, in the recently evolving nation-states, loyality to the nation became primary. It does not amount to worship of the nation, but supporting the nation for collective benefit and survival. At various stages of history, Britain, France, Germany, Italy, United States evolved into nation-states in the western hemisphere ; there were also the latecomers like the Soviet Union. In the eastern hemisphere, Japan emerged into a strong nation-state under the Meiji, leadership in the 19th century.

So also People's Republic of China a little later. India breaking away from the shackles of colonialism resolved to become a strong nation-state.[2]

Education has gained utmost priority in the State and Tami Nadu has the second highest percentage of literates among States. Since the present government came to power, innumerable portals of education have been born. New universities such as the Bharatiyar University at Coimbatore, Bharathidasan University at Tiruchirapalli, Tamil University at Thanjavur, Mother Teresa University for Women at Kodaikanal and Anna University of Technology at Madras were opened. To imporve the number of trained personnel in the State, self-financing Medical Colleges, Engineering Colleges and Polytechnics are encouraged apart from increasing the seats and facilities at the Government institutions.

Tamil Nadu now has 193 colleges of Arts, Science and Commerce. Before the commencement of the Sixth Five Year Plan (in 1979-80), 1,36,000 students were studying in these colleges. Now the strength has touched two lakhs.

In 1985-86, as many as 85 new high schools and 49 new higher secondary schools were opened.

The State has attached great importance to vocationalization of education. In 1983-84 itself, Tamil Nadu had more than half of the 1,600 vocational training institution in India. Out of the 3.32 lakh higher secondary students in Tamil Nadu, 61,502 were studying in vocational courses. Vocational courses have been introduced in 969 out of the 1,541 higher secondary schools.

During the year 1984-85, 355 new elementary schools were opened.

With an outlay of Rs. 468 crores, Education in the state accounts for 20 per cent of the revenue expenditure in 1985-86. School education accounts to Rs. 384 crores.

740 school improvement conferences have been conducted since the inception of the programme. About 13 lakhs of poor pupils in Standards 1.3 are given text books free. This scheme costs Rs. 1.6 crores every year. During the current year, (1985-86) the Government has extended the scheme to poor

children studying in Standard 1 to 8. Apart from this, 36,553 schools have book, banks that benefit 13 lakh of pupils. 1,123 high schools have been equipped with science laboratories.

How rightly Venkataraman has said at the convocation of Osmania University, Hyderabad that learning should be sharing ethical and moral principles and not a mere passport to employment.

It is true that universities should not function merely like factories, producing graduates but should turn into true temples of learning and workshops of wisdom. Apart from acquiring knowledge in various subjects, the students are to be cast in various moulds of noble qualities and fabricate them with the components of values and virtues so as to emerge from the portals as full-fledged citizens. It is said, education devoid of wisdom is a like a flower without fragrence.

The only comparative study of Tulsidas and Kamban—the Tamil poet of the tenth century, who wrote the Ramayana in Tamil—has emanated from the university of Madras, oddly enough. This again is due to the fortuitous circumstance that the author, Shankar Raju Naidu, was a resident of Agra for many years before he took up a teaching assignment in Madras. If literature and literary appreciation were to flourish, especially in a multi-lingual society such as ours, the relevance of comparative study must be recognised. When the literary output in Hindi and Tamil is placed side by side, it will not take long to realise how baseless and absured is so much of contemporary comment, on either side of the Vindhyas. The "Padavalis" of Vidyapati, for example, have much in common with "Padams" in Tamil today as well as with the great Sangam poetry of the dim past. The languages is different, but the thought is dientical. Similarities of this kind must remain meaningless until we recognise our cultural history in proper light. That perception begins to dawn when we delve into facts of history that have eluded us, thanks to the dynastic accounts of our history by historians who failed to know that emperors and dynasties mattered little to the cultural tradition of India. Thus it is that the early migration of saints with missionary zeal from Magadha to the region of Madurai has seldom been noticed as of tremendous cultural significance. These Buddhist and Jaina monks who looked upon travel as a sacred mission disigamana reached the Tamil region well before Christian era, as attested by caves and inscriptions in and around Maduria. Sangam poetry, the earliest anthology in Tamil, has indeed been their contribution: for, they believed in propagating philosophical truths and ideas by means of love poetry. The early classic in Tamil Silappadikaram, is manifestly a work of Jaina proselytisation: the next Manimekhalai is what the Buddhists produced in order to extol their way of life. All this is documented history, for those concerned with culture in the pan-Indian context.[3]

Ideas and conventions apart, there is great similarity in the poetic devices that Tamil and Hindi employ so richly. Quaint expressions such as 'woman of elephant gait' occur alike as *gajagamini* and pidi nadaiyal: a radiant girl is likened to a flash of lightning as in Vijurilata (Vidyapati) and minnal kodi (Kamban). Man, the porfligate, is metaphorically referred to as the bee in the classical poetry of Hindi and Tamil, as indeed of all other Indian languages. The southtern breeze, *dakhina pavana* is what acts as stimulant to lovers, who are for ever goverened by the conventions that belong alike, whether love is depicted in Tamil or Hindi. The ten *awasthas* of the classical heroine which Kesavadasa details in Hindi in the 'Rasikapriya' (16th cent) have their parallel in 'Tolkappiyam' in Tamil (7-8th cent.). All this cannot be meaningless to us, what with our claim to better knowledge and speedier communication. Linguistically too Hindi and Tamil have much in common as anyone with knowledge of both languages knows full well. To cite the most important point, both languages follow the same syntax, word sequence. Thus any sentence in Hindi can be written word for word in Tamil in the same order as it proceeds. (The problem begins only when we try to translate from one language to another via English). The neglect of bi-lingual scholarship within the Indian context is proving costly, day by day. If modern Hindi is a product of Sauraseni Prakrit, as linguistics would show, it is not insignificant that until two centuries ago the

Indian tradition knew Tamil as Dravidi Prakrit, Prakrit being a generic name of language widely spoken (as compared to Sanskrit) to those obsessed with the problem of script, it would be of interest to know that until the 8th cent. AD, the Brahmi script was the only one in use: it served both Sanskrit and Tamil. Modern ingenuity must seem in poor light if a common script—any script—cannot be agreed upon or evolved for communication between the inhabitants of this sub-continent where cultural unity is writ large at every turn. To achieve that, it is imperative that we rise above the din and dust of populist speeches.[4]

The full-time community nutrition worker in Tamil Nadu plays an important role by providing simple, health services such as providing Vitamin A, iron and folic-acid, deworming and diarrhoea control. He also promotes use of health centres through regular home visits.

"Beyond obvious humanitarian considerations, malnutrition affects labour productivity, motivation and the activity levels and improving capacity of children and thus both the well-being and earning capacity of the poor," the report asserts. Although malnutrition is clearly linked with poverty, "much nutritional improvement is possible without major income increases." The experience of the World Bank team is that nutrition programmes can be affordable by meeting some costs by restructuring the existing programmes.

Successful experiments in Tamil Nadu show that nutrition projects may not be confined to one sector. Some early projects which were planned to last four or five years were too short to demonstrate the expected charges in nutritional status.

Education is a specifically human activity. Our minds are like handles to which alternative system of culture can be fitted. In most human societies, in most times and places so far, education in the broad sense of the transmission of a cultural heritage has been an unself-conscious and unorganised activity. People here mostly acquired their ancestral culture in the way in which they learn their mother tongue.

India is a country of continental size and diversity. In fact, the physical, social and cultural diversity of India is so stupendous and fascinating that many a superficial observer has remarked that India is a mere "georaphical expression" devoid of any semblance of national unity. However, most historians who have studied carefully the endless and fascinating diversity of India agree that despite the diversity of physical features, climate, races, castes, religions, cultures and languages, our ancient seers, philosophers and poets were conscious of the unity and oneness of India. The fundamental unity of India lying beneath its immense and colourful diversity was very well expressed in the epics and puranas. For instance a *sloka* in "Vishnu Purana" says :

"Uttaram yatsamudrasya himadreschaiva dakshinam
Varsham tadbharatam namabharati yatra santihi".

It means that "the country that lies north of the ocean and south of the snowy mountains is called Bharata ; there dwell the descendents of Bharata". Another puranic *sloka* used for sacrificial purification of water also brings out the idea of the unity and oneness of India. It says :

"Gange Cha Yamune chaiva Godavari Saraswati
Narmade Sindu Kaveri Jalesmin sannidhim kuru".

That is : "O Ye Ganga, Yamuna, Godavari, Saraswati, Narmada, Cauvery ! Come Ye and enter this water of my offering" Thus, as Jawaharlal Nehru wrote in his "Discovery of India" : "Some kind of dream of unity has occupied the mind of India since the dawn of civilisation. It was something deeper, and within its fold the widest tolerance of beliefs and customs was practised and variety acknowledged and even encouraged."

Fight against illiteracy is the call of the day. We cannot hope to catch up with the industrially advanced West without waging a relentless war against illiteracy and the deep-rooted ignorance and backwardness that result from it. The problem is as complex as it is urgent. Its solution is beset with formidable obstacles which have to be overcome before we can step into the 21st century with confidence and dynamism which is our key national features today. India enjoys one great advantage over many developing countries. It is traditionally known as a land of sages and the learned ones. Learning is held in great respect by the masses of people. This respect for learning needs to be transformed into an effort to acquire, it. It is for the state and the society to provide the people with reliable and tested means of overcoming their reluctance to benefit by education. Moreover, the co-relation between education and national advance must be explained to them in easy-to-understand terms. Their urge for being enlightened will be more easily whetted when they grasp the fact that love for one's country cannot be complete or effective without being educated. Patriotism is in the prime quality that can be profitably utilised as one of the incentives for education.[5]

It seems pertinent to go into the question of how best to attain an optimum level educational facilities, in even the remote parts of our country. No doubt, the number of educational institutions has increased manifold since Independence. Still, they are not enough to take every child or citizen into their fold. This leads us to the need of non-formal educational bodies in every settlement. To being with, teachers should be induced to reach out even to the far-flung places. They should not only impart the knowledge of the 3 R's to the young as well as adult pupils, but also familiarise them with the history and geography of India, her cultural variety and social diversity. At the same time, these resident-teachers as we might call them, should also create, cultivate and train local cadre of teachers who should take over from them in due course of time. This, however, is to be done without weaning them away from the economic pursuits of the pupils. The need, in other words, is to integrate sound education into their pattern of life and do it in a way that ultimately raises their pattern of thought and life itself.

In the years since Independence, Indian bureaucracy has simply been a continuation of the colonial administrative system. But changes in the political system generated a groundswell among the people as the Founding Fathers decided to establish a parliamentary democracy. All the constraints of caste, class and illiteracy were suddenly swept away. *A Harijan* (scheduled caste) could become a Minister and a small-town boy could get into the Indian Administrative Services (I.A.S.).[6]

For several years a strong and sustained demand has been made by different sections of society, the educators, planners, social workers and even the politicians suggesting that educational degrees should be delinked from jobs. In fact, the new educational policy laid down by the government has also stressed it. It has been argued that the former colonial rulers of this country had introduced this system to create a section in our society which would suit and benefit their own interests. But regrettably, even after forty long years, since the British left India, nothing has been done in this respect and the same old craze to secure a general degree continues among our young generation. Our students, for long, have been pressured by circumstances to in for a degree to get a job. Not that the educationists or administrators are unaware of the futility of such a requirement. Yet the situation has not changed and the old theory that whoever wants so earn a living must secure a degree still persists, no matter whether his mental faculties are sufficiently equipped to have it. No wonder, there has been a steady rise of half-baked intelligentsia who can neither deliver the goods nor be productive in making any meaningful impact on the cross-currents of life.

Today, our educational institutions are by and large much more equipped than ever before with more qualified persons joining the profession, thanks to better pay-scales and improved service conditions. Several educational reforms have also been put through. How come then that the standard of education, both at the lower and higher levels, is falling year by year ? More and more new colleges, too, are coming up along with a mushroom growth of universities. But the steady deterioration in standards has not been arrested. One ready answer is the unwidely number of students which our schools and colleges find impossible to hold. The intake of students has become disproportionate to the optimum capacity of an educational institution. It is yet to be realised that higher education is still a luxury in India and that only through a very careful and selective process its doors should be opened for those who are really capable of making the grade. But for a guardian sending his ward for higher education involves a matter of prestige while the politicians will certainly like to have a large contingent of students to satisfy their narrow and selfish ends. Similarly, those running colleges are naturally too keen to have a large enrolment, for the greater the number the fatter get the college coffers. And for a recipient of higher education, there seems to be hardly any choice as he has to accept whatever is available in the market. So, this process has continued and will possibly go on and on unless a radical change is made. Requisite skills rather than a general degree should form the basis for employment for which a drastic reorientation right from the school level in the educational system has to be made. The emphasis has to shifted from mere academic learning to vocational training and instruction in a planned manner while the current system of recruitment policy has also to be changed with an eye to face the problem.

In the broad perspective, the New National Policy on Education envisages an all-round development—physical, intellectual and value-based—of learners at all levels of education.

Efforts will be made evolve a national system of education which will provide far greater access to education of a comparable quality to all students irrespective of caste, creed, location or sex.

The national system of education will be based on a national curriculum framework. This framework, while having a common core, will have sufficient flexibility so as to meet local requirements and to suit the local environment. Minimum levels of learning will be laid down for each stage of education. Special emphasis has been laid on the removal of disparities and equalization of educational opportunities keeping in view the specific needs of the disadvantaged groups and girls.

In order to create conditions for success, a general programme of improving all primary schools will be taken up under the scheme entitled, "Operation Blackboard". Also, for those who are not in the school network for any reason, a massive programme of non-formal education of a quality comparable to school education, will be made available. Considerable changes in the content and process of education have been envisaged, particularly in the area of work-experience, mathematics and science education. Lots of emphasis has also been laid on sports and physical education, arts, music, community singing and other cultural aspects. For gifted students from rural areas, the Navodaya Vidyalayas will provide very good all-round education in residential schools.

Education, has had little impact over the years beyond treating employment as an objective and eradicating illiteracy as a pipe-dream. The Constitution had laid down clear diretives for free and compulsory education for all children. But the data of its realisation has been advanced decade after decade. Enrolment at primary school level is still only 32.2 per cent in the country, while the drop-out rate in the very first year of schooling is at a staggering 40 per cent. In 1965, a young Indian from Cambridge came to our famous Doon School ; Dehradun, Uttar Pradesh, and remarked that the pattern of public schools established in England had been most remarkably transformed into something totally different in India. He was immensely impressed with one major achievement : Doon School had created the Indian. The new proposal for creating the Navodaya Schools is an extension of the same concept ; top class schools for the brilliant child in every walk of life in every district. Could this be a move to create a cadre of administrators and citizens as Britain had done in the 19th century ?

The late Prof. Humayun Kabir once said that in India democracy had created divisions rather than unity. It is a significant remark. Followership in the Indian democratic pattern of politics that emerged election after election proved the leaders had to depend upon caste and regional followers rather than upon national issues and objectives. In the process, our "Indianness" has been severely eroded giving place to a disquieting separation both national and religious.

Whatever changes the new education policy might undergo, its basic features should be retained. The main purpose of the policy is to bring about a transformation in education at different levels. The objectives spelt out in the policy—eradication of illiteracy, improvement in the quality of education, vocationalisation and non-formal education—are aimed at continuing a process that has already been initiated but there is a subtle shift of emphasis towards excellence in education. This objective is commendable but is it attainable? For instance, Operation Blackboard may help to fight illiteracy but how can the problem of children dropping out of schools be solved? Until the socio-economic factors that stand in the way of poor children are removed, they are unlikely to be benefited by the new policy. Even if there are teachers to teach them and benches and blackboards are provided in their classrooms, where is the certainty that children will go to school so long as they live in poverty and ignorance ? It remains to be seen how far the new education policy will improve the lot of these unfortunate sections, whose basic needs are not met in their homes.

Prime Minister Rajiv Gandhi refuted the contention that the new education policy was elitist. In fact there is nothing more elitist than the present education policy. The new education policy would infuse dynamism in youth's thinking process and help develop manpower to match India's requirements in the 21st century. The country's education system should be so redesigned as to produce more "employable" youths. The present education system, shorn of an accent on "dignity of labour," had failed to develop probing minds the country required and stifled excellence. Educating India for the 21st century, must not be limited to a mere technical or economic education. It must not be limited so that the younger generation only look for a university degree for earning their livelihood without looking to their prospects for the future. It is to be much more than that. It must develop the individual, the development of human being inside that individual and it is this that we would like to try through the new educational system." The country would have to try to find excellence in every individual. The excellence was there is in every individual and it was for the teachers and professors to find in which area, in which path the society that individual could excel, in which he could contribute most. The Indian society under the banner of socialism was today having mediocrity as the norm. No nation could develop and progress if mediocrity was the order of the day." "And we must allow that excellence to develop and not suffocate it."

Prime Minister Rajiv Gandhi made a policy statement in his national broadcast on 5 January 1985, promising a new "National Policy on Education" that was to include, inter alia, an expansion of the "Central School System" at the rate of one school per district. The intention was to make quality education accessible to meritorious students in each district of the country, irrespective of their economic and social positions.

In the course of an exercise, it was discovered that the Central Schools which were intended to impart un-interrupted education mainly to the children of the Central Government employees, including para-military personnel, liable to frequent transfers from one language area to another in the exigencies of their services, would be misfits. The extension of the concept of Central School had, therefore, to be abandoned.[8]

An altogether novel idea of such schools which would serve as trend-setters and pace-setters was conceived. A scheme to that effect was formulated. It was approved by the Cabinet on 5 August 1985. In the context of the nation wide debate on the "New Education Policy," this scheme was also extensively discussed. In the light of the views expressed the scheme was revised, and it was approved by Prime Minister on 25 April 1986. Under this, the schools are known as Navodaya Vidyalayas. According to the finalised version of the scheme, these Navodaya Schools are to come up—one in each district—as free, residential and co-educational schools, admitting students, from the sixth class onwards. The students who will be admitted on the basis of tests conducted at the *tehsil* or block level, will be mainly from rural areas, though there may be urban children up to a maximum of one-fourth of the strength.

Prime Minister Rajiv Gandhi said on April 8, 1987, in New Delhi, that the challenges that "we will be facing from now on are going to be much more than the challenges in actually making the new education policy because this is where the inertia is going to hit up. This is where all the vested interests which went to keep their heels dug in are going to cause us problems. This is where it will need a really big push to see that it gets through. I have no doubt that the Ministry for Human Resource Development and all the allied agencies will have the energy to do this."

In 1985, Prime Minister Rajiv Gandhi said, "I had felt that education, as we were giving it to our children, was not tailored to the tasks they were asked to face when they were coming out of the system......We had to tailor the education levels to match the needs of the country in the coming years. Economic changes will happen automatically if we can bring about a positive change in the attitude of our people to development in the country. That is why such a big thrust on the education system."

Children must be taught to imitate the noblest things in life, and what is more noble than truth ? A true thing is not necessarily truth of fact in a world where truth in fact is so often believed or made meaningless, but truth to the universal, the superior demand of our conscience. In the Indian context it means the teaching of harmony in variety that is India. Harmony is the Universal Truth. Variety is the truth of fact. That India is one is true in essence and in significance. The regional varieties may be significant but cannot at best be better to us than broken ends and shards. The greatest need of the hour is to establish a system of elementary education which encourage the child's instinctive desries for imitation and harmony and teach him to realise himself as an Indian in all that he learns to do and in all that he learns to know.

Nowadays when there has been much debate on delinking degrees from jobs, there is much more left to ponder over. While students do study and we have umpteen number of bright and intelligent youths passing out every year from different universities, the questions that stand out before our eyes are—can students he confined only to their studies ? Dont's they have a more comprehensive and constructive role to play in a society which, amid much publicised rhetories, aspires to enter the 21st century ? Are we becoming educated in the real sense ? Do we realise our contribution that we have to make for the development of country and its society ? Will we be satisfied even if we get a job without graduation or post-graduation ? These are only a few questions that haunt those students who seem to lose their way in the maze of political, social and cultural wilderness.[9]

On the intellectual field, Venkataraman has been the founter-editor of the Labour Law Journal since 1949. He got a *tamra patra* (a medal) of participation in the freedom struggle, won the Soviet Land Nehru award for travelogue in Tamil on the late Kamaraj's visit to the socialist countries. Besides his many accomplishments in letters, arts and science, he was given the title of "Sat Seva Ratna" (a diamond of true service) by His Holiness Shankaracharya for service to the temple.

Venkataraman has deplored the practice of collecting capitation fees or donations by educational institutions for admission.

It would be preferable to shut down an educational institution rather than to perpetuate it through capitation fees or forced donations. "India cannot afford an education which demands a price," he said.

The only price that education could and should demand was the "price of standards," he said.

Venkataraman said with the government's policy to give a thrust to computerisation, there was a lot of scope for employment in this new field. The area of programming offered enormous scope for employment not only within the country but also for services abroad. Hence computer education at the college level had become apt and timely. But computerisation should not become an objective of a goal in itself.

To be worth the name education should train children in values, Venkataraman has rightly stressed the importance values teaching occupies in education : "It is the duty of every right-thinking citizen interested in the future of this country and in the preservation of our great cultural heritage to extend the fullest cooperation for the successful implementation of such programme of introduction of value-oriented education."

Education alone, if imparted in the right manner, teaches man how to live. We need value-oriented education to pull the present generation out of the quagmire. An educated man without good values is a body sans soul.

India today stands on the threshold of a mighty leap into an era of progress. As Prime Minister Rajiv Gandhi has often stressed, a great contribution has to be made by every individual. This can be done only when their vision has been broadened and mind enriched by education. The everage Indian of the 21st century, whatever walk of life he may belong to, will have to handle or cope with complex kinds of technological mechanical and electronic equipment. So, a scientific awareness and orientation must be cultivated among the masses. At the same time, as Prime Minister Rajiv Gandhi has said on several occasions, the Indian of the future must not be delinked from his heritage, tradition, culture and moral values. The cause of the malady having been identified, remedial steps should not be hard to find. What is of paramount importance is that the Government, beside initiating steps for the regorous implementation of its blueprint for education, should also devise ways of involving a large number of the literates, the educated, the social workers and even certain kinds of institutions in its efforts. Prime Minister Rajiv Gandhi has already given a call for mass participation of the people in eradicating obstacles to progress. It is time for action now [10]

The quality of education can be achieved only when it is provided to all. There could be a talent in that person who remained away from the doors of the school due to certain deprivations. Only by absorbing all into the formal school system, will not it be possible to utilise their intellectual skills for raising the standard of education. The goal of universalisation of elementary education is still a distant one. The problem of poverty and economic development can be tackled only if education reaches every citizen. Our education must become scientific-social oriented which will launch a drive against superstition, obscurantism and dogmatism. These issues must be ideologically and rationally tackled. Various national problems like population, disease, poverty, ignorance and un-employment can be overcome with the help of such a strong, well-knit education system.[11]

Venkataraman emphasised the imperative need of making school education compulsory and free for all children throughout the country. Free education, meant not only exemption from fees but positive assistance necessary to enable the children to get the right kind of education ; such assistance should be in the form of provision of books, mid-day means and even clothes. He realised that this would entail cost, but he felt that the country should be able to find funds for the purpose.

He is also in favour of the idea of free education at the university stage and expressed the view that if the idea is vigorously pursued for some tiem, necessary funds for the purpose will be found. In view of the prevailing disparity in the socio-economic life of the country, he sees no alternative to giving free education at the university stage. He appreciated the fact that in faculties such as those of science, technology, medicine, admission is restricted because of physical conditions, but in regard to other fields of university education he was not sure that there were dependable methods of selection for restricting admission.

Venkataraman was not unaware of some of the reported malpractices in the administration of education by the *Panchayat*. He also realised that there was a sense of concern that the *Panchayat* elections were conducted on the basis of casteism and of local factions, and that there was absence of social purpose in the election campaigns. The role of some of the teachers, themselves was not in-variably laudable. Nevertheless, the *Panchayats* a had come to stay and one had to learn to live with them. The *Panchayats* were a step in the right direction. The growing pains were no doubt real in the new system and one would live in the hope that time would cure them. It was hoped that healthy public opinion will grow in the course of time and provide correctives. There was, indeed, a fear that the society may accept the malady itself as a fact of life, and it would be a pity if this happened.

He appreciated the difficulties in teaching three languages to all students and the burden it imposed on the curriculum. He was aware of the difficulties of learning three languages by children who had no linguistic aptitude and whose interests in life as well as whose career ambitions did not require study of all the three languages. He was also conscious of the difficulty of finding adequate teachers to teach all languages at the earlier stages of school education. The vast population may not also require the use of all languages. He, however, favoured the three languages as the basis of education of all and the felt that even those who were to work on the farm and in the factories would benefit by being able to communicate with others as well as derive advantage in the helds of their work through the knowledge of other languages. He felt that languages, if properly taught, were not a burden. He realised difficulties in conceiving of a system of education which would require knowledge of a single language only. In the special circumstances of the country, it was desirable to know three languages, though the medium of instruction should be the mother tongue.

It was not, however, necessary to learn all languages at the same time or to learn them all through the educational career. The programme of teaching the three languages should be properly phased and this was a task for the educations.

He is in favour of raising the standard of education in all schools. He does not appreciate special schools which cater only for the rich who can afford it. While he favours special encouragement to the poor and talented to get the best education, he is doubtful about the value of special schools reserved only for the talented.

He has realised that the problem of suitable wages for the teachers is an issue of grave national importance. If the nation agrees to pay the right kind of salary to the teachers, it will be unable to afford sufficient number of teachers it needs. The salary of the teacher is associated with the problem of national economy which in different spheres allows very high levels of personal incomes. He feels that even so great a leader as Mahatma Gandhi was unable to persuade some of his followers of the importance of lowering levels of personal incomes and to symbolise it by ceiling the maximum salary to Rs. 500 per month. He feels that the nation should be prepared to facts and the economic realities, though as a practical proposition, he would not expect any immediate results.

He wishes education in the country to help to build up a strong healthy united nation and a society organised on the principles of democracy and socialism. India is a country with rich cultural heritage and traditions, which reveale a significant unity in the midst of a wide variety in the ways of life and thought of the people. He wishes that from the earliest school stage the children should have understanding and appreciation of the ways in which people in other parts of the country live and think. National unity is best cultivated through understanding of other peoples in the country. Cultivation of mutual understanding and appreciation of other people's attitudes should be the special concern of education. While the best elements in the national cultural traditions should be retained, education should be forward looking and must essentially be concerned with the good of the masses of people. It must derive fullest advantage from the benefit made available by the progress of science and technology.

He has deplored the fact that sufficient attention is not given to eradication of illiteracy in the country after independence. Whatever efforts were made were feeble and did not produce much effect. He is of the opinion that a massive effort to eradicate illiteracy is absolutely necessary. The slow progress is due to the fact that people and even the politicians have accustomed themselves to leaving everything to be done by the Governments. The problem of adult education can not be solved by normal routine administrative methods and it can not, therefore, be left to Governments. The challenge presented by the problem of liquidation of illiteracy required a bold resolve on the part of national leadership and an all out massive national effort to eradicate illiteracy within the shortest period of time.

REFERENCES

1, S, Raman. priorities in primary education *Hindu* 3 March 1987 ; p. 19

2. Vikram Simha Rao. Role of schooling in nation-building *Hindu* 13 January 1987 ; p. 19.

3. K. S. Srinivasan. K. S, Shadow-boxing in Tamil and Hindu *Times of Indta*, 25 November, 1986.

4. *Ibid.*
5. V. P. Chawla. Education : Entering the twenty-first Century *Democratic World* & February 1987, pp. 14-16.
6. Tara Ali Baig Tools and Schools *Hindustan Ttmes* 8 February, 1987
7. Tara Ali Baig. *op. cit.*
8. See Deep R. Kapool. Operation blackboard and Navoday School. *Patriot* 13 March, 1987
9. Prashant Saxena. are we really becoming educated ? *Patriot* 1 Mav 1987.
10. V. P. Chawla. *Op. cit.*
11. K. Vikram Simha Rao. *Op. cit.*

12

THE FRIENDLY VISITS

In 1966, amidst diplomatic pleasantries came an invitation to visit the Soviet Union. Kamaraj, now a national leader emerging gradually into international recognition, accepted the invitation, and this invitation was followed by similar invitations to visit the other East European countries. Venkataraman also went with Kamaraj to the USSR. These visits were to make Kamaraj the ever first President of the Indian National Congress to have been officially invited abroad. So far, there had been exchanges on government to government basis, this was an exchange—an informal diplomatic visit in every sense between governments and a party and it recognised, inter alia, the historic role of the Indian National Congress in the life, liberation, and governance of India. The Communist Party-the Right wing or the Left Wing—could draw its own conclusions.[1]

Just a week prior to his historic departure from India, Kamaraj set the tone for his forthcoming visit by sending a message to the Soviet Union in which he described the Soviet

Union as "a beacon light" for developing countries. Thus said Kamaraj :

> "The Soviet Union is like a beacon light to all those countries that are striving to develop themselves rapidly and raise the standard of living of their peoples. The Soviet people have, through their tireless and persistent efforts, overcome immense obstacles, and in less than 50 years risen to the pinnacle of human progress. The Soviet Union has shown to the world that a determined people with the help of a planned economy can achieved astounding progress."
>
> "Long before our country became free, our people had entertained the most friendly feelings towards the Soviet people. We watched with great interest the immense changes and the rapid developments that were taking place in the USSR. This filled us with bright hopes and was a source of inspiration to us, who were then in the midst of our freedom struggle under the leadership of Mahatma Gandhi."

The assent, therefore, was on the determined Soviet people and India's friendly feelings towards them.

Delhi, the seat of the Congress, gave Kamaraj an enthusiastic send-off but before his departure, Kamaraj sought to soften the impact of the hammer blow he had himself, though indirectly, administered to his party government. Kamaraj had been unhappy at the abrupt decision taken by the Indian Government to devalue the rupee. Kamaraj was genuinely convinced that devaluation would not achieve the desired end; the desired and coveted end being to boost exports and solve India's foreign exchange malaise. Kamaraj was also irked by the fact, however, persistent be the denial of the Government, that the decision to devalue the rupee—the symbol of India's prestige abroad—had been taken, if not at the dictation of the American Government, atleast at their persistence in the past many years, in direct contacts or through indirect means. Kamaraj, a very proud Indian he is, felt unhappy that Indira Gandhi, whom he had so fondly set up as a Prime Minister, partly as a memory to her father, Jawaharlal Nehru, had not been able to withstand the pressure and had given way to temptation; the temptation of getting some foreign exchange. The press made out that Kamaraj had not been consulted in advance; that was not true. Kamaraj had been consulted but Kamaraj had thoroughly disapproved of the step and yet the Indian Government had forced it through; that was the gravamen of the charge though in fairness to Kamaraj, it has to be said that he made no such charge publicly. Typical it is of his discreet ways that he just made his disapproval and displeasure known and felt through his confidant. R. Venkataraman, the Industries Minister of Madras, who was to accompany him on his forthcoming visit abroad. The ignited match-stick did rest of the political havoc; there were wild rumours that relations between Kamaraj and Prime Minister Indira Gandhi, were strained and the prestige of the Government naturally slumped. Kamaraj had not waited it all that way but at the same time, the iron man had enough iron in him to make the Government and the country feel the impact of his personality and thinking. He knew the power of his voice, may it be solitary at times, though this time it was not solitary either; he knew that he was echoing the woes and needs of his country and of the masses, who would feel the dire consequences of devaluation.

Kamaraj's indirect censure of the Government ultimately did good. Indira Gandhi, with mounting criticism all round and with the promised American dollars not in sight, herself felt irritated at the let-down and, with a woman's intuitive grasp of things, she was herself convinced that Kamaraj was a more dispassionate counsellor than the self-appointed counsellors around her. Ultimately, the devaluation issue, by bringing to the surface the reality of the latent relationship between Kamaraj and Indira Gandhi, restored working relations between the two. That was all to the good and so, before taking off, on his three-week absence abroad, Kamaraj counselled his countrymen "to stand united and give massive support to the Union and State Governments".

With that parting kiss, Kamaraj, accompanied by the affable Venkataraman, proceeded to Moscow to unfold and unfurl a new chapter in his life. Time alone will, however, reveal whether what was achieved in Moscow and the Kremlin will be the historic foundation for the years to come or will be a passage in time. Time for pre-science was not yet.

The Russians kept the visit at an officially unofficial level as the guest of the Soviet Parliamentary Group.

At the Sheremetyevo airport in Moscow, Kamaraj was given a warm welcome. He was received by Ivan Spiridonov, Chairman of the Soviet of the Union of the USSR Supreme Soviet, who was also Chairman of the USSR Parliamentary Group, Jan Pejve, Vice-Chairman of USSR Parliamentary Group, S.K. Romanovasky, Chairman of the USSR State Committee for Cultural Relations with Foreign Countries, and others.

Throughout his USSR trip, Kamaraj kept his thoughts to himself. Visiting a kindergarten he would say :

> "I find that in the Soviet Union great attention is paid to children's education. When children are happy, it means that the entire country is happy."

Visiting Volgograd, he would say :

> "Your victory in the last war was of great importance to the whole world. The people of this city have been courageous in the war and they are heroic in their peaceful labour. A brilliant proof of that is what you have done to rebuild your city.
>
> We know that the Soviet people are striving for a life in which all the peoples in the world would be happy, and there would be no wars. This coincides with the aims of the Indian people."

And after a ninety minute talk or rather a hard to earth discussion and exploration with Leonid Brezhnev, General Secretary of the C.P.S.U. Central Committee, which, in its implications, could be far-reaching in the time to come, all that the laconic communique said was that during the meeting :

> "Views were exchanged on the cardinal questions of the

international situation and on questions of the further strengthening and developing of friendship and cooperation between the peoples of India and the Soviet Union."

That is typical of Kamaraj ; action and not speech is what matters and even action should be unostentatious, as when the action later unfolds itself, the impact is tremendous. Thiruvalluar taught him :

"Call not him a man who parades forth his empty words. Call him the chaff of men."

Thiruvallur or Thiruvalluvar, as the Tamils respectfully call him, is the respectful *guru* (master), of Kamaraj, from whose fountain of wisdom he was drunk to satuartion throughout his life. Kamaraj was living or trying to live what Thiruvallur taught.

The same pattern of discretion Kamaraj had observed when meeting the Muscovites in the Moscow Friendship House. It was not in his nature to play to the gallery and he needed no reminder that there had been criticism, especially in America, of the joint communique. Indira Gandhi had signed on the conclusion of her preceding visit to Moscow.

Nina Popova, President of the Union of Soviet Societies for Friendship with Foreign Countries was all praise for Kamaraj and said : "The Soviet people know you well as a Staunch fighter for India's independence." The staunch fighter, in a subdued reply said :

"The friendship of our countries is important not only for us but also for all other peoples who strive to live in peace and to achieve progress."

Speaking to the Soviet Parliamentary Group Committee at a luncheon, Kamaraj, though he spoke at length, said :

"I have been to many places in your country these last few days. This gave me an opportunity to feel the kind sentiments which the Soviet people entertain for us.

Our country was for a very long time deprived of its freedom and it was only a comparatively short time ago that it acquired its independence. Therefore, if we want to achieve economic progress, we must work perseveringly for the advance of industry and agriculture.

You not only care for your progress, but are also lending extensive aid and technical cooperation to all countries which recently gained their independence. Your ideal is that all people should be able to live happily and enjoy the fruits of prosperity. We also strive for such a life.

Seeing what great effort you have exerted to make progress in your country and what successes you have scored, we grew confident that, we too, could achieve big successes.

But if all countries strive to enhance the well-being of their people, it is necessary then for a peaceful situation to exist in the world. That is why we, like you strive to create a situation without war, to create a peaceful situation throughout the globe.

We would like very much to see that the war now going on in Vietnam does not expand. In fact, we wish for an end to it. If this war continues to expand, nobody can say to what dimensions it will grow. It can ultimately lead to a world conflict, which will bring incalculable disaster to the peoples of the entire world. Therefore, all the peoples in the modern world who really care for the well-being, for the future of the nations should exert every to stop this war.

I wish to say that our India-Soviet relations play a big role in the world today and that we together will be able to work in the contemporary world for the development of friendly relations, and to put an end to war.

We have grown convinced of the great sympathy and affection which you, the Soviet peoples, entertain for us. It will not be an exaggeration to say that your souls are brimming over with friendly sentiments and affection for the Indian people. In conclusion, I once more express to you our deep gratitude."

Thiruvalluar again guided the diplomat Kamaraj :

"When pleasant words are easy, bitter words to use, is leaving sweet ripe fruit, the sour unripe to choose."

In his reference to Vietnam, there is nothing that would hurt anyone anywhere. Kamaraj was not an exhibitionist ; he could say exactly the same thing before an American audience or to an audience of British dreamers of the imperial glory that was. Kamaraj was sensitive to the fact that each country, conditioned by its environment, geographical and psychological had its limitations ; that harsh words and hardening attitudes might break stones and bones but would solve no problem and, therefore, the essence of statesmanship was in steering the path of "great acceptance" and in trying to solve, rather than perpetuate problems. Kamaraj was in essence, the great common denominator in India and, in time to come, may be one abroad.

Summing up Kamaraj's visit, A. Maslennikov wrote in the *Pravada* :

"This summer will go down in the history of Soviet-Indian relations as a period of fruitful visits of prominent Indian statesmen and public leaders to our country. In the middle of July Muscovites warmly received Indira Gandhi, Prime Minister of friendly India. The arrival of the Premier was preceded by the visits of a number of Ministers of the Government of India to the U.S.S.R. At present, Kamaraj, one of Jawaharlal Nehru's prominent comrades-in-arms and the President of the Indian National Congress, is in our country. Soviet people consider these visits an expression of the development of traditional relations of friendly cooperation existing between our countries."

During his stay in the Soviet Union Kamaraj showed profound interest in the most diverse aspects of our country's political, economic, public and cultural life. He was received by the leaders of the CPSU and the Soviet Government. Kamaraj met Soviet and economic executives in Moscow, Leningrad, Volgograd and Dushanbe. Appraising what he had seen in Tajikistan, Kamaraj said that the progress achieved in that Republic should inspire Indians in attaining similar progress in their country. In Volgograd he paid homage to the heroism displayed by the people of that city during the war and their persistent creative work in times of peace.

Speaking in Leningrad, Kamaraj highly appraised the influence, and instructive experience of the Great October, 1917 Revolution for the struggle of the Indian people for national liberation and social progress.

Cooperation between India and the USSR in the struggle for peace and in achieving a relaxation in international tension is of special significance today when the American imperialists are stepping up their aggressive actions in South-East Asia. The concern for strengthening peace throughout the world found its reflection in the Joint Soviet-Indian Communique signed by A.N. Kosygin, then Chairman of the USSR Council of Ministers, and Indira Gandhi, Prime Minister of India, during the latter's visit to the Soviet Union. The same idea was also time and again expressed by Kamaraj during his stay in the USSR.

On July 30, 1966, Kamaraj received Soviet journalists. During the warm and friendly talk, he shared with them his impressions of his stay in the Soviet Union as a guest of the USSR Parliamentary Group. Kamaraj said that he had interesting meetings with Soviet leaders L.I. Brezhnev and A.N. Kosygin. These meetings, he said would still further facilitate the development of friendly relations between the two countries.

"Kamaraj is leaving our country. While seeing off the distinguished guest, Soviet people believe that his stay in the USSR will become another contribution to the cause of Soviet-Indian friendship, to the cause of the world peace," *Pravada* wrote.

Venkataraman, on a three-nation tour of East Europe (Bulgaria, East Germany (GDR and Yugoslavia), paid an official visit to Berlin from November 5 to 9, 1985 at the invitation of the ruling State Council. Earlier he visited GDR in 1966 in a delegation headed by the Congress Party President Kamaraj.[2]

General Secretary Erich. Honecker, Chairman of the GDR Council, received Venkataraman for a friendly exchange of view. In two rounds of official talks with Deputy Chairman Egon Krenz, member of the Political Bureau of SED, international issues and bilateral relations were discussed. There were no differences, India and GDR are on the same wavelength.

Venkataraman addressed a mass rally of Berliners at a ceremony in which an avenue in the Capital was named after Indira Gandhi. He presented Honecker an anthology on Indira Gandhi, containing contributions of world leaders, including Honecker. The German leader with great feelings, recounted to Venkataraman his memorable meetings with Indira Gandhi.

The Vice-President visited GDR's most modern steel plant at Eisen-huettenstadt, and was given a ceremonial reception at the headquarters of the County Council on the Polish border.

According to Venkataraman; "These Socialist states have made monumental achievements in building a new society. I saw Berlin changed beyond recognition—houses, city-centre, people's appearance. They respect India, our people, they honour our leaders, understand our problems and never run down our country as "backward", "poor" or "inferior". Most important characteristic of our relationship is mutual trust and regard. GDR leaders appreciated the recent initiatives of our Prime Minister Rajiv Gandhi and the Government of India to strengthen India's unity and accelerate economic development. They support the New Delhi declaration of six nations and the recent letter to General Secretary Gorbachov and President Reagan to stop nuclear explosions for 12 months, and wish the Geneva summit every success.

Indo-GDR relations is a model for East-West and North-South. Venkataraman said: "We have no conflicts, no quarrels with GDR. We have, on the other hand, identical or similar views on important international issues. In my talks with Chairman Honecker, we agreed that at present no task is more urgent than to preserve world peace and ward off the danger of a nuclear war. We appreciate GDP. efforts to encourage the forces of goodwill into a "worldwide coalition of commonsense and realism", against the threat of nuclear war and further expansion of arm race. Myself and Honecker believe that in the context of the present complicated international situation, a further strengthening of Indo-GDR friendship and cooperation would provide an important contribution to improve the international climate. We have renewed the invitation, India is looking forward to receive Chairman Honecker. The GDR statesman said, he would be glad to visit India."

GDR is against nuclear arms race in any part of the world. They have opened their entire territory to be a corridor free from the battle-field of nuclear weapons, if FRG also join a treaty, creating a zone in Central Europe free from nuclear arms. GDR has prepared a treaty jointly with West German Opposition Social Democratic Party (which may come to power) for removal of chemical weapons. GDR is for complete abolition of all nucleus arms and banning of star-wars. In every sense, GDR is a peace state, like India, and we have much in common.

"We are satisfied that longstanding, fruitful relations between the two countries have been developing successfully on the basis of the principles of peaceful co-existence. We are interested in strengthening and expanding political, economic, cultural and scientific-technological cooperation. Trade has increased (according to GDR statistics), from 600 million marks (about 2,400 million rupees) in 1984, to about 800 million marks (3,200 million rupees) in 1985. We hope to push it forward to a still bigger volume in coming years. The Indo-GDR Joint Commission was meeting in Delhi while I was here. Many things India wants for its industrial and technological progress are available in GDR. They also welcome Indian private sector trade, GDR can buy many more things from India, from traditional goods to manufactured items and machines. Transfer of technology on a bilateral basis could be the next in the development of economic relations. The promises are great.

"It is not anything special, but normal. It is a relationship to preserve world peace, to prevent war, to promote progress, to avoid international conflicts, to free Namibia, to end apartheid, for international recognition of PLO, for a new world economic order, to respect non-alignment. I found a genuine desire on the part of GDR leaders to work with us on all international issues in the UN, in world organisations, in bilateral and multilateral work."

Meanwhile, Venkataraman has described the Festival of India, opened in Moscow on July 3, 1987 as an event of unparalleled significance in the bilateral relations of India and the Soviet Union.

In a message he say 'the deeply-felt' affinity of the people of India for the people of the Soviet Union is to find, through this festival, its most vivid articulation. There have been between the two nations, many contacts—political, economic, scientific, cultural and academic. These, however, have necessarily had to be confined to individual or group interfaces. Now, for the first time, a mighty pageant of the heritage, the talents, the diversities, the faith and the life-styles of the people of India is to reach the people of the Soviet Union.

"This convergence, moreover, is not going to be presented with the usual distance, real and metaphorical, that lies between the artiste and audience. The representatives of India participating in the festival are to meet a cross-section of the people of the Soviet Union, travelling in a number of cities and towns. These representatives carry with them India's culture at its most authentically natural and typical levels. This is as it should be because culture and life are in-extricably blended. And so the Soviet Union will see both the magnificence of India's ancient arts as well as the vibrance of its present."

The Festival of India in the Soviet Union is to be followed by a festival of the Soviet Union in India. According to Venkataraman, "together these two manifestations will constitute a conjoint pulsation that rearticulates the spirit of the great Treaty of Peace and Friendship signed by the two nations in 1971. May the song *Maithrim Bhajata* which Madam M.S. Subbulakshmi rendered at the inaugural meet reverberate from Moscow to show the way of friendship to our strife-torn world."

REFERENCES

1. For this chapter I am much obliged to Mr. R.P. Kapur and his work on Kamaraj.
2. India and GDR share identical views : An Interview by Kunhanandan Nair. *Blitz* 23 November 1985 ; p. 17.

13

THE LABOUR UNIONIST

Venkataraman owes his early success in politics to K. Kamaraj, the dynamic leader of the Congress in Tamil Nadu. A shrewd judge of men, Kamarj saw in the young *Brahmin* advocate a dedicated and highly intelligent party worker who could be useful in building up the Congress as a mass party in the South faced as he was with the growing challenge from anti-north, regional sectarian forces. He placed him in charge of the Labour department of the Tamil Nadu Congress Committee (TNCC) and, in a short time, Venkataraman was able to establish a network of trade unions owing allegiance to the Congress. Kamaraj was not favourably inclined towards the Indian National Trade Union Congress (INTUC) which he suspected owned its inspiration to Sardar Patel. Venkataraman, who had earlier been with the Congress Socialist Party, was an ideal choice which Kamaraj could have made for organising the labour movement under TNCC auspices. A lawyer by training, his long experience in handling labour matters made him an expert in industrial law and came in handy when he established the *Labour Law Journal*, a prestigious publication, in 1949. He also led the labour delegation to the Metal Trades Committee of the International Labour Organisation (ILO) in Geneva in 1952. In 1958, when he held charge of the Labour portfolio in Tamil Nadu, he headed the Indian Delegation to the 42nd Session of the ILO.

While organising trade unions, Venkataraman practised law for a living. He became known for bringing out the niceties and nuances of the law and when World War II ended he was selected to go to Singapore and Malaysia to defend the Indians who were accused of collaborating with the Japanese—an extension of the Indian National Army (INA) trials at Delhi's Red Fort in which the leading defence lawyers were Bhulabhai Desai and Jawaharlal Nehru.

The injury we do and the one we suffer are not weighed in the same scales.

The thrust of policies in the field of labour and employment since independence has been mainly focussed on organised labour and the urban unemployed, who register themselves at the employment exchanges, and of whom, not a very significant percentage get placed. A central element in the development strategy of the Seventh Plan is the generation of productive employment, and the 15-year perspective envisages that by 2,000 A.D. jobs would be found for all the labour force. This is an ambitious goal but there are few signs to show that determined efforts are being made towards the attainment of this laudable objective.

Taking labour first, the Central and State Governments show concern mainly for the organised working class, in both the public and private sectors, and are consequently engrossed in problems relating to industrial relations, wages, social security etc. and providing some training in technical skills for youths with a view to facilitating their absorption. The rural and unorganised labour force in this country is so numerous that it merits very much more attention than is presently paid to it. Prime Minister Rajiv Gandhi announce in his Budget speech about the appointment of a National Commission on Rural Labour to look into the working conditions of the vulnerable sections of society and the implementation of social legislation for their protection is a welcome step. But it may take some years for the Commission to complete its work and for the Government to go into action to alleviate the problems of unorganised labour.

Even in the enforcement of minimum wages for agricultural and other scheduled employment covered by legislation, there has been much slackness and indifference. Although the contract labour system legally stands abolished and the Government has set up tripartite study groups to examine the conditions of workers in some of the decentralised sectors, there are few visible signs of striking progress. While it is easy to promote legislation guided by social objectives, the plethora of enactments suffers in implementation.

In 1986, according to Labour Minister there was distinct improvement in the industrial relations situation, and in support of his contention he said the loss of mandays,—a little over 22 million was the lowest in ten years. However, as between strikes and lock-outs, there has been increase in the loss of mandays through lock-outs by employers, which is deplorable.

In matters relating to wages and working conditions, the organised sections of the working class have, by and large, been successful in forcing their demands through and getting the employers concede them, if not fully, at least substantially. However, in many ways the existing labour laws are often violated by employers in both the private and public sectors and this again reflects the weakness of the industrial relations machinery of the Government, at the Centre and in the States.

The Labour Minister has promised more labour laws, including amendments to the major pieces of legislation like the Industrial Disputes Act and the Trade Unions Act. Efforts at the tripartite level to arrive at consensus on the important amendments have so far failed. The Labour Ministry has yet to finalise its proposals for amending these two enactments in the light of the known views of central trade union and employers organisations.

Some proposed laws such as one to provide for grievance redressal machinery in hospitals, educational, scientific and other training institutions, another to simplify procedures for small establishments, and a third to ensure safety of workers in the building and construction industry are desirable and should be put through without delay. While membership of the unions has always been a contentious issue, especially with multiplicity of unions in industrial establishments, it is a matter for satisfaction that there is now consensus among central trade union organisations on an improved procedure for general verification of membership strength.

What is of greater cause for concern, however, is the problem of unemployment. The number of job-seekers on the live registers of employment exchanges, at the end of December 1986 was 30.13 million, of whom over three million were graduates. Though large numbers of those who register themselves manage to get employment on their own and do not notify the employment exchanges, there is nc doubt that the number of unemployed is rising alarmingly. Nor is registration in the exchanges the real index of the problem of unemployment in the country.

According to figuers given in Parliament, there were more than 35,000 engineers on the employment exchange registers waiting for jobs on December 31, 1985 and over 1,60,000, unemployed engineering technicians. The data on employment and the unemployed that is compiled at present is deficient and can provide only rough estimates. The additions to the labour force are rising faster than absorption and the backlong is becoming larger. Thus, unempolyment, particularly in the rural areas, poses a big challenge. Employment generation must, therefore, become the principal focus of development activities.

Efforts should be made to settle all disputes between labour and management, keeping constancy in mind that the mode of settlement should help to bring about maximum welfare of society at large.

Even if disputes linger on, both the parties should not behave in such a way as to create doubts in one's bonafide actions. They should be in a position to agree to disagree on points of view and yet earn respect from each other.

Giving a glimpse of the Gandhian technique trade unionism Venkataraman has said that genuine respect for mutual views in settling disputes was in total consonance with the cardinal principles of truth and non-violence practised by Mahatma Gandhi.

An earnest approach of mutual trust and respect creates a congenial climate for genuine appreciation of each other's points of view and for finding out a common ground, which can accommodate interests of both the parties.

What is the way out of the present predicament of about a dozen sick textile mills in Tamil Nadu and a similar number in Bombay ? What is the role of labour in this context ? What should be done with the mushrooming of powerloom units, which produced cheaper cloth outmarketing the products of the organised mills ? What should be done about people's craze for highly durable textiles like manmade cloth, which is said to be the root cause of the textile industry's sickness? Don't we think today's pitiable situation of the textile industry has been the direct result of a basic contradiction between propagation of both the unorganised sector and the organised sector ?

It was not beyond one's capacity to realise what ensured the maximum welfare of the people on such honest realisations. If one prepared oneself for the changing times, one would have no reason to plead that changes came about like a bolt from the blue. Both labour and management should view the forces of the changing times dispassionately and work out solutions in their mutual interest. Times were bound to change, and so were people's tastes and needs. One would be foolhardy if one thought one could stall the changes. The only wise course was to adapt to the new situation without coming into conflict with the larger interests of society.

In the face of new problems arising due to the tide of changes sweeping society it was not wise for aggrieved people to blame each other for one's woes. Instead, they should view the happenings dispassionately and co-operate with each other in tackling the difficulties. The accent on production of textiles in the unorganised sector is a basic necessity not only for providing jobs to the vast multitude of unemployed people, but also for providing cheap cloth to the poor masses. The accent on this sector is in the larger interests of the people in the prevailing situation.

Mahatma Gandhi's techniques, whether in regard to industrial disputes, the freedom struggle, the removal of untouchability or the propagation of *khadi* and village industries, were identical and all based on the firm foundation of an all-pervasive love for the people, truth and non-violence.

The touchstone, which decides correctness of otherwise of any step, is whether it is designed to bring about maximum welfare of people. If this criterion is adopted by all parties, there will be no scope for conflict of interests. It is only because of this approach adopted by Venkataraman and most industrialists in Tamil Nadu that the state could make speedy headway in industry.

Venkataraman is very keen that all agitations are non-violent and free of rancour. If any industrial dispute is riddled with rancour and vengeance as a result of violence and such other extraneous human factors, it would obstruct consideration of merit of the issues involved in a dispassionate manner, and hence would prove counter-productive.

It was at Champaran that Gandhi proved his mettle in India. Soon, there were other causes which received his attention. He stepped in to negotiate a just settlement of the dispute between the mill-owners and the striking workers of Ahmedabad. He told the workers not to get dispirited.

He asked them to take a pledge binding themselves to stay out of work till they got at least 35 per cent wage increase. He told them not to take to arms, not to resort to looting or stealing of property, to put up with inconvenience with courage and determination.

The owners of the mills offered an increase of 25 per cent in wages. Many workers were willing to return to work. Gandhi knew that any increase less than 35 per cent would really leave the workers in great economic distress. He called upon the workers to hold on to their resolve.

He also told them that he would undertake a fast unto death for getting the workers what he considered was their right. Three days after he began his fast, the owners of the mills came round. They agreed to grant the workers the increased wages.

This was another feather in Gandhi's cap. He told the owners of the mills to look upon themselves as trustees, to care for the well-being of the workers. This was a new concept. It was put across forcibly by Gandhi through his fast. It was the first fast he undertook. Later, he resorted to fasting several times to bring people round to his point of view.

It was Champaran which made Gandhi a national leader. Ahmedabad proved that he had the quality of the mind and the body to make it to the top as a servant of the people. And the nation watched the rising star with great expectation.

Mahatma Gandhi considered a trade union to play a mojor role in the education of workers. At the instance of Gandhi, Venkataraman's mentor Kamaraj played an active part in propagating the virtues of abstinence from liquor, abolition of child marriage and dowry, development of home industries to supplement their meagre incomes and other constructive activities.

It is because of Gandhi's influence, in addition to trade union Venkataraman remained engaged in conducting multifarious constructive activities like popagation of family planning, occupational programmes to widows, blind and handicapped people, co-operatives for spinning, weaving and marketing *khadi* and for other products of home industries, education of children, adult education, maternity homes and dispensaries, sewing classes, and hostels for girls especially from backward communities.

In an appraisal of Lenin's achievement the then British Prime Minister Winstin Churchill once said that Lennin's aim was to reform the world and his method was to blow it up. It would not be inappropriate to say in an assessment of the Union Government's labour welfare policies that its aim is to improve the situation and its method is to sit tight on the plethora of proposals. Take the case of bonded labour. A national survey conducted at the instance of the Planning Commission has estimated the number of such labourers at 3.45 lakh. As many as 2.14 lakh of them have been "identified". And of this "identified" mass 1.75 lakh persons have been rehabilitated. Rehabilitated whose, when, and by whom ? The Planning Commission plans and conducts surveys. The survey give estimates. There are amorpious "slave labour" just as there are variously tagged sectors of employers and employment. However, is not there a definite law applicable to bonded labourers ?

The members of Parliament ask : "Is there no bonded labourer in Haryana ?" Nobody knows the answer ; rather everyone does but no one wants to give an answer. The Labour Minister, says : "Money will not be a problem in the rehabilitation of the bonded labourers." But who will execute the formulated proposals and use the allocated money ? Thus, again, is nobody's concern. So, the bonded labour "system" continues. And so does the Government's method of sitting tight on its own proposals.

14

THE GREAT HUMANIST

The moment has clearly arrived when different hands will begin the task of evaluating the political method of Ramaswami Venkataraman and the impact which it has made on our time. This biographical study concerned is primarily with the Hero of this book—Venkataraman, to some extent with the promise of our national leaders like Mahatma Gandhi, Jawaharlal Nehru, Indira Gandhi, Rajiv Gandhi, and only incidentally with the potential importance of K. Kamaraj. They should be considered separately, but it is impossible not to consider them also as one. At five successive decades of the Indian National Congress, all have in turn been prominent in the national chronicles, representing not the hope of a few, but a national expectation.

Mahatma Gandhi, Jawaharal Nehru, Indira Gandhi, Kamaraj—are legendary figures, and their names will be sung as long as men tell stories to each other about their past. The legend is today being questioned, but it is likely to remain the source of a powerful mythology, if for no other reason than that the lives of Gandhi, Nehru, Indira Gandhi, Kamaraj were cut short the unfinished National Integration task of the Mahatma, the unfinished Premiership of Nehru and Indira Gandhi and unachieved economic salvation of Kamaraj may tempt the Indian people to believe that, just as their nation was deprived of four unusual chances of salvation in the past, so their best hope in the future, as tribals beset them, is to find and to follow another deliverer. It is the promise of Venkataraman, unrealised but remembered, which is itself a source of expectation. Each was the saviour of his country.

At 77, with more than 50 years of political career behind him, Venkataraman has to decorate the highest office of President on July 25, 1987 in terms of range and impact. The great humanist which he is, Venkataraman is a true friend of the poor. He is unique, he has the force, the true patriotic character. "I am the humble servant of the people," is how Venkataraman puts it. No one has even seen him in bad mood or angry.

It was only by 2nd October 1948, that total prohibition was introduced in Madras State. Tamil Nadu has given the lead in prohibition. Its history will bear ample testimony. The British Indian Excise Policy was laid down in 1790. About this time Tipu Sultan had released his prohibition policy. This was on the lines of other Muslim rulers, who believed in prohibition.

Emperor Ashoka had debarred drink and harmful drugs. The British rulers of India were faced with paucity of funds. They introduced love of liquor to earn money. The evil took roots in our economic growth. The income from liquor was one-fourth of the total revenue of the State.

In 1912 late Gopalkrishna Gokhale while leading a deputation to wait on Secretary of State for India, condemned the British Liquor Policy and urged for total prohibition. This led to steady growth of public opinion. The rulers were indifferent to the demand.

Raja Ram Mohun Roy, Kesab Chandra Sen, Gilder and many others were the earliest supporters of prohibition, so also Dr. Annie Beasant and Lokamanya Balagangadhar Tilak. Mahatma Gandhi, when he entered the Indian political scene, incorporated the policy of total prohibition, in the eleven major issues taken up by National Congress in 1921. Prohibition was one of his instruments to achieve Independence. In 1923 under his leadership, Liquor Picketing Movement gained impetus. Thousands of men and women went to jails. This attracted a countrywide attention.

British rulers were clever. Their aim was to gather as much money out of it as possible. Hence to circumvent Congress propaganda for prohibition, many a Commission was appointed to sidetrack the demand. Nothing succeeded till Congress came into power in 1937. This, however, does not mean that the individual efforts were non-existent. In 1922, Dewan Bahadur M.R. Rao introduced a Bill on Prohibition in Madras Legislative Council. Punjab had already passed this measure in 1921. Bombay in 1923 by an Act reduced 50 per cent liquor consumption. Bengal, Uttar Pradesh and Assam followed the lead. In 1937 when Congress came in top ower, it was Rajaji, who had identified himself most with Gandhiji, who made a declaration in the Madras Legislative Assembly, that all toddy and liquor shops in Salem, his home town, would be closed. He emphasised that the loss of Rs. 26 lakhs in revenue is equal to putting Rs. 1 crore in the pockets of poor people. His decision was welcomed by all.

Tamil Nadu was the first State to introduce prohibition. Prohibition was introduced in three stages. Rajaji's policy of Prohibition was sincerely and truly followed by K. Kamaraj and M. Bhaktavatsalam, who followed him as Chief Ministers. The success of Prohibition in Tamil Nadu largely depended on the pains taken by the Chief Ministers to implement it. They continued the policy unabated. C.N. Annadurai, the D.M.K. Chief Minister followed the Prohibition Policy, with same courage and dedication.

The Congress (I) politics in Tamil Nadu, as in many other states, was marked for some time by ruthless in fighting, growing cynicism among partymen and public disbelief in motives and intentions of leaders. Though the Congress (I) was not a major political force in the state, factional strife among Congressmen reached alarming dimensions. At the centre of the controversy was the AICC General Secretary G.K. Moopanar, who had emerged as the most powerful leader in the state. Venkataraman, then Defence Minister had been so frustrated over the then "goings on" in the party that he was said to have decided to retire "gracefully" from politics. He was unlikely to offer himself as a candidate in the next parliamentary elections.

Moopanar's rise in Tamil Nadu politics had been spectacular. An unknown Congress worker 15 years back, he shot into prominence in 1980, owing to his proximity to Sanjay Gandhi. Since then he has not looked back. He has fitted into Prime Minister Indira Gandhi's scheme of things to sideline tried and popular leaders and replace them with political lightweights. Gundu Rao in Karnataka, and JB Patnaik in Orissa and Antulay in Maharashtra, were the types she chose to build up as her *satraps* in the states. Strong-willed people like Devraj Urs, Venkataraman and Chenna Reddy, with a stature of their own, were not of much use to her.

The first major blow to the Congress in Tamil Nadu was administered by the scheming Kamaraj who successfully ousted stalwarts like C. Rajagopalachari from power. He, however, surrounded himself with able administrators and politicians like Venkataraman and C. Subramaniam. His only condition was that they should be loyal to him. Moopanar, unfortunately, lacks Kamaraj's shrewdness and ability to carry the partymen with him After. Kamaraj died. Venkataraman and Mrs. Margarathan Chandrasekhar were regarded as his political heirs. But Indira Gandhi, and more particularly her son, Sanjay, had other ideas. They found Venkataraman inflexible in his outlook and a stickler for traditional Congress values. It is said that he was one of the few ministers who did not allow official files to be sent to Sanjay. He was later shifted from Finance to the Defence Ministry. Not only that, his trusted men were gradually eliminated from all important party positions. M. P. Subramaniam, one of his prominent supporters, was thrown out of the TNCC presidentship on the plea that under his leadership the party had lost the Periakulam by-election. Moopanar then wanted his expulsion from the party and had served him a show cause notice why he should be removed from the organization for his criticism of the leadership at the Madurai conference.

Moopanar's overbearing attitude (though in New Delhi he projected himself as a "simple and modest" political worker), had turned important Congressmen of the state against him. Sivaji Ganesan, the popular Tamil Film Star, whom the Congress party had been building up to counter the matinee idol M.G. Ramachandran's influence among the Tamil masses, had turned against Moopanar. Earlier, he was hostile towards Venkataraman. Party MP, Era Ambarasu, had presented a memorandum seeking withdrawal of the show cause notice served on Subramaniam. Another Congress (I) MP, K.T. Kosalram, who was earlier in Moopanar's camp, went against him.

At the regional conference of the Congress (I) in Madras, the in-fighting in the state Congress reached a new high. Men from rival factions abused each other and exchanged blows. Giant posters outside the conference venue depicted Moopanar as a rich landlord sitting on a pile of black money and distributing party offices to his yesmen. The police had to intervene to rescue Indira Gandhi from unruly Congressmen who squatted in front of her jeep. The grouse of the anti-Moopanar group was that he had cornered the bulk of party offices with the help of his money and power. According to Subramaniam, the 19-sub-committees set up for the regional conference were packed with Moopanar's men. This provoked fival factions to boycott the conference. They later agreed to participate in it as they did not want to be misunderstood by Indira Gandhi. The wordy dual between the pro and the anti-Moopanar factions at one stage ended in a brawl and the police had to be called.

No dobut, supporters of Venkataraman were able to show how isolated and unpopular Moopanar was in the state Congress. But this was unlikely to gain them much. Gresham's law operates as much in politics as in economics.

Tamil Nadu's inescapable fixation with filmi politics was amply reasserted when the Congress (I) MP and veteran of the Tamil screen, Sivaji Ganesan, paraded his political power through the streets of Madras on February 25 and 26, 1984.

Under the guise of a "political conference" organised by the Sivaji Fans' Association, the actor collected around him a handful of dissident MLAs and MPs, including the Defence Minister, Venkataraman, and staked his claim for the presidency of the State Congress (I) unit.

Dubbed by the official leadership of the state unit as anti-party, the conference, preceded by a huge procession on the first day of the two day meet, was the dissident group's retort to the southern region conference of the AICC (I) organised by the Tamil Nadu Congress (I) committee on January 17 and 18, 1984 and buycotted by the dissidents headed by the former state unit president, M. P. Subramaniam. It was only at the instance of the party president, Indira Gandhi, that Sivaji chose to attend the regional conference on the second day. His complaint was that he and his followers had been ignored by the organisers, who belong to the Moopanar faction.

Dissidence in the state unit really came to a head when Subramaniam was served with a show-cause notice for indiscipline and his group, in turn, came up with a memorandum charging the local leadership with choking the party with the covert backing of the two general secretaries— G. K. Moopanar and the late C. M. Stephen. The dissidents, however, performed a volte-face, posthumously patching up with Stephen by naming the conference venue after him.

The difference of opinion ultimately boils down to : with whom the Congress (I) should align itself in the state-while the Sivaji MP's group backs the AIADMK, the Moopanar faction finds the DMK a more dependable ally.

Of late, the dissident group has been orchestrating a "make Sivaji TNCC (I) president" compaign and the matinee idol reciprocated with the announcement of his full-throated entry into politics after cutting short his film commitments. Well past his prime and having entrenched his son, Prabhu, as his successor in Tamil Cinema, the head-on plunge into state politics should prove a respectable way out of the film world for the aging star, though he continues to strike an incongruous combination with teenage actresses.

Coming to the February 1987 show, it proved to be a

veritable *tamasha*, providing Sivaji yet another chance to put on one hell of a live act before thousands of fans who had poured in from all over the state. Sivaji did not disappoint them.

In an hour-long speech full of theatrical aplomb and verbal gusto, he castigated his tormentors in the party, complained how his children (members of the fans association) had been ignored and threatened, cried for a *Harijan* fan killed in a road accident on the way to the conference, adopted the women present at the venue as his mothers, reiterated his unswerving loyalty to "Mother Indira" and called upon his fans to be disciplined and work for the party.

Even before the echoes of his speech had died down, about 1,000 fans wreaked violence near the Egmore railway station after they had been prevented from travelling home ticketless by train.

Venkataraman and other MPs and MLAs stuck to the "Sivaji for state president" refrain to the delight of the fawning crowd. If crowd-pulling were to be the main criterion, Sivaji should be the next TNCC(I) president, what with the Congress (I) losing its committed crowd and a comple of deposits in by-elections. And if the Congress (I)—AIADMK Combine does fructify, it certainly would be a star-studded cast what with M.G. Ramachandrans Miss Jayalalitha, Sivaji, Vaijayanthimala and Bhagyaraj, nominated by M.G. Ramachandran as his heir in filmdom, arrayed on one side.

The 4th century Latin poet, Claudius Claudianus said : "But when I observed the affairs of men plunged in such darkness, the guilty flourishing in continuous happiness, and the righteous tormented, my religion, tottering, began once more to fall."

Venkataraman is against all forms of corruption. Despite being in active politics for over five decades, he has been free from the taint of corruption. His name did not figure in any controversy

We live in times that try men's souls (not to mention also their bodies all the way from head to sole). More so, the souls and bodies of ordinary people with no strings to pull, no names to drop, no funds to raise. In a country of close on 800 million people, a thousand families or so rule the national roost. While some others in their frantic bid to gatecrash into the club trample unmercifully on the bodies of the rest that form the macro majority. All is fair in love, hate and the rat-race, with the wicked flourishingly exceedingly and the good and the honest going to the wall. More: the successful specialise in mocking the meat they feed on. In the moments they do not do so, they sermonise. Or patronise. Or advise. Even—perhaps to break the tedium once in a while sympathise. (After a fashion). In fact they are willing to do anything except get off their victims' aching, breaking backs.

Democracy was devised as a system in which the strong would help the weak. But what we see today is an order that makes for the former continually adding to their offensive strength at the cost of the latter. A democracy that exists largely only in form is hardly the answer to the people's prayer for a policy polity that would give them security (physical, economic), and the freedom to cultivate their gardens and their souls. (and, as most have no gardens of their own, at least the right to stroll around in public gardens without having to pay a fee). A dictatorial or near dictatorial regime dressed up in democratic garb can do more harm than a naked dictatorship, because of its claim to the people's authority at its back. When a democratic scheme of things fails to improve the condition of the people the failure may be traced to the leaders. This must be so more especially in a country such as India where the people are humble, respectful, tolerant and obedient to the leaders. The latter have the powers and call the tune, and must own the responsibility for the state of affairs.

The state of affairs is anything but what it shonld be. It may be said that the mother of all trouble is the corrupt way of life engendered by people at the top, followed blindly and enthusiastically by those below, crushing those at lower levels. The curious (and appalling) thing about it all is that the haves, having all and more, still manage to take from the have-nots who curiously, while not having the visibly desirable things of life, still seem to possess an inexhaustible *akshayapatra* whose contents continue to sustain and strengthen their masters. As a result corruption sports a great variety of *avatars* besides the giving and taking of bribes. Luxury, comfort, well-being, security, survival itself demands unceasing compromises and surrender of self-respect, honesty, principle, and right conduct that demean and debase the men at both ends of the transaction. The requirements of life generated by the ethos at the top make failure a nightmare, because one failure can only lead inexorably to another, making the pressure unberable. To avoid failure, therefore, is the grim *sumum bonum* of this kind of existence, an end that takes all the manhood out of men.

Mankind has never before so endangered its very existence as in this epoch, dividing itself into two vast, hostile blocs struggling for world domination. The rival camps embody the great polarization of values and societies in modern civilization: Liberal Democracy and Communism, Individualism and Totalitarianism. An intractable dogmatism or absolutism surrounds the opposition between the self-glorifying, contrasted social and economic systems, provoking a world wide cold war that destroys global peace and threatens the annihilation of the species.

Tolerance, compromise and harmony are Eastern rather than Western values. These are conspicuous badges of humanism in all cultures and epochs. Intellectually speaking, humanism believes that truth may be set forth in various and even opposite ways, and is tolerant and open-minded rather than dogmatic and uncompromising. In its rebellion against intellectual, and especially ecclesiastical authority, it brings forth a flexible system of thought. It cherishes and promotes several and complementary truths and values in life, society and culture in consonance with its overall conception of human fulfilment, dignity and freedom. True humanism is embodied in Cromwell's historic admonition in seventeenth-century England: "My brethern, by the bowels of Christ, I beseech you, bethink you that you may be mistaken." It is expressed in Jefferson's famous warning in nineteenth-century America :

> "Let us restore to social intercourse that harmony and affection without which liberty and even life itself are but dreary things. And let us reflect that having banished

> from our land that religious intolerance under which mankind so long bled and suffered, we have yet gained little if we countenance a political intolerance as despotic and wicked and capable of as bitter and bloody persecutions."

Love, harmony and social goodwill stimulate and strengthen, while intolerance, hatred and violence jeopardize democracy, freedom and humanism.

The humanism of Cromwell and Jefferson is entirely incompatible with the kind of fanaticism or closedness and the double standard of morality, rampant in both capitalist and socialist worlds of today. In the democracy the principles are humane, but deception and violence are found in practice. Beyond that propaganda has a field day. The meaning and passion of the new radiant humanism now sweeping across the world is the vast social meaning and passion for mankind and world as a whole, and not for mcre capitalist or socialist man and culture.

The peace and solidarity of mankind should not be a smoke-screen, nor mere abstention from overt of disguised use of force. It should not be deemed an intolerable burden for the affluent nations, nor be a collective reaction of terror of the nations against the common atomic doom. It should rather be a true, constructive global feeling and enthusiasm based on a revival of humanism and its idealistic fight for freedom from misery, injustice and exploitation anywhere on the earth. The universal neighbourship of all peoples, due to advances in technology and communication and economic interdependence, leads today to unexpected universal suspicion, fear and ill-will. These can only be dissipated by progressive mutual understanding, trust and cooperation on a world-wide scale. The nations all over the world, governed by justice, goodness, love and compassion, must meet together in the valleys of human needs. Humanism always speaks in language and accent, accessible to the under-privileged, whether individuals or peoples, to man, absolutely every man, as man. *Jaspers stresses that in the future even more than in the past, no spiritual reality will remain unless carried by the masses.* He remarks :

> "Achievement at a high level will always be a matter for a few individuals, for the elite who educate themselves. Yet the coming humanism will, while the scaling summits, also have to discover the simplest forms which become approachable and convincing to everyone. An effective humanism would, in principle, have to be a humanism for all."

A global devastation can be averted today only by a vital cosmic humanism that can rise to universal truths and complete values through a dialectical reconciliation balance of the antinomic or complementary principles and values of mankind: Freedom and Organization, Community and Individual and Liberty and Social Justice in modern civilized living.

No humanistic synthesis is, however, possible as long as the pernicious phase of World Capitalism conditions whole peoples to competitiveness and aggressiveness, and hinders the growth and spread of the spontaneous normal impulses of self-transcendence and altruism; or as World Communism thwarts the true community or communion by social coercion and regimentation, and nurtures a profound distrust of the higher spiritual goals and values. Both social systems depend largely on specialized social practices, arrangements and institutions rather than on moral and spiritual factors and trends for human progress. It is a curious tragedy in the history of civilization that when mankind's productive forces and technology are at their peak, and a completely industrialized, automated world is round the corner, promising an undreamt of leisure and freedom from want, the problem of the spiritual values and destiny of man has ceased to be of principal concern for him.

Man's basic values, loyalties and obligations in the contrasted social systems of World Capitalism and Communism are directed to the class or mass. to the institution and to the nation rather than to mankind. The generic sense of oneness and solidarity of mankind, the higher and deeper spiritual values and strivings that bind man and man, class and class and nation and nation are sacrificed at the alter of efficiency and power individual and collective. Simultaneously, due to the excessive complexity and elaboration of group organization and collective tools and techniques, both the biological instincts of human survival and the psychological impulses of human fulfilment are socially conditioned and canalized in a thorough-going fashion, and, so to speak, 'de-individualized'. The self is the class or mass-self; social institutions and morality are 'closed', not 'open', in Bergson's sense; values and allegiances cease to be species-values and allegiances; and the community of mankind is broken up into bits and fragments. The absolute sovereign State of the modern age that supersedes mankind as a whole places wealth and achievement above goodness and wisdom, and toughness and aggressiveness above conscience and compassion.

A pugnacious, war-like nationalism, born and bred in the West during two centuries of European wars and world expansion, is a global arch-enemy of humanism. In the mid-twentieth century it is reinforced throughout Asia and Africa by the accrual of freedom and independence in former colonial territories and by the replacement of imperialism by neo-colonialism and the struggle for world ascendency among the more advanced nations. Today the cleavage between the rich and the poor peoples of the earth, created since the Industrial and Commercial Revolution of Europe and maintained by the global spread of colonialism and imperialism has become much greater than in the past. This fans the flames of nationalism, chauvinism and racialism. As long as a few advanced nations can pressurize the backward nations, free and awakened, and yet dependent and miserable, human freedom and dignity cannot accrue for the considerable part of mankind. Oppressing societies and cultures defend this by their opaque and mischievious doctrines of cultural and ethical relativism and of subjectivism of all human values and standards.

Political power, cultural supremacy and economic suzerainty of the more powerful nations are today conjoined together for global mastery, and contribute towards the denial and suppression of the universal or absolute values and rights of mankind, in spite of these being eloquently set forth in the U.N.O. Charter of Human Rights. This is aided and abetted by the false Westerns social-science postulates of relativism of human behaviour, values and culture. An outmoded nineteenth-century philosophy of man and culture continues to challenge cosmic humanism and human fulfilment on a global scale in this century.

True, cosmic humanism rests on the universality and transcendence of each of the philosophical triad in dynamic, reciprocal interchange or 'transaction', in Dewey's vivid phrase: Person-Values-Community, or Being-Norms. Cosmos. A humanism that does not underline the universalization or 'cosmicization' of all the three enduring and universal realities is myopic, self-stultifying and disintegrative. It can be either religious-theological, materialistic-astheistic or scientific-empirical and its closedness and lopsidedness become of serious detriment to civilization. It can, no doubt, believe in an ideal solidarity of mankind which man, due to his religious alienation springing from the economic one, can project outside of himself and hypostatizes as God or the Supreme Principle. In Marxism man or being as and entity does not exist, but only men in the collective exist, formed or transformed by the society in its historical situation. Contrasted with Marxist humanism is Indian humanism that grounds itself in the metaphysics of the Real Self, God or *Brahman*, The basis of Indian humanism that is religionful is formulated in the Mahabharata as follows: 'I assert this, the secret of the highest Truth (Brahman or Reality), there is nothing superior to man." "Service to man is service to God." Again, in the epic God declares :

> "Know that *Dharma* (righteousness) is my beloved, first-born spiritual son, whose nature is to have compassion on all creatures. In this character I dwell within all men, both present and past, through many varieties and forms of existence for the preservation and establishment of righteousness".

But this traditional Vedantic humanism, which Indian civilization derives from the *Upanishads*, the *Gita*, the epics and the *Puranas*, lost its fine balance and harmony and undervalued the infinite status and dignity of the individual in actual social practice. Neither liberal nor Marxist, neither Vedantic, Buddhist nor Confucian humanism can rebuild civilization without full acknowledgement by each of all aspects and dimensions of the metaphysical Real as embodied in the interdependent triad. Man-Values-Society. No humanism can ignore the claims of anyone of the triad, tied to one another in endless interpenetration and unity, manifesting unforeseeable, transcendent potentialities.

It is only in the self's relation to the other-selves and to the unlimited and unknown community that man can achieve the absolute humanistic values and the spiritual freedom, unity and wholeness of the Real Self, Being or God. Real Self or Being and norms are both attained in the most extensive society conceivable—the community of the earth and cosmos that belongs to all men. There are greater epistemic justification, psychological motivation as well as moral commitment for man if he discerns his values as embedded in the very structure of his Real Being and cosmos. This is the transformation of values into norms. Truth, goodness and love then become absolutely certain and supremely obligatory beyond and above the relativities and contingencies of life and world, because human nature and cosmos are what they are.

Humanism may be defined as an integrated system of human meanings, goals and values and harmonious programme of human fulfilment, individual and collective. It seeks to clarify and enrich man's goals, values and ideals and achieve his full humanness through bringing him in ever deeper and more intimate kinship and harmony with the surrounding life and society. It is obvious that humanism rests on 'value-realism' which is not an abstract notion but involves the concrete fulfilment of human life and potentialities that is itself invested with the highest value by, and for man's self. Mankind's universal experience at the level of both the self and society is that the real value of human fulfilment—the aim of all humanisms—is supreme. This is connected by philosophy with the universal quest of being for unity, wholeness and transcendence. Many humanisms identify these with the

Ultimate Reality or Being at the ontological and transcendent dimension. The absolute fulfilment of human life is not possible; it ever recedes because of the transcendence of being, values and cosmos. Another way of saying this is that human fulfilment has its source and foundation in the ontological or transcendent dimension, in metaphysical and transcendent Being or God.

Unity, wholeness and transcendence are as much within the being as in the community and in the cosmos. Man comprehends the order, unity and transcendence of the community and the cosmos, to the stuff, quality and process of which he belongs, through his science, art, ontology and religion. His contemplative mind's function and experience are dual and linked together, viz :

(a) the interiorization of the community and the cosmos within the mind or self. As the community enters into the self, we see the rise and maturation of human values and conscience. The internalization of the cosmos-total embodies itself in the transcendent or cosmic dimension of the self-superposed on its biological and psychological dimension; and

(b) the extension of his affiliating, extending and transcending self into the community and the cosmos. Man's self-transcendence—the outcome of his memory, imagination, abstraction and symbolization—is his unique fundamental impulse and capacity by which he constantly overcomes his finiteness and creatureliness, actuality and contingency. The diminution or suppression of this is the attenuation or denial of his true self-realization. The internalization of the community and cosmos and the penetration of the community and cosmos into his mind or self are complementary, dual processes comprising the most potent instruments of the refinement and complete realization of his life, values and potentialities—the aim of humanism. The creativity of humanism in civilization's long, chequered course depends on the strength or feebleness of its commitment to his belief and faith in both experiences.

Man by his nature is a living, affiliating and expanding link. He is not fundamentally the ego-centric and aggressive animal as he is often made out to be by a natural science-oriented psychology and soicology. Affiliating and self-transcending dispositions and intentions are inherent in his inner nature, growth and fulfilment. All his reason, intuition, memory and imagination urge him to look forward to opportunities and potentialities of more open, wider and more integrated and harmonious forms of existence. True human existence is transcendence. True humanism is transcendent or cosmic.

Man seeks to identify himself with the other-selves, to merge the society and the vast cosmos in his mature, transcendent self. The human mind or self is infiniteness and transcendence to itself. The greater the accord of the self with openness, infiniteness and transcendence, the deeper, richer and more authentic it is. This is the way of truth, goodness and love, man's relating his consciousness to the whole and real self or infinite Being and his creation and pursuit of the absolute values, embodied in Being and immanent in all social relations. Jaspers remarks :

> "Through the presence of the absolute and the infinite, man's finiteness does not remain merely the unconscious datum of his empirical existence, but through the light of transcendence becomes the basic trait in his consciousness of his created nature. Thus though man cannot annul his finiteness, he does break it."

Humanism stresses that man neither adjusts nor integrates, nor shapes, but transcends and expresses himself, or seeks for the meaning of self-transcendence and self-experience. Such meanings or principles of meanings are expressed by him dialectically. This is because he encounters the cosmos as a pattern of opposites—chaos and order, part and whole, break and restoration, actuality and possibility, value and contingency

This polarity or opposition rules not only his outer adjustments to the cosmos and the community but also his inner feelings, values and experiences. The goals and values he seeks confront him as denial and fulfilment, frustration and gratification, constraint and freedom, attraction and repulsion. Finally, he seeks and achieves a harmonious, balanced unity of such opposites and antinomies, marking his mental and spiritual fulfilment—complete ontic knowledge and ontic transcendence. All values and truths, whatever the dimension he finds, are likely to be well-founded when these correspond with the tension and opposition within themselves. The polarity and unity of oppsites are universal, belonging to the very structure of human mind and experience.

The philosophical theory of humanism postulated certain central ontological principles or categories that are dialectical in character, i.e. implying each other as antinomic or complementary. These comprise, indeed, the foundations of an adequate philosophy of humanism a that embraces the whole evolutionary process from atoms, stars and galaxies to organisms, minds, values and civilizations.

Humanistic science philosophy ought to abandon the static and 'eternal' traits of the older metaphysics, but should be in full accord with the ascent of cosmic evolution at the successive dimensions of matter, life, mind and values and with temporal concepts. The above categorization in a philosophical theory of humanism would perhaps meet the findings of modern science as well as stand the test of rigorous philosophical reasoning.

Humanism rejects the sterile logic of an outgrown naturalism that reduces human meanings and experiences to that segment of human behaviour and experience that is externally controlled and determined. It discards a naive and opaque psychologism that distorts the self of man, its unity, harmony and transcendence and the values and possibilities of the self-in-relation to mankind and cosmos-as-a whole. It reveals the total self of man with its functions, meanings and values at the three successive dimensions of the environment, physical-biological, psycho-social and ideal-transcendent. It hence formulates a general philosophical rather than psychological and sociological view of the self in dynamic, multidimensional relations to fellow-man, to the universe and to values.

Both man and cosmos are foci of dimensions and polarities. Matter, life, mind and values are the four successive dimensions of the structure of the cosmos. Man is the constant bridge of the tension towards the realm of matter and life on the one hand and towards reason, imagination, intuition and values on the other. The notion of the four successive dimensions, and of the polar or complementary principles, dialectically resolved in human self-transcendence, is fundamental in a philosophical theory of cosmic humanism. The everlasting antinomies or complementaries (that fall into twelve categories indicated above) direct and govern man's activity located within the realm of values and Being. Self-transcendence of fusion of self with the Real Self, All-Being or God is the fundamental process—man's creative, detached and universal knowledge, love, altruism and compassion which constitute the vast, over-spreading single thread that binds cosmic existences into a transcendent harmony of harmonies. The core of humanism is its acknowledgement of the essence and truth of transcendence that progressively and dialectically achieves harmony.

Hence the unrelenting search for an impregnable social-security by way of insurance in the shape of strategically placed friends and high connections ; servility to upstarts and disdain of the good ; and general acquiescence with wrong and opposition to the right. Running dubious errands and doing the questionable behests of those whose favours one craves, standing up for evil-doers while fearing to "speak for the fallen and the weak"—all these are among the launching pads and staging grounds for what we identify formally as corruption. They are corruption no less ; and unless we combat it at the source, this hydra-headed monster will eat away enough of the Indian body politic to render its recovery a near impossible exercise. But those who have the frontile role in the effort to make such an exercise unnecessary are busy grimly defending their fortresses against forces they have themselves created by their own actions.

In all the hullabaloo created by the different "deals" and

connected problems, some of the basic and vital issues touching our very survival have taken a back seat.

Venkataraman has suggested the need for continuous production and more production as a means of checking corruption.

In the final analysis, the expansion of production and an enlargement of the area of operation, leading up to the substitution of the class economy by a mass economy, is the real answer to the problem of corruption and the various ills that it spawns. The runaway spending of the government can be one of that prime causes of the evil of corruption that presently rages like a fire across India.

The government, which ought to be a model in the utilisation of the money at its disposal, has been going haywire throwing it away on unproductive and unnecessary.

These ventures have an undesirable effect on the public, both in monetary and psychological terms, with prices ever overtaking earnings in a vicious circle created by artificial scarcity conditions not to say artificial requirements.

A government equipped with a monopoly of money supply and of power to deploy it, in addition levies indirect taxes through which 40 per cent of the national income goes back to the government machinery where a minuscule minority of persons lays down the law for millions.

As a result, millions of people who would be active and productive participants in the growth of the economy are denied the opportunity and reduced to the role of mute witnesses to a process that stalls their progress as well as the country's. An enlightened liberalisation policy that would enhance production and discourage corruption is the need of the hour.

15

THE CHALLENGE

Many of us knew the mind of the leadership that who would be India's next President ? And this writer had already started collecting reading materials on R. Venkataraman. Most people within the Congress and outside it believed that "Venkataraman will be the ruling party's candidate for Presidentship when Giani Zail Singh retires on July 1987". His stewardship of the Rajya Sabha has been so fair and just that he evokes friendliness from many quarters. He has given adequate opportunity to Opposition members to express their views fully. Some people fear that age is against Venkataraman but he is in good health and quite active. Should Congress choose some other candidate for Presidentship, it is practically certain that Venkataraman will opt out of Vice-Presidentship and go home to live as a private citizen. That was the stand of Dr. Zakir Hussain also. What kind of a President will he make ? Venkataraman, as those who know him well, is not an uncritical person. He will not be a rubber stamp President. He will offer his considered advice to the Government and others, to whichever political party they belong who wish to consult him. But having done his duty he will stay within the limits the Constitution of India allows. He will not try to embarrass anyone because that is not his style of functioning. Venkataraman is a worth successor to Dr. Radhakrishnan. The two can be compared in some ways even though Dr. Radhakrishnan was a towering scholar and Venkataraman started out as a lawyer. But dignity and fairplay are common traits. Dr. Radhakrishnan commanded respect and so does Venkataraman. If the Congress Party settles for Venkataraman, then it will have to find a suitable candidate for Vice-Presidentship.[1]

We asked an Opposition politician whether there was any truth in a combined opposition move to back the possible candidature of Giani Zail Singh. He replied it was much too early to take a decision on the subject. Much would depend on the outcome of the elections in various States. At that point the Opposition parties would decide whether they should put up a candidate who has a good chance to win particularly if the Congress position is weakened. If no, then they may merely want to put up somebody to embarrass the Congress Party. At that time it will be seen who may be available to the opposition for the candidature for Presidentship.[2]

Giani Zail Singh was the choice of Indira Gandhi. In private conversation Zail Singh never underestimates the fact that he owed much to her. Perhaps it is not generally appreciated that R.K. Dhawan lent great support to him in this matter. Dhawan was his great advocate. And since Dhawan and Pranab Mukherji were good friends and both worked closely with Indira Gandhi, they were looked upon as friends by Zail Singh whose feelings for them did not diminish with their having gone into political wilderness, for whatever reason. Zail Singh may believe that he paid back the debt he owned to Indira Gandhi for all her favours done to him by elevating her son Rajiv to Prime Ministership, but was it not also expedient that he should have done so? Arun Nehru pointed out to Zail Singh looking out of a window in 'Rashtrapati Bhavan' the rising smoke from burning taxis and some shops soon after the assassination of Indira Gandhi. Would it have been possible to control the fires, keep people in check and restore peace and normalcy if Rajiv Gandhi had not been immediately installed as Prime Minister? Zail Singh has been a politician for the better part of his life. He knew the odds. He had to save the people, including people of his own community. There was no alternative.[3]

There have been unfortunate references in a section of the Press to a strained relationship between the President and the Prime Minister. Matters have to an extent been aggravated by 'Rashtrapati Bhavan' activists spreading tales calculated to embarrass the Prime Minister and blowing up even routine matters out of proportion. A recent instance is of the President being requested to return to Delhi a day or so earlier from Calcutta. A Cabinet reshuffle was expected. The President, it appears, had some engagements of import which he wanted to fulfil in Calcutta, among them a ride on the metro. One newspaper commented that somebody had at last got his priorities right. Friends of Zail Singh who wish to generate a measure of sympathy and support for him may actually be harming him. People are beginning to wonder why there is lack of rapport and why so much chill all around? All the blame surely cannot stick to the Prime Minister. Much is made of it that the President is not given opportunity to travel abroad. He will in fact be going to four countries in Europe in November 1986. The decision was taken some weeks ago but that story did not emanate from 'Rashtrapati Bhavan'. Zail Singh is expected to visit West Germany, Yugoslavia, Poland and Greece. Will 'Rashtrapati Bhavan' try to create a real crisis some time before the President retires? This is an apprehension which is being talked about. The Government certainly is giving no cause for it and the Prime Minister has maintained a dignified silence on anything connected with 'Rashtrapati Bhavan'. He has never encouraged the Press to write on the subject.[4]

Interestingly, Venkataraman's name was projected as the future President as far back as in June 1982, as a successor to Sanjeeva Reddy. When asked how he felt about becoming the next president, the then defence minister replied, "Such questions should be asked to immature politicians."

I had assumed that Venkataraman would be the next President. I had seen him in action as a Minister and Chairman of the Rajya Sabha. There were very few Ministers of his calibre : he did his homework, he was clear-headed, his speeches were short and to the point. As Chairman of the House of Elders, he re-imposed discipline among members without being discounteous to anyone. There was this other consideration which also went in this favour : it was time we had a President from the South. He had the three qualifications Allama Iqbal required of a leader of the caravan : broad vision (nigah buland), heart winning speech (sukhan dil-nawaz) and warmth of personality (jaan pur soz). I was, consequently somewhat bewildered and amused to find so many names being mentioned by politicians and the Press as likely candidates. Some were admirable characters but did not have national stature. Amongst them was the name of a joker whose chief qualification was having served as a kind of *khidmatgaar* (household servant) in the Nehru household. I am relieved to see that the choice has narrowed down to a few worthies, the worthiest still being R. Venkataraman.[5]

The Constitution confers very few powers on the President of the Indian Republic. The Constitution 42nd Amendment Act modified Article 74 and made the advice given by the Council of Ministers binding on the President. The Janata Government (1977-80) which restored the old position in respect of many provisions changed by the 42nd Amendment, did not restore the old clause(1) of Article 74. It only modified the clause by empowering the President to send any matter decided by the Cabinet for reconsideration. This does not amount to a veto ; if the Cabinet upon reconsideration—no matter how perfunctory—resolves to reaffirm its previous decision, the President is obliged to accept it.

There is also Article 111. It again does not amount to a veto such as the American President can apply to Bills passed by Congress. The President can only require reconsideration of any Bill or its clause or clauses. He can even suggest an amendment. But if Parliament proceeds to re-enact the Bill in the same form then the President is helpless and has no choice, but to append his signature. It is not known what course the President has adopted in the case of the interception of post : Whether he has acted under Article 74—this is not extra-constitutional but perfectly constitutional—or under Article 111 ? Should he proceed under Article 74, he would get another "opportunity" to send the matter to Parliament under Article 111. In either case the action is truly unprecedented.[6]

Rajendra Prasad was indeed toying with the idea of returning Hindu Code Bill under the original Constitution, but since further consideration of the Bill was dropped the crisis was averted. The confrontation between the President and the Prime Minister was transformed into a harmless exercise of an academic debate on the powers of the President. Mrs. Gandhi was always obsessed by a Presidential coup d'etat (and so was to a lesser extent Morarji Desai). Like Indira, Morarji Desai too, was afraid of interference by 'Rashtrapati Bhawan' which would inevitably weaken the Prime Minister's authority, although he did not hesitate to impose on Indira Gandhi in 1969 a presidential candidate she distrusted. Now the action of President Zail Singh on the Postal Bill has certainly revied memories of the President—Prime Minister conflict, although it is an exaggeration to say that the confrontation has begun. The President has acted, ostensibly, in defence of civil liberty, of privacy and freedom. He has obviously cogent reasons for seeking reconsideration of the policy underlying the Bill. Nor can it be said that he has violated any constitutional principle or propriety. Yet I cannot but feel that if Rajiv Gandhi had maintained a correct and cordial relationship with the incumbent President, if he had not ignored him and slighted him, perhaps the matter could have been talked over without much publicity. But Rajiv Gandhi never bothered to develop warmth in his relationship with Zail Singh who had invited Rajiv Gandhi to form a government even before his election as leader of the Congress Parliamentary Party. There is no doubt that the Presidential action, though constitutionally proper, is so unusual that it is bound to embarrass the Prime Minister.

Rajiv Gandhi accorded priority to the Anti-Defection constitutional amendment, because despite "his" massive mandate, he seemed like a frightened chick. He wanted to be sure that no member even dared think of defying him. But in the eventuation of a real crisis, Rajiv would find that the Act is no help at all. In fact it would aggravate the nature of the conflict, since the safety valve of conscience voting and mild protest has been eliminated by the Anti-Defection law. With the accords in a shambles, grave doubts having arisen about Rajiv's capacity to deal with the growing threat to the nation's integrity, and, further, with Kamalapati on the war path, Arun Nehru sulking, Jagannath Mishra and Madhav Singh Solanki dissatisfied, the scenario cannot but be called grim. The President's action can be interpreted as the overture of the campaign for a second term. It can be said that the Postal Bill has been used by Zail Singh as a launching pad. But it would be premature to do so. Should the conflict between the President and the Prime Minister go out of hand, untoward consequences might result. An adamant and badly advised Prime Minister and a hurt President can produce great harm. It is about time Rajiv Gandhi gave up his arbitrary ways and become a constitutional Prime Minister who does not disdain a proper and mannerly relationship with the President, the Cabinet members and Party colleagues. He should also meet the President, taking his Law Minister with him, and sort out the question of the modification of the obnoxious provisions of the Bill. To stand on prestige is to invite trouble. This is not an issue on which the Prime Minister should "take on" the President so to say.[7]

Professional news analysts were industriously engaged for several days during January 1987 to fathom the motives for the President's reluctance to sign the Postal Bill passed by Parliament which seeks to strengthen the Government's hands to intercept private mail. The fig leaf of "clarifications" has not deceived anyone. In actual practice under the Constitution the President's desire to ask for "clarifications" of a legislative measure or a Government order and to have this desire made public (through whatever channels) amount to clear hesitation to give his consent. But he cannot, under the powers vested in him, refuse consent and stay in office without causing a serious crisis. What then were Giani Zail Singh's motives for his controversial action that has won him much applause from the public and the news media other than Doordarshan and All India Radio? Was it only his constitutional conscience that prevented him from registering formal approval of a document already passed by the people's representatives in the Lok Sabha and the Rajya Sabha? Or was his action a gesture of indirect political protest in response to the extensive opposition to the Bill already expressed in both Houses of Parliament and outside? The questions acquire a special edge in view of Giani Zail Singh's impending retirement from office. One simple way of making an assessment of the President's motives would be through a comparison of his past attitude in an uneasy situation during the Prime Ministership of Indira Gandhi with his reactions and responses under the present dispensation. It is possible that there were occasions when he did not see eye to eye with Indira Gandhi (as, for instance, over Operation Bluestar), but the difference of opinion was not calculately given the appearance of a serious dispute in public. This can hardly be said about his relations with Rajiv Gandhi. Within a few weeks of the latter's taking over as Prime Minister 27 months ago the souring of relations had become public knowledge. There is no need to recall the series, of illustrative episodes in this connection.[8]

In other words, the President has repeatedly expressed his dissatisfaction over the manner in which his position as Head of State had been undermined for the past two years, not through aggressive disrespect to his person but largely through blatant indifference. He was, at last, recently shown a copy of the Mathew Commission report on Punjab but, presumably, he has to want for a look at the findings of Justice Misra in respect of the anti-Sikh riots in November, 1984, until Parliament is informed at the coming Budget session, as promised by the Prime Minister. The "cuts" made in the draft of his Independence Day message to the nation last year still rankle. The draft of his Republic Day broadcast was sent to the Prime Minister's Secretariat earlier this month. It is not known yet whether this too has suffered from censorship.[9]

All in all it has been a most unsatisfactory relationship between the Head of State and the Head of Government for two years, and presidential request for "clarifications" of the Bill under reference was only the latest example of a serious difference of opinion. The fact that the question-answer session was limited to the President's Secretary and the Secretary of the Law Ministry did not make the constitutional rumpus any the less noticeable ; and the further fact that the dispute came out in the open inevitably gave the matter a political meaning. Giani Zail Singh has been heard to say that if the President of India is to be treated only as a museum piece, worthy of being seen but not heard, he should appropriately be given the same position in the Constitution as that of the Queen of the Netherland in her own country : she attends Parliament for ceremonail occasions but never addresses it.

Going by the conventional criteria, the current Vice-President, Venkataraman, would appear to be a readymade choice for the new occupant 'Rashtrapati Bhawan'. He is from the South, politically mature, socially gracious and intellectually accomplished, apart from having served the ruling party with consistent loyalty. He has done nothing so far to offend the Prime Minister or the ruling party, and has 'carried himself with great dignity and self-confidence. His stewardship of the Rajya Sabha has left nothing to be desired. Thus this 77-year-old lawyer, politician and administrator from Tamil Nadu would appear to be an automatic choice for 'Rashtrapati Bhawan'.[10]

A current compromise suggestion is Venkataraman for President. Whichever way Rajiv Gandhi decides, he cannot afford to make a slip over the choice of his nominee for the office of President. There is already more genuine dissatisfaction over his leadership (even in his own party) than he probably realises. After the present mess in the Prime Minister's relations with the Head of State he cannot and must not go wrong again. Giani Zail Singh was his mother's choice, and he did not like it. The next President will be picked by him and he must choose wisely.

He will not be allowed easily to get away with an error of judgment for which the nation will have to pay until 1992.

Venkataraman, on June 13, 1987 entered the contest for the

office of the 8th President of India, with more than 50 members of Parliament (MPs) and Members of Legislative Assemblies (MLAs) sponsoring his candidature.

Two sets of nomination papers for Venkataraman papers for Venkataraman were filed. Prime Minister Rajiv Gandhi, led the list of 15 proposers for the first set of nomination papers and Union Minister for Human Resources Development, P.V. Narasimha Rao, led the list of the seconders.

The second set of nomination papers had 12 proposers and 12 seconders. Rajasthan Chief Minister, Hardeo Joshi, headed the list of proposers, while Union Minister for Parliamentary Affairs, M.M. Jacob, led the seconders.

Narasimha Rao walked into the office of the Returning Officer, Dr. Subhash Kashyap, in Parliament House at 1.45 p.m. with the nomination papers. He was accompanied by Union Home Minister Buta Singh. Deputy Leaders of the Congress (I) in the Rajya Sabha, N.K.P. Salve and Congress (I) general secretary, Nawal Kishore Sharma. At 1.49 p.m. Narasimha Rao handed over the first set of nomination papers, while the second set was delivered ten minutes later by AICC (I) general secretary, Bhagwat Jha Azad.

The Returning Officer's room was packed to capacity with Union Ministers, members of Parliament, media men and the security staff. Venkataraman's signature was on the form but he preferred not to come to the Returning Officer personally.

According to the rules, it was essential that members from different States were included in the list of proposers and seconders in both the nomination papers. The lists were changed several times to arrive at the correct combinations.

Minister of State for Parliamentary Affairs, Madam Sheila Dikshit, went to the Prime Minister's residence to obtain his signatures on the first set of papers. She returned to Parliament House accompanied by Narasimha Rao and M.L. Fotedar, political aide to the Prime Minister.

After the proposers and seconders had signed the nomination forms. Narasimha Rao, went to Venkataraman's house to obtain his consent.

The fifteen proposers in the first set include, besides Rajiv Gandhi, Buta Singh, P. Shiv Shankar, Arjun Singh, Vasant Sate and Minister of State for Rural Development Ramanand Yadav.

The seconders' list includes, besides Narasimha Rao, the Congress (I) general secretaries, G.K. Moopanar and A.K. Anthony, N.K.P. Salve, Sunderwati Nawal Prabhakar, Tourism Minister Mufti Mohammed Sayed, Madam Omem Deori, Rajasthan Pradesh Congress Committee President, Ashok Gehlot, Harubhai Mehta, Hari Krishan Shastri, the Minister of state for Surface Transport. Rajesh Pilot, AICC (I) Joint Secretary, Mehandresh Kumari, Ajeez Sait. Deputy Welfare Minister, Girdhar Gomango and Pratap Bhanu Krishnagopal.

Former President N. Sanjiva Reddy welcomed the Congress (I) Parliamentary Board's choice of R. Venkataraman as the presidential candidate.

In nominating Venkataraman, as the party's candidate in the presidential election, the Congress (I) has stuck to one convention and discarded another. After Dr. Rajendra Prasad's long innings of 12 years at 'Rashtrapati Bhavan', first as interim President and then as elected President for two terms, a convention of alternating the Presidency between north and south India was developed. The convention is fortified by a quarter-century of unbroken adherence. After Giani Zail Singh, it is the turn of a leader from the south to be the country's President, and in nominating. Venkataraman the Congress (I) leadership has upheld the convention. At the same time, the party has broken a convention almost equally old. All three Presidents of India after Dr. Rajendra Prasad were Vice-Presidents before their elevation to the highest office in the land. It seemed that Vice-Presidency was a stepping stone to Presidency. Before this practice could develop into a firm convention it was nipped by Indira Gandhi. V.V. Giri was the last Vice-President to become President, but he was a distress choice, not her first choice. That was in the fateful year, of 1969 and the ruling Congress (I) party has, after 18 years nominated a Vice-President for Presidentship.

Indira Gandhi broke the tradition by first denying the chance to Dr. G.S. Pathak. It is no accident that the presidential chair lost much of its aura and majesty with the ruling parties in Delhi plumping for pliable politicians (Sanjiva Reddy was an exception) rather than choice non-controversial persons of eminence.

The announcement of Venkataraman's name as the Congress (I) candidate implies that the efforts for a consensus candidate have been unfruitful. Several other names cropped up in subsequent discussions, but his remained on top of the list. Now the Congress parliamentary board has put its seal of approval on his nomination. He fulfills the criterion suggested by the founding fathers of the Constitution that the President should "represent the dignity of the State."

The choice of the Congress party is excellent and should elicit broad support not only from every Congressman but also from various other sections of the political spectrum. Venkataraman embodies dignity, decorum, intellectual depth and personal charm, all the qualities that the country can hope for in its first citizen. Even though he would be a Congress nominee, respect and regard for him cut across party lines. Above all, he is best-equipped to keep up the high traditions of the office established by distinguished predecessors like Dr. Rajendra Prasad, Dr. Radhakrishnan and Dr. Zakir Hussain.

Electoral contests ase a democratic exercise and there is no reason to fear that contests for Presidency will affect the prestige of the office. Nevertheless since there has been a search for a consensus candidate, is it necessary for the Opposition to put up a candidate against Venkataraman, knowing full well that in the present situation there can be no better choice ? The search for a consensus began when the Prime Minister himself announced that he was in favour of one. The Opposition also indicated that it too was keen on consensus. Unfortunately, there has not been an adequate exchange of views between the ruling party and the Opposition with the result that there has been no agreement on who should be the next President May be, the Congress-(I) should have made known its preference for Venkataraman a few days earlier.

Nevertheless, it is difficult to discover even one valid reason why the Opposition should not support him. Even now it is not too late for the Opposition to welcome Venkataraman's choice and pave the way for his unanimous election. Such a gesture will not only ensure that the next President assumes office on the support of all parties but also improve the political climate.

In the parliamentary system of government India has adopted, it stands to reason that a presidential candidate must be acceptable to the Prime Minister. It is, of course, to the advantage of both the Prime Minister and the country to have a person of eminence who enjoys national esteem. A good President will have the respect of the Government he should quietly advise, and can tell the people about the nation's failings and requirements outside the ambit of partisan politics. But the political atmosphere is too charged to make such a desired denoument possible. The very nature of the President-Prime Minister controversy makes Rajiv Gandhi wary of selecting any but the "safest" candidate, and he is hardly likely to move out of the circle of Congressmen.

The qualifications prescribed for the office are simple. Any citizen of India who has completed 35 years of age and is qualified for election as a member of the Lok Sabha is eligible to contest provided his nomination is backed by not less than 10 electors as proposers and at least 10 electors as seconders. The question is not who is eligible for nomination, but who should be elected ? The position of the President in the constitutional scheme and the nature of his functions provide enough guidance to the members of the electoral college for exercising their franchise.

There is no office more exalted than that of the Rashtrapati in our country. The fact that the powers conferred on the President are ordinarily exercised on the advice of the Prime Minister and the Council of Ministers which, in turn, is collectively responsible to the Lok Sabha, does not diminish the importance of the office. His powers of appointment are wide ranging. Most of the constitutional functionaries, including the Prime Minister and other Central Ministers, Governors, the Chief Justice of India and the Judges of the Supreme Court, the

Chief Justices and the Judges of the High Courts, the Attorney-General of India, the Chairman and the Members of the UPSC and the Chief Election Commissioner are appointed by him. Ambassadors, High Commissioners and the Service Chiefs and other important officers and dignitaries are also appointed by the President. A warrant of appointment signed by an eminent President gives immense satisfaction to the appointee. N.C. Chatterjee once mentioned to me that his warrant of appointment as Judge of the Calcutta High Court was signed by no less a person than C. Rajagopalachari, the then Governor General of India.[11]

The President is a constituent part of Parliament. He summons the Houses of Parliament, prorogues the Houses from time to time and dissolves the Lok Sabha on the advice of the Cabinet. The power to dissolve the Lok Sabha assumes importance only when no party commands the majority support in the House. The power to appoint a Prime Minister also assumes importance on rare occasions. So long as the leader of the ruling party enjoys the confidence of the Lok Sabha, the President has no choice but to make him the Prime Minister. Following the death of Nehru, Dr. Radhakrishnan swore in G.L. Nanda, the seniormost member of Nehru's Cabinet, as interim Prime Minister pending election of a new leader by the Congress Legislature Party in Parliament. He repeated it in 1966 on the death of Lal Bahadur Shastri and his decision was appreciated. However, in 1984, Zail Singh straightway administered the oath of office to Rajiv Gandhi. It was a bold decision based on a shrewd assessment of the prevailing situation. Rajiv Gandhi's land-slide victory at the polls shortly thereafter fully vindicated Zail Singh's decision. In contrast, N. Sanjiva Reddi landed himself in a serious controversy in 1979 by calling upon Charan Singh to form the Government after the fail of the Janata Government headed by Morarji Desai, Charan Singh could not face Parliament and bowed out within a few months. The President should be a person of sound judgement so that his decisions may not spark controversies.[12]

The Constitution vests in the President the supreme command of the Defence Forces of the Union with the rider that the exercise of this power shall be regulated by law. The

Service Chiefs maintain formal contacts with the President. The President, visits the Defence establishments, holds investiture ceremonies, presents awards, medals, colours and decorations to the gallant members of the Armed Forces. As the Head of the State, he receives invitations to visit foreign countries and at times, to address the legislature there. He receives all Heads of States visiting India. All Ambassadors and High Commissioners posted in India present their credentials to the President. It is, therefore, essential that the President should not only be a well-read and well-informed person, but should also be able to hold his head high and conduct himself with dignity in any gathering. In this respect, Dr. Radhakrishnan was an outstanding President. He was a renowned philosopher with a rare gift of speech and an impressive personality. He was Nehru's choice. Whether it was an address to Parliament or to the nation through the State media. Dr. Radhakrishnan was heard with rapt attention.

Dr. Rajendra Prasad, the first President of the Republic, was one of the most popular and highly respected Presidents with a distinguished record of service to the nation. As the President of the Constitutent Assembly he was one of the architects of the Constitution. Although he differed with Nehru on some issues he did not precipitate matters. He was the only President to have two terms.

Issues involving the Centre-State relations, the role of the Governors, particularly in the context of the imposition of President's rule in States, etc., tend to be sensitive and need delicate handling. The three rights of a constitutional Head of the State articulated by Walter Bagehot—the right to encourage and the right to warn—come in handly on such occasions. Rising above party politics, the President can use his good offices for building bridges of understanding between the Centre and the States. As B.N. Rau said, the voice of reason is more readily heard when it can persuade, but no longer coerce. Conceding that the titular Head has vary limited scope for exercising his powers all by himself, we cannot overlook the fact that he can easily cause serious embarrassment to the Council of Ministers if he fails to appreciate his role in the constitutional set-up.

The recent controversy over the powers and functions of the President vis-a-vis the Council of Ministers underlines the need to make a careful choice of the President in order to ensure harmonious working of the Constitution. As Dr. Ambedkar said in the Constitutent Assembly, however, good a Constitution may be, it is sure to turn out bad because those who are called to work it, happen to be a bad lot. However bad a Constitution may be, it may turn out to be good if those who are called to work it happen to be a good lot.

Having regard to the relative strength of the political parties in Parliament and the State Legislative Assemblies, it is obvious that the Congress (I) is in a position to get through its nominee. The responsibility for making a proper choice rests largely on the Prime Minister who is also the party chief. There is nothing unusual if the ruling party wants to set up one of its members as a candidate for the high office, as the Janata Party did in 1977. Even so, it is always desirable to strive for a consensus among all prominent political parties on a common candidate. They all seem to agree with Dr. Ambedkar regarding the position of the President that "he is the Head of the State, but not of the Executive. He represents the nation, but does not rule the nation. He is the symbol of the nation". To look for a person who is as popular as Rajendra Prasad, as famous as Radhakrishnan, as cultured and softspoken as Zakir Husain and as amiable as V.V. Giri, may be difficult.

In the ruling party can suggest a candidate who is fairly well-known, non-controversial and reasonably good, one may hope for a consensus. Consensus adds to the stature of the candidate and may help him to eschew party politics. Much depends on the members of the electrol college. It is their responsibility to give the nation a good President capable of ensuring political stability and discharging his multifarious, but largely ceremonial functions to the satisfaction of all concerned.

"I am very happy that the (Congress) party has reposed confidence in me. I endeavour to justify it."

Thus replied Venkataraman when asked for his reaction to the Congress party's decision to field him as its candidate for the Presidential election on 13 July 1987.

Told about the possibility of facing an opponent sponsored by the Opposition, the suave and mild-mannered Venkataraman said it did not matter to him. "I will contest the election", he said.

Would you resign as Vice-President before contesting the election ? "Well, it is not necessary at all. There have been people who did not resign to contest", he replied.

When would you launch your election campaign ?

He said that he would take a decision shortly. Moreover, he pointed out, there were Presidents like Dr. Rajendra Prasad, Dr. Radhakrishnan and Dr. Zakir Hussain who did not have to campaign at all. Others campaigned for him.

A correspondent told him, "Some leaders have been saying that your health is not good."

"You are seeing me", replied the smiling politician pointing out that when one is a candidate all sort of things are said.

Asked what would be his constitutional relationship with the Prime Minister, he replied : "all this comes later. At the moment I am only a candidate."

The veteran politician told a questioner, "I can read and write Hindi and also understand it without any difficulty. But I cannot speak it fluently and correctly."

He said he had delivered speeches in Hindi several times. But admitted that while talking in Hindi he often got the genders wrong. For instance, "I find it difficult to differentiate between '*aata hai*' (he coming) and '*aati hai*' (she coming).

Prime Minister Rajiv Gandhi had no doubt that the Congress candidate for the presidential election, Venkataraman, would get much more votes than the Congress "strength." He doubted if Congress legislators would vote for the opposition candidate. There was no difference of opinion in the Congress party over Venkataraman's candidature.

The Chief Minister of Sikkim, Nar Bahudur Bhandari on June 19, 1987 extended the support of the Sikkim Sangram Parishad for the Congress (I) candidate in the Presidential election, Venkataraman.

Bhandari did so when he met Prime Minister Rajiv Gandhi.

He was the fourth non-Congress (I) Chief Minister to offer his party's support for Venkataraman's candidature. The three others were M.G. Ramachandran (Tamil Nadu), Dr. Farooq Abdullah (Jammu and Kashmir) and Laldenga (Mizoram).

In a statement, Bhandari said that Venkataraman, an erudite scholar, veteran Parliamentarian and eminent administrator and one who is endowed with many qualities of head and heart" was the most suitable person for the exalted office of President.

"I would appeal to all irrespective of their party affiliations, to support the candidature of the Vice-President R. Venkataraman in the Presidential election and ensure that his election is unanimous", Bhandari added.

The nomination of Venkataraman, by the Congress for the presidential election made it hard for the opposition Dravida Munnetra Kazhagam (DMK) to make its choice.

The DMK would face a dilemma if the opposition nominee were to be from the Hindi belt, as it would then have to vote against Venkataraman and for a non-Tamil.

The DMK party was awaiting the announcement of the opposition choice for the presidential poll and was expecting a communication from N.T. Rama Rao, the Andhra Pradesh Chief Minister, in this regard. It was to take a decision on its choice later.

The DMK could hardly be expected to support a candidate for whom the All India Anna Dravida Munnetra Kazhagam (AIADMK) voted. Besides, Venkataraman was a Congress nominee and a Brahmin.

The political commentator, 'Cho' Ramaswamy, said DMK would have to go along with the opposition. "It has various shelters and could use one (for opposing Venkataraman)", he quipped.

Ramaswamy felt there was no alternative to Venkataraman. He was a good person to occupy the high office of President and keep up the dignity of the country, he said. Looking at some of the names mentioned by the opposition, one could not sit in comfort, he said.

Paying a tribute to Venkataraman's ability as an administrator, he said the veteran politician had somewhat lost his balance only twice in his long career—first when he changed his stance on the emergency and then when he compared M.G. Ramachandran with the Shankaracharya. Among the available choices, he was the best choice, Ramaswamy added.

The ruling AIADMK's support to the Congress nominee had already been announced by the party's leader Ramachandran.

Congress circles were happy over the choice of Venkataraman. The President of the Tamil Nadu Congress Committee, M. Palaniyandi thanked the Prime Minister for the choice, while expressing the hope that Venkataraman would bring glory to the post of President. O. Subramaniam, Congress legislature party leader, and Tindivanam Ramamurthy, MP, are among those who have welcomed the party choice.

Venkataraman, incidentally, will be the first Tamil to hold the high office. The others from the South who have held the august office, like Dr. Radhakrishnan, V.V. Giri and Sanjiva Reddy, are technically from Andhra Pradesh. Venkataraman, like Giri is also a labour leader.

The Dravida Kazhakam (DM), a movement for the Scheduled Caste, accused Venkataraman being involved in the submarine scandal when he was Defence Minister. Was Venkataraman really involved in the submarine deal ? No the deal was signed before Venkataraman became Defence Minister. It was signed in December 1981—when Indira Gandhi was herself Defence Minister. She handed over charge to Venkataraman only the following month, in January 1982. He was left with the responsibility of defending the deal in Parliament—defending a decision in which he hadn't in the least been involved. The decision to buy the subs from Germany (and not Sweden, reportedly one of Sanjay Gandhi's last wishes) was made in June 1980, when Venkataraman was Finance Minister. All he signed as Defence Minister was an expansion of the deal in February 1984, for the indigenous construction of two more submarines.[13]

As a Presidential candidate Venkataraman, refused to solicit country-wide support for his candidature.

He did not think it necessary to go on a campaign tour all over the country. The first two Presidents did not campaign and Venkataraman said he did not feel that electioneering was befitting the high post.

Also Presidency was not the kind of post where a candidate could educate his voters about any policies that he would follow, if elected, Venkataraman said.

On his part, by refusing to canvass for his candidature, Venkataraman gave evidence of the conviction that the office of President is too august for its aspirant to be have like a petty politician in a by-election. At the other end of the spectrum, what was positively disgusting about the antics of the Opposition leaders was that they proved that the path from anti-Congressism to unity among non-Congress parties continued to be indistinct even after the thumping electoral sucess achieved in Haryana by a non-Congress party. That they had managed to persuade so widely respected a person as Justice V.R. Krishna Iyer to be their candidate did not seem to have made the slightest difference to their thinking. As a result, all that could be said of the "Left-democratic" Opposition leaders was that, having achieved a hard-won but seemingly wasted triumph in getting, Justice Iyer to agree to be their candidate, they could not be certain that the rank and file of the parties they represent would not find themselves out of sympathy with their particular brands of frivolity, and at the time of voting ;

Sponsors of Venkataraman enjoyed a combined strength of over 60 per cent of the total votes in terms of valued in the electoral college for the presidential election slated for 13 July, going by the latest party position in Parliament and State Legislatures.

About 40 per cent of their support, provided there was no cross-voting, comes from Parliament alone, where the Congress and its allies in the Presidential election had about 600 MPs behind them.

The Chief Ministers of four non-Congress rules States, namely, Jammu and Kashmir, Tamilnadu, Sikkim and Mizoram has also publicly announced their support to Venkataraman.

Venkataraman's main rival was Justice V.R. Krishna Iyer who was being backed by a combined opposition with a vote bank of over 30 per cent of the total value in Parliament and various State Legislatures. The third candidate in the race was Mithlesh Kumar sponsored by 20 Bihar MLAs.

For Venkataraman, the ruling Congress had a tally of 562 MPs in both Houses of Parliament. The AIADMK (22), National Conference (4), Kerala Congress (3), Muslim League (3) and Sikkim Sangram Parishad (1) and some of the 16 nominated and unattached MPs had announced their support for the Congress nominee.

There were 26 vacancies in Parliament. With value of votes per MP having been worked out as 702, Venkataraman should poll over four lakh votes in terms of value in an electoral college of 1,089,751 votes from Parliament alone. On the basis of the strength of the Congress and its allies in various State Legislatures, Venkataraman should get another over 2.50 lakh votes. The votes in terms of value which Venkataraman might get in the absence of any cross-voting should be over 6.75 lakh.

Strength of the combined opposition backing Krishna Iyer in Parliament was 147 which in terms of value came to 1,03,194. This, however, did not include the unattached MPs who might lend their support to Krishna Iyer.

Nothing would be better than if the President, the Vice-President and the Speaker of the Lok Sabha were always unanimously elected and there was no intrusion of partisan considerations in their choice. In the new political climate in India this does not, unfortunately, seen possible.

REFERENCES

1. Prmoila Kalhan. Who will be next President ? *Hindustan Times* 6 October 1986.
2. *Ibid.*
3. *Ibid.*
4. *Ibid.*
5. Khushwant Singh. Choosing a President *Hindustan Times* 20 June 1987.

6. Madhu Limaye. The President's intervention *Patriot* 20 January 1987 ; p. 4.
7. *Ibid*.
8. Prem Bhatia. Choosing the next President. Tribune 24 January 1987 ; p. 4.
9. *Ibid.*
10. *Ibid*.
11. See *Hindu*, 8 June 1987.
12. *Ibid.*
13. Jyoti Punwani. Everyone's goodman. *Sunday Observer* 21 June 1987.

16

THE OFFICE OF THE PRESIDENT

The current controversy about the powers of the President in relation to the Prime Minister can serve no useful purpose at the present juncture. It is too late in the day to revive the theory literal construction of Articles 74 and 78 to make out a case for inherent or independent Presidential power under the Indian Constitution. The controversy must be deemed to have been finally settled by the 42nd and 44th Amendments negating such a power and making the President only a titular head of the State.

In the Constitutent Assembly Jawaharlal Nehru declared ; "We did not give the President any real power but we have made his position one of great authority and dignity." The distinction drawn by Nehru between "real power" and "great authority" was characterised as a hair-splitting distinction by Justice P.B. Mukharji in his Lectures on "The Critical problems of the Indian Constitution" delivered under the auspices of the Bombay University in 1968. After a meticulous examination of the elaborate provisions relating to the President, the learned judge concluded that the Indian President is no mere figure head. On a literal reading of the Constitutional provisions a learned Constitutional Writer, Prof. Alan Geldhill in his work. "The Republic of India" felt that an ambitious President can easily establish an authoritarian system of government in India. B.N. Rau in his "India's Constitution in the making" opines that "The Constitution does not impose any legal obligation upon the President, to act upon the advice of his ministers." A similar view was held by K. Santhanam in his article on the "President of India" published in the *Journal of Constitutional and Parliamentary Studies,"* (1969).[1]

The view that the President has discretionary powers and is no rubber-stamp has been held by several other eminent Jurists also : See Justice Ismail "The President and the Governors in the Indian Constitution" : page 10, K.M. Munshi "*The President under the Indian Constitution*" page 12.

The other view is that in appreciating, the scope of the powers of the President the literal reading of the relevant Articles would be misleading. This was realised by Prof. Alexandrawicz who in his "Constitutional Developments in India" published in 1957 observes : "The provisions of Chapter 1 of Part V of the Constitution convey *prima facie* the impression that the President of India is the real Head of the executive and the Ministry is only there to aid and advise him. However, a careful examination of constitutional practice in the post-independence years shows that the position is exactly the reverse and the President is by convention reduced to a mere figure-head". This view accords with that of Dr. Ambedkar also. According to this view the Articles of the Constitution vesting various powers in the President are really meaningless since by conventions of Parliamentary Government the real executive power resides in the Ministry, Prof. Jenning noted that the "Indian Constitution lacks self-confidence in defining the nature and extent of its executive power." Jennings : *Some Characteristics of the Indian Constitution*, p.6.

The two contending views were considered by the first Attorney-General of India, Chimanal Setalvad when Prime Minister of India Jawaharlal Nehru subscribing to the Second of the aforesaid views and the then President Dr. Rajendra Prasad subscribing to the First of those views requested him to elucidate the matter. The correspondence on this subject is reproduced by K.M. Munshi in his "Pilgrimage to freedom." Setalvad's opinion was that the President should in all cases act of the advice of the Ministry. It is true that this view of the President's function reduces him to the position occupied by the King in the Constitution of the United Kingdom. Dr. Rajendra Prasad specifically claimed that as the Supreme Commander of the Army he had the right to call for information directly from the service Chief and individual army officers. Setalvad advised him that he had no such right. This is revealed in his autobiographical work of Setalvad. *"My Life, Law and Other Things" published in 1970.* Setalvad further states "A few years later the Supreme Court in a division by and large endorsed the view that I had expressed in my opinion."[2]

The decision of the Supreme Court about referred to by Setalvad is reported in 1955 S.C. 549 Ram Jawaya vs. State of Punjab. This view has been confirmed subsequently by the decision in U.N.R. Rao vs Indira Gandhi (1971) SC 1002 and Shamsher Singh vs State of Punjab (1974) SC 2192. All these decisions hold the view that the real executive power is only in the Cabinet and that in all matters the President is bound to abide by its advice.

Further confirmation of this view was supplied by the 42nd Amendment, 1976, which amended Art. 74 to provide that the President shall in exercise of his functions act in accordance with the advice of the council of Ministers. The 44th Amendment of the Janata Government in 1978 did not touch this matter. It only gives the President power to request the cabinet to reconsider their advice but the advice tendered on such reconsideration is made binding upon him.

It is thus beyond controversy that under the Constitution as it stands now the President is bound by the advice of the Prime Minister. If the latter advises the President not to call for particulars relating to the Fairfax or the Bofors deal or not to call for particulars regarding developments on the border, the President has to respect such advice. Otherwise there will be Constitutional deadlock and chaos in our Parliamentary system of Government. That is why every Prime Minister has been keen to have his own nominee as President. Jawaharlal Nehru at first could not have his own way as the first President of India Dr. Rajendra Prasad was really the candidate of Sardar Patel and not of Nehru. Only after the demise of the Sardar he could have his own way and Dr. Radhakrishnan emerged as his candidate. Indira Gandhi preferred to have V.V. Giri as President and not Sanjiva Reddy and this led to a split in the Congress Party. Ex-President Sanjiva Reddy has recently stated that the nomination of the Presidential candidate by the party in power is the prerogative of the Prime Minister. There is no question of any prerogative here. It is merely a question of practical politics. There canot be two opposing centres of political power. This explains the anxiety of the Prime Minister to have his candidate on the Presidential chair. The people want to have a smooth and efficient government and are not interested in theoretical dialectics about Constitutional intricacies. They have reposed their trust in the Prime Minister and it is for the Prime Minister to choose proper tools to ensure a safe voyage for the ship of State in the turbulent sea of acrimonious politics surrounding India at the present day. The President has no power to call for any information beyond what the Prime Minister submits and the Prime Minister is not bound to supply any information or details. Actually there is no controversy. The founding fathers clearly spelt out the powers, duties and responsibilities, of the President and the Prime Minister in the Constitution. The King does no wrong, because he does nothing. The President of India is nothing more than a titular, dignified, ornamental Head of State. Hence only experienced, elderly people are chosen for this post.[3]

The USA is the oldest modern democratic republic. Its first President, George Washington, was Commander-in-Chief during the War of Independence. The U.S. Constitution provides for the President to be Commander-in-Chief but no President has functioned as such in a professional sense. Being both the head of state and head of government, as also Commander-in-Chief, the President of the USA exercises ultimate political control over the U.S. Armed Forces. The Indian Constitution, by providing for the President to be also the Supreme Commander, follows the American pattern, but the President of India does not function as head of government. There is also a difference in terminology but not in the content of the appointment. The U.S. Presidenl is a Commander-in-Chief while the Indian President is a Supreme Commander. The latter term really came into vogue during World War II. In this regard, our system is different from the British whose sovereign is not specifically designated head of the armed forces. Prior to 1947, the Viceroy of India functioned as head of state and both reigned and rules, but he too was not designated head of the armed forces. Article 53 (1) of our Constitution vests the executive power of the Union in the President and Article 53 (2) stipulates that "the Supreme command of the defence forces of the Union shall be vested in the President and the exercise thereof shall be regulated by law." The proceedings of the Constituent Assembly show that various aspects connected with the appointment and functioning of the President were discussed at length in that august body. An amendment was put up to Article 53 (2) regarding the President having the right to hold a referendum, declare war, and so on. This amendment was rejected and Article 53 (2), as it stands today, was duly approved by the Assembly. At no stage was the role of the President as Supreme Commander discussed. We have to draw our own conclusions as to why the founding fathers deemed it necessary to specify that the President was also to hold the supreme command of the defence forces. Was this not inherent in his being vested with the executive power of the Union under Article 53 (1)? The fact that it was found necessary to have a special provision to this effect suggests that a special relationship between the head of state and the defence forces was visualized. In the context of the spirit of our Constitution and the President-Prime Minister controversy, that special relationship calls for discussion. The defence forces, like any other organ of the Administration, function under the head of government. They must at all times loyally carry out the orders of the government. However, considering the fact that, unlike other organs of the state, they have to be prepared to make the supreme sacrifice in the service of the nation as part of their duty, it is only right that a special ceremonial and emotional link be provided between them and the head of state. In this context, the President, also being the Supreme Commander of the defence forces, has a special meaning. All officers of the defence forces hold the President's commission. Parchments signed personally by the President are given to each officer calling upon him loyally to serve the nation and faithfully carry out the orders of his superiors. At mess dinners, which, at one time, were supposed to be held four times a week, officers are required to drink a toast to the President as a symbolic act of loyalty. It is to be noted that the toast is not drunk to the head of government or even to the nation or the country. The President presents colours to regiments and the President's Colours are the most cherished and sacred possession of a combat unit. In the old days, colours used to be carried into battle and had to be defended to the last man. Now-a-days, colours are not required to be carried into battle but elaborate ceremonies are prescribed for showing honour to the colours, Soldiers joining the Army take their oath of allegiance under the colours awarded to their regiment by the President.

Apart from the ceremonial links between the President and the defence forces, it is expected that, being the Supreme Commander, the President will take a personal interest in the defence forces. The style of our Presidents in this regard has varied with different incumbents of that high office. The first President, Dr. Rajendra Prasad, took a paternal interest while visiting defence establishments, but generally remained aloof. It is note-worthy that he took no interest in the Krishna Menon-Thimayya dispute which rocked the nation in 1958, nor did General Thimayya exercise his right of pleading his case before the Supreme Commander. Dr. Radhakrishnan showed concern for the defence forces during the Sino-Indian war of 1962. He visited troops in the forward areas and went round the hospitals to cheer the wounded soldiers. In fact, he was the only President to do so. In 1971, V.V. Giri did nct mak such visits.[4]

Giani Zail Singh has in his own way been taking an interest in the defence forces. In this connection two incidents deserve mention. The Military Secretary to the President used to be an appointment which could be held only by army officers. Giani Zail Singh rightly felt that this appointment should rotate between the three services so that, apart from Generals, Admirals and Air Marshals could also serve as Military Secretary to the President. He informally discussed this matter with General Krishna Rao who advised that no change be made in the then existing arrangement. General Krishna Rao then put up a formal note giving detailed reasons why no change should be made and this note, duly endorsed by the Government, was put up to the President. Giani Zail Singh ruled that as Supreme Commander he had only consulted the Army Chief and it was wrong of the latter to put up a formal note on this subject through the Government. As the constitutional head of state, he had of course to be guided by the advice of the Government, but he could exercise his own discretion in selecting his personal staff. He selected an Air Marshal to be his Military Secretary and Indira Gandhi did not object to it.[5]

This then is the well established political-constitutional practice governing relations between the President of the Republic, who should hold, and be worthy of, a place of high respect but who has a constitutional function which is strictly limited and the Prime Minister and popularly constituted Council of Ministers whose decision-making authority should be treated as substantively decisive and pre-eminent. Ironically, some of the very same jurists and intellectuals who argued a doctrine of no off-his-own-bat powers for the President of the Republic vis-a-vis the Prime Minister and the Government of the day during the period of the Sanjiva Reddi—Morarji Desai controversy of the late Seventies are now advocating the specious case of constitutionally overriding powers for President Zail Singh vis-a-vis Prime Minister Rajiv Gandhi, who is alleged to have lost his "right" to govern. At this point, the dangerous basis idea may be floating around in the form of whispers, informal talk, lobbying, speculation, innuendo and gossip with no precise boundary lines drawn between these but we would earnestly urge upon. Zail Singh himself, and also the Rashtrapati Bhavan' (which has not been shy in issuing clarifications and denials on a number of matters, big and small), to clear the air decisively of the whiff of any such thinking.

It is indeed amazing that the constitutional purists who seem to be alarmed that presidential assertion would wreck the system, watched quite benignly while President of the Republic was being reduced to the position of a bartender who must cheerfully put up with offensive customers. A liberal political arrangement is marked by the absence of arbitrarianess in the exercise of authority. Those who are elected to wield legitimate authority are necessarily hemmed in by institutions and indus-titutional procedures and traditions, and this is applicable to the Indian situation as well ; there is nothing in the Constitution of India that countenances the assumption of a monarchical role for a Prime Minister. After an election, terms of bargain-ing between a President and a Prime Minister may change, but the need for bargaining and trading influence cannot and need not be eliminated altogether. The 42nd amendment or on amendment, the basis of Prime Minister—President relation-ship can only be one of mutual trust and esteem ; either one who reneges on deeping up his part of the relationship is guilty of undermining a very kecessary and delicate constitutional balance. The burden of maintaining an esprit de corps cannot rest entirely and unilaterally with the President. Whether or not the President of the republic should have the kind of powers Rajendera Prasad asked for in his March 1950 note to Jawaharlal Nehru apart, the experience of the last many years has been that there are no effective institutional checks on the Prime Minister, should he or she be inclined to behave imperi-ously. This position has become all the more acute because the judiciary has abdicated much of its role of slowing down the executive's juggernaut and our Parliament no longer attracts men and women of eminence and courage who can say "no" to the insatiable demands made in the name of the Indian state.

In the circumstances, an active and alert President remains the only source of much needed resistance to executive waywardness and insolence. Whatever then be President Zail Singh's personal and political motives, the Indian system has been served well by a bit of presidential assertiveness. It will do any Prime Minister a lot of good to know that in the 'Rashtrapati Bhawan' sits a man who will ask a few inconvenient questions.[6]

Pranab Mukherjee has said: "Being a genuine Congressman, I am opposed to the presidential form of government. When we joined the Congress, we pledged to strengthen and uphold the parliamentary form of government. So how can I think otherwise? A developing country like ours, with its diverse religions, languages, and economic levels, is more suitable to a parliamentary form of government. There may be no rationale in the method of functioning now, but still I am not convinced of the benefits of a presidential form of government. No doubt, both forms of government are democratic, but in the presidential form the largest single group would have in advantage more than in the present system. Moreover, an elected president cannot be removed easily if need be. The parliamentary form, on the other hand, is more responsive to the change of mood of people as has been evident from the pattern of power in our country. It is not generally known that in a parliamentary form, there is nothing to stop the Prime Minister from inducting outside experts. A Prime Minister is supposed to be the first among equals but now Cabinet members are treated as subordinates. After all is said and done, we do not need to switch over to another system. In fact, the debate is a non-issue".[7]

The plea for a presidential form of government has been made by many. It is believed that the presidential system would secure a federal structure. Direct election of the President could project leaders who represent the entire country unlike the Prime Minister representing just one constituency or enjoying the confidence of just a single party. A directly elected chief executive would transcend regional, communal and caste divisions and if the electoral process is properly devised he would have secured a majority of the vot es. Therefore he will be not only the symbol but a true representative of the entire nation. He will also not be subjected to the day-to-day pulls and pressures of party politics, legislators and others. The term of office would be secured constitutionally and this would lend a lot of stability. Limiting the terms of the President to a definite period would also have a salutary effect. However, I am conscious that even this system is not free from flaws. There is an apprehension that since democratic institutions are less developed in India compared to other countries that have the presidential form of government, the system could result in greater centralisation and possible abuse of power. It is also argued that this system may not be the answer to the use of money power in elections. It is pointed out also that this system may not automatically develop a two-party or multi-party system.[8]

It is vital for the functioning of Indian democracy that the most exalted office of the nation is always kept above controversy and at all times shown the highest respect. Any attempt by anyone to denigrate that exalted office is not only showing dis-regard for the Constitution but is an insult to the nation as a whole. It is indeed a great pity that the Government chose to deny information about the Bofors guns to the Supreme Commander. The plea that the details are secret, and known only to a few Generals and the foreign arms supplier, is too preposterous to call for any comment.[9]

As the President of the Republic, Venkataraman will be obliged to defuse the controversy and doubts over the extent and nature of authority the President enjoys under the Constitution of India. Fortunately, Venkataraman has given every indication that he understands unambiguously that there can be no two centres of authority in New Delhi. While the office is one of great dignity, to which Venkataraman will no doubt add his own share, he can also be banked upon not to convert 'Rashtrapati Bhavan' into also be banked upon not to convert 'Rashtrapati Bhavan' into a centre from where to wage a war of nerves against the Prime Minister. As it is, relations between the Vice-President and Rajiv Gandhi are most cordial and one of mutual esteem. The country can remain assured that while Venkataraman would spare the polity, much tension and uncertainity, his sage counsel would be available to the Prime Minister and his colleagues. The presence of this great believer in parliamentary democracy would be best antidote in the days of turbulence that lie ahead.

Venkataraman prefers to avoid any discussion on the controversy over the constitutional rights of the President. The only remark he volunteers is that the founding fathers of the Indian Constitution had visualised the role of the Indian Presldent as that of the Crown in England.

Asked about the possible differences between a President and the Prime Minister, Venkataraman preferred not to express any views except and that too under persistent goading temperamental differences. But they should never be made public.[10]

In the words of Venkataraman : "The President's advice (to the Government) can't be made more effective (than it is) because that would create another centre of power. And, in a democracy, there can be only one centre of power."

Summing up his overall position, he recalls his ruling in the Rajya Sabha where he has noted that the President occupies the same place under the Indian Constitution as the Crown under the British.[11]

"Under a democratic Constitution, sovereignty rests in the people. They exercise it through their elected representatives in Parliament. And, the Council of Ministers in responsible only to Parliament", he stresses.

Candour, for example, characterises his comments on the subject of declining standards in public life. "Politics is not longer a mission. It is a profession and a career."

He contrasts this situation with the days of the freedom struggle "when we went to jail without thinking of becoming ministers, when independence was not even a distant dream."

The veteran leader with varied political experience at both the State and Central levels also says that "your political career does not depend upon your qualities". He thinks the situation could be improved by "a sober, responsible" electorate "a person with a sullied reputation should not be able to get elected."

Venkataraman, however, deprecates cynicism. "Developed

democracies have taken centuries to achieve a sound functioning. You want to achieve it in 40 years?"

Laughing, he quips "That's the difference between us and you journalists. You won't agree that a tree takes time to grow, a fruit takes time to ripen. We, as a nation, also tend to exaggerate these things."

REFERENCES

1. P. V. Ranga Rao. President, PM and powers. *Deccan Chronicle* 16 June 1987.
2. *Ibid.*
3. *Ibid.*
4. S. K. Sinha. The supreme commander : President as symbol of national pride. *Statesman* (New Delhi) 22 June 1987 ; p. 6.
5. *Ibid.*
6. Harish Khare. President-Prime Minister : No acquiescence, no confrontation *Times of India* 2 March 1987 ; p. 6.
7. Jo Anand. Is the Presidential form of government desirable ? *Mid-Day* (New Delhi) 3 February 1987 ; p. 7.
8. Ramakrishna Hegde. This present system will not do. *Times of India* 18 January 1987.
9. S. K. Sinha. *op. cit.*, p. 6.
10. See *Amrita Bazar Patrika* (Calcutta) 26 June 1987.
11. J. Sri Raman and V. Shankar. President no centre of power ; RV (An interview)*Patriot* 28 June 1987.

BIBLIOGRAPHY

A pity both can't win. (RV and Justice Iyer) *Blitz* (Bombay) 4 July 1987 ; 2.

Anand, Jo What attributes should the President possess? *Mid-Day* 1 July 1987 ; 4.

Attar Chand. A right choice *Newstime* (Hyderabad) 28 June 1987 ; 7.

Attar Chand. National choice : Venkataraman. *Madhyo Pradesh Chronicle* (Bhopal) 30 June 1987 ; 4.

Attar Chand. Next President. *Pioneer* (Lucknow) 25 June 1987.

Attar Chand. The right choice. *Mid-Day* (New Delhi) 23 June 1987.

Attar Chand RV : A leader *Patriot* (New Delhi) 2 July 1987 ; 4.

Attar Chand. RV not involved (in the Submarine deal with West Germany) *Patriot* 29 June 1987 ; 4.

Attar Chand. Venkataraman is clean. *Indian Nation* (Patna) 3 July 1987 ; 4.

Attar Chand. Venkataraman has a clean track record. *Mid-Day* 8 July 1987.

Battle of giants. *Northern India Patrika* 26 June 1987 ; 4.

Bhandari's support (Nar Bahadur of Sikkim) for Venkataraman *Statesman* 20 June 1987 ; 7.

Bhaskara Rao, N. RV as 'active' President favoured. *Hindustan Times* 6 July 1987 ; 1,22.

Bhatia, V.P. Ramaswamy Venkataraman. *Organiser* (New Delhi) 5 July 1987 ; 13.

BJP sticks to 'neutrality' in Presidential poll. *Patriot* 6 July 1987 ; 1.

Chakravarty, Nikhil. Will this controversy ever end ? (President-PM conflict). *Times of India* (Sunday Review) 5 July 1987.

Charade. *Indian Post* (Bombay) 15 June 1987 ; 6.

Charlu, V.S. New President. *Financial Express* (New Delhi) 6 July 1987 ; 5.

Choice, wise and proper. *Tribune* (Chandigarh) 16 June 1987 ; 4.

Chopra, V.D. Significant of Presidential poll. *Patriot* 29 June 1987 ; 4.

Communists bale out Rajiv to blackmail him (on RV's nomination. *Organiser* (New Delhi) 5 July 1987.

Congress (I) Choice. *National Herald* (Lucknow) 16 June 1987 ; 6.

Consensus Candidate of conscience—*New Wave* 14 June 1987 ; 3.

Contest for Vice-President's office. *Industrial Times* (Bombay) 20 August 1987 ; 7.

Dhar, M.K. Congress-I, may select Venkataraman. *Hindustan Times* 14 June 1987.

Expert on labour laws. *Newstime* (Hyderabad) 15 June 1987.

Fifty years of public Service. *Hindu* (New Delhi) 15 June 1987.

From trade unions to politics—a long career. *Indian Post* 15 June 1987.

I will endeavour to justify confidence in me : RV *Patriot* 15 June 1987.

Isidore, S.J. Venkat is the apt choice. *Daily* (Bombay) 9 July 1987.

Iyer against Iyer. *Times of India* (Sunday Review) 5 July 1987.

Iyer versus RV. *Democratic World* (New Delhi). 28 June 1987 ; 4.

Iyer's call to install dynamic President. *Times of India* 4 July 1987 ; 4.

Joga Rao. Foreign forces foul-up presidential poll. *Blitz* (Bombay) 4 July 1987 ; 4.

Joshi, B.K. R. Venkataraman : Winning friends and influencing people. *Free Press Journal* 12 August 1984. *Newstime* (Hyderabad) 19 August 1984 ; 3.

Kalhan, Promila. 'The President is not a second seat of power.' *Hindustan Times* 5 July 1987.

Kalhan, Promila. RV—portrait. *Hindustan Times* 22 June 1987 ; 8

Kamaraj, K. Nation's leader and his legacy. In *Nehru legacy*. (New Delhi), National Book Club, 1966 ; pp. 1-73.

Kamaraj, K. *Towards Socialism*. (New Delhi), A Congress Forum For Socialist Action Publication, 1966. p. 108.

Kamath, M.V., R. Venkataraman *Mid-Day* (New Delhi) 27 June 1987 ; 6.

Katyal, K.K. Choosing a president. *Frontlinte* (Madras) 27 June 1987 ; 4-8.

Katyal, K.K. Venkataraman : A low profile. *Frontline* (Madras) 27 June 1987 ; 6.

Khushwant Singh. Choosing a President. *Hindustan Times* 20 June 1987 ; 9.

Maniam, V.S. 'A Mahatma can check communalism' (RV's views). *Statesman* 6 July 1987 ; 4.

Mathur, Girish. Left's pro-Congress stand riles opposition. *Link* 3 July 1987 ; 8-9.

More a statesman than ever a politician. *Times of India* (Sunday Review) August 1984.

Namboodiripad, E.M.S. 'The battle is worth fighting.' *Hindustan Times* 5 July 1987.

New Vice-President *Deccan Chronicle* 24 August 1984.

New Vice-President *Economic Times* (New Delhi) 24 August 1984.

New Vice-President. *National Herald* 23 August 1984.

New Vice-President. *Pioneer* (Lucknow) 24 August 1984.

Next President. *Northern India Patrika* (Allahabad) 17 June 1987 ; 4.

New President : P.M. begins fresh round of talks. *Hindu* 9 June 1987.

No rift in Cong. over RV : Rajiv *Times of India* 21 June 1987.

Pandit, C.S. PM—President differences may only be temperamental—Venkataraman. *Amrita Bazar Patrika* 26 June 1987.

President or pensioner ? *Statesman* 17 June 1987 ; 6.

Presidential election : An anti-climax. *India Today* 15 July 1987 ; 39-41.

Presidential poll : Need for consensus. *Hindu* (New Delhi) 8 June 1987 ; 6.

Presidential poll. *Amrita Bazar Patrika* 6 July 1984 ; 6.

Presidential poll. *Northern India Patrika* 7 July 1987 ; 4.

Presidential poll. *Indian Nation* 28 June 1987 ; 4.

Punwani, Jyoti. Everyone's good man. *Sunday Observer* 21 June 1987.

RV for ahead of Iyer. *Deccan Chronicle* (Secundrabad) 4 July 1987 ; 13.

R.V. hails Festival of India (in USSR) *Hindu* 3 July 1987.

R.V. : The most suitable choice. *Democratic World* (New Delhi) 21 June 1987 ; 3-4.

RV as President. *Sunday]Mail* (New Delhi) 14 June 1987 ; 1,8.

RV is Congress (I) nominee for Presidential poll. *Hindu* 15 June 1987.

RV's choice dilemma for DMK. *Times of India* 17 June 1987 ; 4.

RV's futuristic plans ? *People's Comment* (New Delhi) 16 June 1987 ; 10.

R. Venkataraman : Always unruffled. *Current* (New Delhi) 20 June 1987 ; 2.

R. Venkataraman. *Madhya Pradesh Chronicle* (Bhopal) 17 June 1987 ; 4.

R. Venkataraman not the obvious choice. *Newsman* (New Delhi) May 1987 ; 8.

R. Venkataraman Role of Planning in industrial development 1969 X9 : 75 : 2 : N6 K9. 77846.

Raghavan, A. The picking of a President. *Blitz* 20 June 1987 ; 7.

Raghavendra. New President *Deccan Chronicle* 18 June 1987 ; 6.

Rajiv (Gandhi) puts up R.V. to defuse the crisis. *Democratic World* 21 June 1987 ; 5-7.

Ramachandran, C.P. He will be in his element. *Hindustan Times* 2 September 1984.

Rangarajan, R. 'RV'—A statesman. *Hindustan Times* 30 June 1987 ; 9.

Rangarajan, R. RV : Evenful public life. *Deccan Chronicle* (Hyderabad) 5 August 1984.

Rangarajan, R. VR no victim of inebriety of power. *Patriot* 6 August 1984 ; 5.

Ranga Rao, P.V. President, PM and powers. *Deccan Chronicle* 16 June 1987.

Rao, Rajeshwara. 'We do not want a rubber stamp.' *Hindustan Times* 5 July 1987.

Rattan, Renu. R. Venkataraman : Able follower of an illustrious line. *National Herald* (New Delhi) 26 August 1984.

Sapling time (RV in President House) *Newstime* (Hyderabad) 5 July 1984 ; 7.

Sarin, V.I.K., Venkataraman assured of easy victory. *National Herald* 29 June 1987.

Sinha, Dharam Bir. RV—best candidate for presidentship. *Mid-Day* (New Delhi) 3 July 1987 ; 7.

Sri Raman, J. and V. Shankar. President no centre of power—RV. *Patriot* 28 June 1987.

Sundar Rajan, K.R. A troubled legacy. *Sunday Observer* (New Delhi) 28 June 1987.

Sunder Rajan, K. R. Final degradation. *Sunday Observer* 14 June 1987 ; 2.

Sundar Rajan, K.R. RV may not be a rubber stamp. *Mid-Day* 3 July 1987 ; 6.

Venkat is Congress (I) nominee. *Tribune* 15 June 1987.

Venkataraman as head of state. *Link* 21 June 1987 ; 3.

Venkataraman Congress (I) choice. *Statesman* (New Delhi) 14 June 1987.

Venkataraman is Congress choice. *Times of India* 14 June 1987.

Venkataraman is Vice-President. *Newstime* 23 August 1984.

Venkataraman sworn in. *Indian Express* 1 September 1984.

Venkataraman, R. *Hazari Prasad Dwivedi Memorial inaugural lecture*. Santiniketan, 23 November 1985. p. 11.

Venkataraman and, K. Kamaraj's unique career. *Hindu* (Madras) 15 July 1964.

Vice-President's advice to politician. *Statesman* 8 September 1984.

Vice-President's call to politicians. *Times of India* 8 September, 1984.

Visiting temples with nomination papers. *Hindustan Times* 28 June 1987.

Viswam, S. Venkataraman as good as elected. *Tribune* (Chandigarh) 15 June 1987.

Warm welcome to Venkataraman (in Rajya Sabha). *Tribune* 19 January 1985.

INDEX